**Native
North
American
Armor,
Shields,
and
Fortifications**

Native
North
American
Armor,
Shields,
and
Fortifications

by David E. Jones

University of Texas Press, Austin

Library of Congress Cataloging-in-Publication Data
Jones, David E., 1942–
Native North American armor, shields, and fortifications /
by David E. Jones.
        p.   cm.
Includes bibliographical references and index.
    ISBN 0-292-70209-4 (cl.: alk. paper)
    ISBN 0-292-70170-5 (pbk.: alk. paper)
    1. Indians of North America—Warfare.   2. Indian
weapons—North America.   3. Indian armor—North
America.   4. Fortification—North America.   I. Title.
    E98.W2J66   2004
    623.4'41—dc21
                                    2003007786

Contents

Acknowledgments

I owe an immense debt of gratitude to my wife, Jane Morris Jones, for encouragement, emotional and intellectual support, and invaluable editorial assistance. I am also grateful to Gil Gillespie for artwork, and to Dr. Michael G. Davis and Dr. Wayne Van Horne for reading an early draft of this manuscript and making crucial suggestions. Of course, the final responsibility for any statement made in this work is mine.

Introduction

The nature of North American Indian cultures at the time of European contact in the fifteenth and sixteenth centuries is poorly understood. Europeans who first entered the New World were, for the most part, untrained in scientific observation. In addition, depopulation from introduced diseases caused rapid changes in traditional Indian lifeways. This drastic reduction in populations forced abandonment of ancient homelands; emptying of towns; and devastating economic, religious, and political restructuring. Warfare against superior numbers of Europeans and advanced military technology shattered the societies that remained.

One fact, however, stands strikingly clear: At the time of contact, warfare was endemic among the North American Indians. (See Holm 1996 for further discussion and sources concerning early Indian warfare.) Hernando De Soto, one of the first to traverse Indian country in the Southeast, found rabid hostilities among neighboring groups. His chroniclers described a semiprofessional warrior caste and fortified villages. Later travelers reported the grouping of Indians into chiefdoms and large confederacies, both to better defend themselves and to aggress against others. The Chickasaw fought the Choctaw, the Creeks fought with the Cherokee, the Calusa battled with Timucuans, and at the time of contact, all northern Florida Indians hated the Apalachee. In the Southwest the Apaches fought the tribes of the Pueblos. On the Plains the Blackfeet fought the Crow, the Sioux fought the Cheyenne, and the Crow fought the Shoshone. Explorers like Henry Hudson in New York, Samuel de Champlain in Canada, and George Vancouver on the Northwest Coast reported a similar situation in terms of Indian relationships. The early accounts of Indian culture also depicted sophisticated offensive and defensive martial technology. The most complex, and to most contemporary Americans probably the most surprising, was the presence of armor among almost all Indian groups.

Given the significance of armoring in warfare and the obvious ubiquity of warfare in native American culture at the time of contact, one would think that historians and ethnologists would have dealt with the subject exhaustively. However, in perusing the past several years of *American Antiquity,* I found no archaeologically related references to armor, and in surveying forty thousand citations in *The Ethnographic Bibliography of North America,* I encountered the word "armor" only once, in Hough's "Primitive American Armor," published in 1895 in the *Annual Report of the Board of Regents of the Smithsonian Institution.* Hough's report simply described the specimens of native American armor housed in the United States National Museum; no systematic survey of the topic was attempted. Frank R. Secoy (1953), in his classic *Changing Military Patterns of the Great Plains Indians,* devoted a handful of pages to Indian armor but, again, drew most of his references from the Hough article. This pattern of dependence on the Hough piece has been repeated in a number of scanty references to armor found in various "dictionaries" and casual accounts of American Indian lore and material culture.

Because a wide-ranging study of North American Indian defensive technology—armor, shields, fortifications—is lacking, this work will seek to fill that void with a systematic survey from the Southeast to the Northwest Coast, from the Northeast Woodlands to the desert Southwest, and from the Subarctic to the Great Plains. I will provide a preliminary step toward a broader ethnological investigation of the relationship among warfare, defensive technology, and the evolution of political entities. Likewise, the focus of this work will assist the understanding of the relationship of subsistence base to defensive technology, as well as to many other ethnological, historical, and ethnohistorical issues related to warfare.

Many questions that rely on a basic survey of information arise. What are possible diffusion routes of armor and general defensive technology coming into native North America from surrounding cultures? Did trade systems in which armor was a major commodity exist in North America? Is armor style related to subsistence activity? Under what conditions do shields evolve—change shape and size—and become mystical accoutrements of the warriors? It is to the service of such investigations that the material in this book is directed.

For example, John Keegan (1994, 139–142), when discussing fortifications in *A History of Warfare,* differentiates among refuges, strongholds, and strategic defenses and suggests that each form relates to a certain type of political environment. Refuges function as short-term defense and only work against an enemy without the means to linger in an area for long periods. Refuges simply have to deter an enemy from organizing an assault. A stronghold, on the other hand, must be able to withstand attackers who can maintain supply lines to the siege site. Strongholds must be large enough to protect and house a garrison when under attack. They typically possess walls, towers, and some sort of moat—wet or dry. In the "strategic systems" type of fortification, multiple strongholds connect, much like a wall, to deny enemies access over a wide offensive front. Keegan concludes that refuges are most likely found in small-scale societies of the band or tribal type, whereas "Strongholds are a product of small or divided sovereignties; they proliferate when central authority has not been established or is struggling to secure itself or has broken down" (1994, 142). With regard to strategic defenses, he writes, "strategic defenses are the most expensive form of fortification to construct, to maintain and to garrison, and their existence is always a mark of the wealth and advanced political development of the people who build them" (1994, 142).

The application of Keegan's observations on fortification and political structure to the North American Indian scene depends, of course, on the presentation of sufficient information to be able to pursue his argument. This book seeks to fill this informational gap.

Throughout this volume I will use the term "warfare" in a very general sense to mean fighting among members of a specific social group or between two or more groups. A more refined rendering might consider "warfare" to mean a state-level form of massed social aggression involved with maintaining and supplying an army in the field, with the ultimate aim of occupying an enemy's territory, while "raids" can be described as military operations which, if successful, require only one strike. A "raid" might be seen as a message to a potential enemy to stop the behavior that is upsetting the attacking group. A "feud" is more or less a family affair. Classically, it is about the vengeance of kinsmen against those individuals who have assaulted the life or honor of the kin group. A "military demonstration" is a show, a display engineered to impress the enemy with the futility of further hostilities or to distract an enemy while the real strategy is being acted out.

Most North American Indian warfare was of the raid and feud variety, although true warfare, in which one group maintained concerted pressure on another for the purposes of genocide or the removal of a people from their territory, existed. In some places at some times, war was unremitting, while in others lack of defensive arrangements or the dilapidation of former stout palisades indicated a low level of hostilities. In some cases thousands of fighters were involved; much more often, however, the number of combatants was much smaller. Martial demonstrations, most often in the form of dancing while brandishing weapons, were widespread. Often, too, the martial demonstrators carried shields and were accoutred in various types of armor.

The near universality of armoring the human body is not difficult to understand. Though humans have over the past millennia risen to dominate the creatures of the earth, they accomplished this not through the strength of their sinews or the toughness of their hide, but through their intelligence and symbolic ability, which enabled them to transmit learning from one generation to the next. Humans are, in fact, quite weak physically, vulnerable because they lack thick pelts or hard coverings to protect their skin from claws and ripping canine teeth.

It is possible that ancient humans first experienced armoring with the animal pelts used to cover their bodies. The earliest skin clothing was, no doubt, crudely produced, with the "finished" skin a stiff rawhide more reminiscent of shoe leather than the finely tanned, almost feltlike buckskin of many Indian cultures. The fine tanning of leather to a clothlike suppleness came later in time. The relative hardness of the earliest leather clothing possibly suggests that one could add harder and thicker coverings to protect the body from punctures, scratches, and cuts. Possibly those who experienced physical confrontation with their fellows discovered that a layer of rough leather offered some protection from harmful blows as well as the chance to fend off attacks and fight back. Perhaps from these early experiences, human armoring unfolded.

Native Americans never developed iron and steel technology and therefore lacked the ability to produce metal-plate battle dress, the type most familiar to Westerners. Their armor was constructed of wood and bone (hard armor), leather (soft armor), and combinations of hard and soft materials. But does that mean it was ineffective as body protection? Police today employ a variety of soft armor against the highly evolved weapons of modern-day criminals. Leather and wood can, in fact, be fashioned into effective body armor and withstand some of the sharpest cutting and puncturing weapons ever produced.

There are many examples of the effectiveness of leather armor. Roman models greatly influenced early European armor. A funereal figure from the Romano-Germanic Museum at Mainz depicts a Roman legionary of the first century A.D. clothed in leather. Records indicate that in Great Britain, Charles the Bald (ca. 850), borrowing ideas from the Roman Praetorian Guard, equipped his warriors with torso protection of hardened leather, shoulder pieces of leather strips, a leather helmet, and half-leggings of leather. The ninth century saw the appearance of the byrnie, a leather jerkin inspired by the armies of the Eastern Roman Empire. The surface was layered with disks of horn and later of copper and iron. It allowed flexibility of movement while offering ample protection from sword cuts, spear thrusts, and even arrows (Martin 1967, 19). Into the twelfth century, only the knights and noblemen could afford the elaborate metal arms and armor which had evolved at that time, while the ordinary soldier continued to fight protected by a leather jerkin and leather helmet.

Records from the time of the Japanese Emperor Tenji (661–671) indicate that the earliest armor was constructed of leather. George Cameron Stone, in *A Glossary of the Construction, Decoration and Uses of Arms and Armor* (1961, 346), describes *kawara* (*kawa* meaning leather), a type of armor made of leather scales sewed on cloth. Hakuseki Arai, in *The Armor Book in Honcho Gunkiko* (1964, 17), states, "Ancient sheep-skin armor and cowhide armor [were] worn by the warriors of Ono-no-Ason-Uyu during the Konin era and given to his two sons, Mutsu-no-Kami-Harueda and Tsu-shimano-no-Kami-Harukaze, who fought in the Jogen era (976–97)."

The history of traditional African battle dress opens with descriptions of leather battle accoutrements. In the first century B.C., Greek geographer Strabo described the Berbers of North Africa using white leather shields. Herodotus, the Greek "Father of History," noted four hundred years earlier the North African shields made of "ostrich skin." In 1275 Ali al-Janahani al-Maghribi visited a town in the northwestern Sahara:

> There are artisans there who make arms such as lances and the *lambda* shields. These latter are made from the skin of an animal called the *lamt* which is to be found only there. It is white in color, like the gazelle, but of heavier build. Its skin is tanned in their country with milk and the shell of ostriches' eggs for a whole year. Iron makes absolutely no impression on it. If it is struck by swords the swords glance off. . . . Shields and cuirasses [front and back torso armor] are made from it worth 30 dinars apiece. (In Spring 1993, 29)

The Language of Armor

Throughout this book various terms relating to armor will be used. In Western Europe metal plate armor was commonplace by 1250, reaching its peak of popularity by the mid-fifteenth century. At that time a full suit of armor, the "white harness" as it was sometimes called, weighed about sixty pounds and was composed of myriad named pieces: the *aventail,* a curtain of mail covering the neck and shoulders; the *besagew,* a circular plate which hung over the wearer's armpit; the *bevor,* a metal piece to protect the lower face; the *charnel,* a hinge to connect the helmet to the breastplate; and the *cuisses,* protection for the thighs. Dozens of other terms described pieces protecting the elbows, kneecaps, feet, and hands.

In the Indian armoring repertoire, gorgets (armor for the throat) occurred in a variety of forms; helmets, both hard and soft, were widespread. There is some evidence of greaves, protection for the shin and calf. The cuirass was common. Leather jackets called arming doublets, which were worn underneath armor, appeared, as did leather bards, or horse armor. Breastplates, as the term suggests, covered the front of the upper body. Shields such as the pavise (a large rectangular shield used in siege warfare) and targets (small round shields) were ubiquitous. Cuisses (armoring for the thighs); cuir bouilli (hardened leather armor); gauntlets (protection for the hands); haute-piece (upstanding neck guard); jacks, jerkins, or doublets (jackets of leather); scale-armor (protection made of overlapping scales sewn to a cloth or leather garment); rod-armor (armor made of wooden dowels); slat-armor (armoring composed of numerous wooden slats sewn together); and the tasset (armor protection for the top of the thigh) were also found in North America.

Offensive/Defensive Spiral

The "offensive/defensive spiral" is constantly alluded to in the historical study of weapons of war: One side invents an effective offensive weapon; the opposing side creates a defense against it. The new defense is then trumped by a new offense, which is defeated by a new defense, and so on. The spiral is slowed only when one side can technologically place its offense and defense outside the technological response range of the opposing forces' offensive/defensive capabilities.

Leather armor in Europe was countered by advanced metalwork, swords and axes which could sunder and pierce leather. In the eighth century, coats of chain mail significantly defeated the cutting and piercing weapons of old. The blade makers advanced their technology to pierce mail. Iron plates responded to the new generation of mail-defeating cutting weapons. The crossbow countered the new plate armor, which increased in thickness and weight to overcome the bolts of the crossbow. The crossbow-defeating armor was then attacked by early firearms, which appeared in Europe at the beginning of the fourteenth century. In response, the defensive armor became even heavier. This advance was topped by advances in the evolution of muskets that could pierce armor plates. At this point offensive technology had outstripped defensive technology. Armor weighed sixty to eighty pounds and actually imperiled the wearer by rendering him slow and inflexible.

For a time armoring technology moved in two novel directions. Lighter armor continued to be designed specifically for the battlefield function of the soldier, and the light armor of the cavalry was modified for archers or cannoneers. Secondly, full "white harnesses," suits of armor which were militarily functionless but which were used by nobility both as a visible statement of wealth and status and for ceremonial events, were created.

In the late nineteenth century, soft armor was manufactured from silk for law enforcement agencies and the Secret Service. First explored by the medieval samurai of Japan, silk armor successfully protected against cutting blades and low-velocity bullets, but, of course, the next generation of handgun bullets pierced it. In the early 1900s, "bulletproof" vests were implemented by the FBI, but they proved cumbersome and ultimately useless against the increased power of criminal ordnance. World War II saw the invention of the "flak jacket," constructed of ballistic nylon. It protected against pistol and rifle fire but was impractical for use outside the military. The failure of hard armor in Europe before advances in gun ammunition was re-created in the United States; the technology could block the bullets but became too heavy to be useful.

A new technology had to be found to break the offensive/defensive deadlock. In the 1970s DuPont introduced Kevlar ballistic fabric, the choice for most law enforcement agencies today. But inevitably, the criminal use of high-capacity semi-automatic weapons and "cop killer" bullets is challenging the most modern ballistic fabric. The offensive/defensive spiral is inescapable.

Defeat of Indian Armor

The armor of the Indians withered before the same forces that defeated plate armor in Europe and at about the same time. If Native Americans had evolved metallurgy and the ability to manipulate iron and steel, the struggle with the European invaders would have been somewhat protracted; but, of course, the end result would have been the same because of the overwhelming population numbers and overall technological, political, and economic complexity of the European culture. When plate body armor confronts the gun, only one possibility results; at some point in the evolving relationship, the body armor will be pierced by the bullet.

Sir Walter Raleigh's Roanoke Island colony in the latter 1500s offers an example of the kinds of weaponry used to ultimately defeat Indians of the area. Indian offensive weapons included the wooden sword, club, bow and arrow, and stone knife. Defensively there was the scattered use of the rod-armor cuirass (wooden dowels sewn tightly together for protection of the upper front and back torso) and wicker, wooden, and leather shields.

The hundred or so military personnel at the Roanoke Island colony carried steel swords and daggers and wielded nine- to ten-foot pikes and halberds, long-shafted weapons that combined the spear and the axe. Neither longbow nor crossbow is mentioned directly, but oblique references allude to their presence. A seasoned bowman could fire six or seven arrows in less than a minute and exceed distances of 200 yards. The longbow could fire farther and more accurately than the firearms of the period.

More significantly, the Roanoke Island colony personnel possessed several kinds of firearms, including wheel-lock pistols. The arquebus was approximately sixteen gauge and was accurate up to 50 yards. The musket of the period weighed up to 20 pounds and usually required two men to operate. The colonists used a variety of small cannons that shot 4-, 5-, 7-, and 9-pound balls, as well as sharpened bolts, large buckshot, and chains.

The soldiers of the colony were armored, wore metal helmets, and carried targets, which were small, round shields. The Indians, after fighting against the metal armor of the colonists, concluded that it had no great value. John White left a metal corselet at the colony when he departed in 1587. When he returned three years later, he found the corselet disintegrating with rust. The Indians had not even bothered to pick it up.

Gonzalo Mendex de Canzo wrote to King Philip III in 1600 and argued for the wider use of *escupil* (quilted cotton armor):

> For war with the Indians no other armor except this is of any value. As for the coat of mail, the arrow could go through it and splinters of it would be very dangerous; the buffalo-leather coat designed to absorb sword-cuts is pierced very easily; and the corslet is very dangerous, moreover, if the arrow hits it will re bound and injure the next person. It is clear that the *escupil* is the best armor because the arrow is stopped by it and sticks. (In Evans 1997, 3)

Symbolic Armor

In almost all cases, when armor outlived its usefulness on the battlefield, it remained in a modified but predictable form: It became a symbol of male military and political power. The overelaboration of functionless "white harness" suits of armor in Europe by the sixteenth century has been noted above. The wearing of such armor signaled status and wealth.

The devolution of the gorget is tracked by Warren Moore (1967) in *Weapons of the Revolution*. Prior to the mid-eighteenth century, the gorget played an important part in defensive armor, but by the time of the American Revolution, though full body armor was rare, the gorget remained regulation for officers in the British army. From about 1702 to 1768, the British gorget was shaped like a wide crescent and hung from the neck by a ribbon. After 1768 it was fastened to the lapel or collar buttons. Moore concludes, "Generally speaking, the gorget was no more than a symbol of rank for officers of all the armies participating in the American Revolution. As such, it has lingered on through the years, and while officially abandoned by the British army in 1830, it is still worn by some armies today" (1967, 185).

Just as rulers in Europe would wear outmoded suits of full armor for ceremonial occasions, so, too, Asanti kings of eighteenth- and nineteenth-century Africa danced with a sword in the right hand and an *ekyem,* or battle shield, in the left when they ascended to the throne. Both weapons had been militarily obsolete for over a hundred years. Elaborate suits of armor were symbols of power and authority in Japan even after the entrenchment of firearms in that country's military. It will likewise be seen among the Indians that certain items which appeared in historic times as mere traditional costume adornment may well have been the last gasp of ancient armor in symbolic form.

Organization of Materials

The following material will be organized for convenience of presentation by culture area. The concept is based on the assumption (not always demonstrable) that certain ecological zones—desert, woodlands, coastal, etc.—seem to correlate with specific cultural types: High Plains tribes are bound to be buffalo hunters, riverine tribes are bound to include fishing in their subsistence repertoire, and so on. These "culture areas" are necessarily abstractions of the ethnologist; therefore, the precise boundaries of the areas vary with the expert. For example, A. L. Kroeber, when preparing to discuss the California Culture Area in *Cultural and Natural Areas of Native North America*, wrote:

> Otis T. Mason made his California area include Oregon. Wissler makes it coterminous with California, except for excluding the southeastern corner

of the state and including western Nevada. My classification gives southern California to the Southwest, the northwestern corner to the Northwest Coast, the northeastern, as just discussed, to the Great Basin, the eastern or trans-sierra fringe also to the Basin. (1939, 53)

Since the main thrust of this work is simply to identify and catalogue Indian defensive technology to create an informational base for later more elaborate and focused studies, my culture areas will be very broadly conceived: Southeast, Northeast, High Plains, Prairie, Northwest, Southwest, California, Basin/Plateau, and North Pacific. In addition, since the accounts of early defensive technology are rare, the conclusions drawn from them are always suspect because the sample is so small. Further, the descriptions that do exist are often vague. Some authors, for example, use the terms "rod" and "slat" interchangeably when speaking of wooden armor even though they are, in fact, two different forms of armoring. "Leather tunic" can mean many things, as can "rampart," "palisade," "bastion," "redoubt," and "stockade" when applied to fortifications.

**Native
North
American
Armor,
Shields,
and
Fortifications**

1 People of the Rivers
The Prairie Culture Area

The Prairie area is differentiated from the High Plains by lower elevation and a higher annual precipitation rate. A key diagnostic defining the western Prairie boundary is the tall, luxuriant bluestem grass which gradually replaces the much shorter grama "buffalo grass," the most common ground cover on the High Plains. The eastern boundary of the Prairie is the Mississippi River; the southern, the Gulf Coast; and the northern, the subarctic forests in Canada, where maize cultivation becomes impossible.

The Indians of this region were centered along the many rivers that run west to east from the Rocky Mountains to the Mississippi River. Their location allowed the Prairie Indians to combine bison hunting and horticulture. In the north the Mandan, Hidatsa, Arikara, and Ponca farmed and hunted along the Missouri River. The Omaha, Iowa, Oto, and Osage ranged through the prairie west of the Mississippi River, while the Pawnee moved west and east in their annual cycle along the Loup, Platte, and Republican Rivers in Nebraska. The Caddo and the Wichita occupied the area between the Red River and the Arkansas River.

Evidence of the earliest known occupation of the Prairie region is found in the Middle Missouri River region, where Clovis points were recovered in a context that dated them to about 10,000 B.C. About 1000 A.D. the Plains Woodland Tradition, stimulated by cultural influences from the Eastern Woodlands, appeared. Maize and beans became part of the subsistence repertory of the riverine people. Pottery was manufactured. Several hundred years later, some of the first evidence of village fortification appeared on the Prairie. The first European to contact Indians of the Prairie, the Spanish explorer Francisco Coronado, led an expedition from Santa Fe northeastward in search of a fabled lost city of gold between 1540 and 1542.

Offensive weaponry of the riverine peoples included the club, lance, knife, and bow. The bow and arrow was, as in most parts of North America, the preeminent weapon. Two accounts describe the power of the bows of the Texas Karankawa (in Newcomb 1978, 69):

He carried a bow as long as he was tall, with arrows of proportional length, with which he could kill game a hundred yards distance. I knew an instance of the terrible force of these arrows which is worthy of note. Aimed at a bear, three years old, that had taken refuge in the top of a tree, it went through the brute's body and was propelled forty or fifty yards beyond.

A second account describes the flight of an arrow shot by a Karankawa warrior across a river at an enemy:

. . . impelled nearly two hundred yards . . . driven to the feathers in the alluvial bank . . . every warrior's bow when strung was precisely as long as his person and as useless in the hands of a man of ordinary strength as was the bow of Ulysses in the hands of a suitor.

An observation concerning aboriginal use of bow and arrows and war clubs is made in the classic account of the Poncas' first encounter with mounted Comanche (Apaches?), whom they called Padouca:

The Padouca had bows made from elk horn. They were not very long, nor were they strong. . . . But the weapon the Padouca depended on in fighting was a stone battle-ax. Its long handle was a sapling bound with rawhide to which a grooved stone head, pointed at both ends, was bound by bands of rawhide. This weapon made them terrible fighters at close quarter. The weakness of their bows and arrows reduced the value of their horse in battle as a means to bring them rapidly up to their enemies, where they could bring their battle-axes into play. (Fletcher and La Flesche 1972, 79)

Fortifications

Archaeologists have found evidence dating between 800 and 1000 A.D. of the rise of the Plains Village Indian cultures (sometimes referred to as the Central Plains Tradition) along the major river valleys of the east-central Plains area. The Plains Village Indian cultures shared a number of general characteristics. The multifamily lodge typified housing, and all groups made use of round-bottomed pottery, bison-scapula hoes, stone arrowheads, and underground storage pits. Permanent settlements were often fortified with dry moats and stockades (Fagan 1991, 151).

At the same time, a slightly more sophisticated culture type was developing farther north in the Middle Missouri River region. These people were the ancestors of the historic Mandan. In the ninth and tenth centuries, the settlements on the Missouri were characterized by a mixed maize-based horticultural and bison-hunting subsistence and settlements with substantial fortifications consisting of deep, dry moats and stout timber palisades. By the 1300s the Indians of the Middle Missouri were building fortified villages on easily defensible sites along steep riverbanks or prominences with dry moats, stockades, and bastions. These defensive towers were situated on the corners and at intervals along walls and could extend 20 to 30 feet beyond the plane of the walls. In some cases these towers, or protruding structures, were raised on mounds of earth and debris. Bastions offered a clear line of sight along the outside of the walls, a crucial feature since a typical attack against a wooden palisade was to set fire to the base of the wall or to undermine it.

As a response to the movement of central Plains farmers northward into the Missouri region, fortified sites became in time even more formidable. Bastions were placed closer together, and moats grew to over 6 feet in depth and 10 to 12 feet in width. In some cases the walls and defense extended around a village for up to a mile or more (Caldwell 1964, 1). A number of sites from this time reveal that the first priority when a new settlement was in the process of being established was to construct the defensive perimeter, including ditch and palisade, after which construction of residential units would commence. The martial pressure was such that some sites show abandonment before any houses were completed or after only a few were partially completed. The relative absence of artifactual materials demonstrates that occupation was short-lived (Bamforth 1994, 105).

The Crow Creek site, located on the Missouri River in central South Dakota, reveals another example of a fortification of the time. The stronghold was constructed about 1325 A.D. and featured inner and outer palisades. The inner walls were fronted by a ditch 20 feet wide and 6 feet deep. The excavators found substantial refuse in the trench and evidence of houses built outside the trench. This suggests a period of peace when the palisades and ditch may have been of little significance. Later, however, a second palisade was erected to encompass the houses once outside the original palisade within the new wall. Twelve bastions were added to the outer stockade as well as a new defensive ditch 12 feet wide and 6 feet deep. The five houses excavated at the site, as well as sections of the palisade, had all been burned. Archaeologists found and excavated the remains of 486 people and stated that fifty or more skeletons remained in place.

A classic example of a fortified settlement of this period was found at the Huff site on the Missouri River south of Bismarck. It was occupied be-

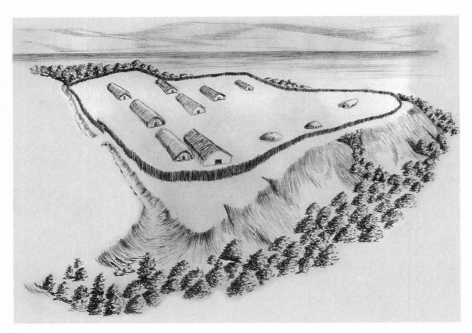

Artist's rendering of the Huff site. Middle-Missouri Tradition.

tween 1450 and 1550 A.D., and its builders were probably Mandan. Over a hundred houses nestled within a massive earthen embankment with palisades and ten bastions set along the corners and the sides (Wood 1967).

During this period smaller versions of the large fortified sites were found scattered through the Missouri River region. In some cases a few houses were surrounded by a simple stockade, one or two towers, a ditch, and a fortified gate. These constructions served more as temporary refuges in time of danger than as strongholds.

The first European to describe one of the forts of the Missouri River Indians was the French explorer Pierre Gautier de Varennes de la Verendrye, who, with an escort of Assiniboine Indians, visited a Mandan town, or "fort," as he called it, in the fall of 1738.

> I gave orders to count the cabins and we found that there were about one hundred and thirty. All the streets, squares and cabins were uniform in appearance; often our Frenchmen would lose their way in going about. They kept the streets and open places very clean; the ramparts are smooth and wide; the palisade is supported on cross pieces mortised into posts fifteen feet apart with a lining. For this purpose they use green hides fastened only

Artist's rendering of the Thompson site. Middle-Missouri Tradition.

at the top in places where they are needed. As to the bastions, there are four of them at each curtain wall flanked. The fort is built on an elevation in mid-prairie with a ditch over fifteen feet deep and from thirteen to eighteen feet wide. Their fort can only be gained by steps or posts which can be removed when threatened by an enemy. If all their forts are alike, they may be called impregnable to Indians. (In Caldwell 1964, 4)

He also noted that the fort was replete with caves, which were used for storage and shelter. Further, he commented on smaller forts built away from the riverbank. "We noticed that in the plain there were several small forts, of forty or fifty huts, built like the large ones, but no one was there at the time" (Bushnell 1922, 123).

La Verendrye's group traveled 130 miles upriver to another Mandan fort a month or so later.

The fort is on the bank of the river . . . the squares and streets are fine and clean; their palisade is in the best order and strength; the whole built in the same fashion as the one in which we were. From what they could hear, all their forts were alike; who saw one saw them all, with this difference, that some were much larger than others; that the last was the largest of all. (South Dakota State Department of History 1914, 179)

5

In the late eighteenth century, Hudson Bay trader David Thompson left an account of a Mandan fortified settlement:

> Except the upper village of the Fall Indians, they were all strongly stockaded with posts of wood of ten to twelve inches in diameter; about two feet in the ground and ten feet above it, with numerous holes to fire through; they went round the village, in some places close to the houses; there were two doorways to each of the stockades, on opposite sides; wide enough to admit a man on horseback. I saw no doors, or gates; they are shut up when required, with logs of wood. (Thompson 1916, 227)

The Arikara were neighbors, allies, and sometime enemies of the Mandan. Both groups occupied villages along the Middle Missouri River and followed similar lifestyles, combining horticulture, trade, fishing, and hunting and gathering. The Arikara, however, spoke a Caddoan language, while the Mandan were Siouan speakers.

One of the first accounts of an Arikara fort was recorded by French trader Jean Baptiste Trudeau, working out of St. Louis, who entered an Arikara village in 1795. The traders were told that the Sioux were sending five hundred warriors against them. The Arikara prepared to defend their settlement as the French observed and chronicled the scene:

> The Ricaras have fortified their village by placing palisades five feet high which they have reinforced with earth. The fort is constructed in the following manner: All around their village they drive into the ground heavy forked stakes, standing from four to five feet high and from fifteen to twenty feet apart. Upon these are placed cross-pieces as thick as one's thigh; next they place poles of willow or cottonwood, as thick as one's leg, resting on cross-pieces and very close together. Against the poles which are five feet high they pile fascines of brush which they cover with an embankment of earth two feet thick; in this way, the height of the poles would prevent the scaling of the fort by the enemy, while the well-packed earth protects those within from their balls and arrows. (Bushnell 1922, 171)

David Bushnell, in *Villages of the Algonquian, Siouan, and Caddoan Tribes West of the Mississippi* (1922, 171), wrote, "Undoubtedly many embankments found east of the Mississippi owe their origin to this method of protecting the villages which they once surrounded."

Another early description of an Arikara fort was offered by the French trader Charles Le Raye in 1802:

The *Ricaras* or *Rus* have three villages situated on the south bank of the Missouri, in the great bend of the river. . . . The town is picketed with pickets twelve feet high and set very close, to prevent firing between them. There is one gate way which is shut at night. (Bushnell 1922, 168)

A month later Le Raye moved to another Arikara village. "This village is situated on an island in the Missouri, and is fortified in the same manner as the lower village, containing about sixty huts" (Bushnell 1922, 168).

The reason that a Stone Age people would need to construct massive strongholds complete with moats, embankments, palisades, and bastions is suggested by the level and intensity of warfare on the Plains during the late prehistoric and early historic periods. An account in Reuben Thwaites' *Jesuit Relations* (in Bamforth 1994, 100) noted an attack on a Mandan fort in 1779 by two thousand Lakota and Arikara warriors.

The necessity of keeping the enemy out of one's village is suggested by what happened when the attackers managed to breach the stronghold. The Larson site on the Missouri River, an Arikara village that was occupied between 1750 and 1785, offers ample evidence. The village was fortified with two ditches backed by palisades which surrounded a town of twenty-nine earthlodges. The archaeologists conclude that when the walls of the Arikara stronghold were overrun, the villagers retreated into their earthlodges to continue the fight. Three such houses were excavated, and the findings reveal the savage violence of northern Plains warfare in the late 1700s. Bodies found in the three houses ranged in age from four years to fifty, at the time of death, and included males and females. Bamforth commented on the findings:

> None of the skeletons is complete, for two reasons. The first, indicated by obvious cut and blow marks on the bones, is that the victorious attackers of the town systematically mutilated the bodies of their victims, with these mutilations including scalping, decapitation, crushing of the skull and face, removal of hands and feet, and disembowelment. Mutilations were carried out without regard to sex or age. (1994, 101)

The French trader Tabeau (Abel 1939, 204), who traded on the Missouri River in the eighteenth century, alluded to Arikara women digging defensive embankments and expressed mock surprise that when an attack was impending, the men would help: "What cannot panic terror do!" Women also dug the defensive embankments found around many Pawnee villages. This role of women is not too surprising because of the almost uni-

7

versal role of women as farmers among North American peoples. With their stone and buffalo-scapula shovels and hoes, they had more experience at digging and earth moving than men. The relationship between the roles of Plains women as horticulturalists and defense builders is found among the Omaha. Fletcher and La Flesche wrote in *The Omaha Tribe* (1972, 45) that when an attack against a village was impending, "The women threw up breastworks with their plant hoes, the word for 'breastwork' later was applied to fences of all kinds."

The Pawnee and their sometime allies the Omaha routinely strengthened their villages militarily in late-prehistoric and early-historic times. Lowie (1954, 29) wrote that the Omaha fortified their permanent earthlodge villages. The Pawnee, though they did not erect the impressive palisaded forts that were found on the Middle Missouri, did excavate defensive ditches that were 3 feet deep and 5 feet wide around their permanent settlements. The Oto, farmers and hunters who lived south of the Omaha, fortified their villages with a deep ditch that fronted palisades about 9 feet high (Bushnell 1922, 172).

In the mid-1700s, a Spanish expedition confronted a fort of the Wichita Indians in north-central Texas along the Red River. Colonel don Diego Ortiz Parrilla wrote:

> We clearly discerned a town of tall, oval shaped huts encircled by a stockade and a ditch. Its entrance road was enclosed in the same manner and in addition it zig-zagged intricately, with its gate at the aforementioned river, whose waters flowed by with a depth of more than a yard and a third. Crowding the front of the stockade were Indians armed with muskets. (Bell et al. 1974, 323)

Six years later, Fray Joseph de Calahorra y Sanz described the Wichita fort in a letter to the territorial governor:

> In the middle of this settlement is the fortress they built to resist Colonel don Diego Ortiz Parrilla's campaign. It is made of split logs, which the Indians have placed separate one from the other in order to make use of muskets, the weapons they use, through them. . . . said fortress is completely surrounded on the outside by an earthen rampart, close to more than a vara [1⅓ meter] and a third in height, which serves them as an entrenchment, and, about four paces to the east and west, a very deep trench made so that no one can come close to the fortress on horseback. Inside there are four subterranean apartments occupying all of its circumference, into which all

the people who cannot help with defense of the said settlement retreat in time of invasion. (Bell et al. 1974, 324)

A similar Wichita stronghold was reported on the Sabine River in 1760. Wichita fortress building seems to have been inaugurated in the mid-1700s when the tribe came under increasing pressure from Spanish and Indian enemies. Several other Texas Indian groups constructed small-scale fortifications. The Waco built an earthen embankment several feet high around one of their villages near present-day Waco, Texas, and evidence exists that the Tonkawa of south Texas built stone breastworks for defense. Álvar Núñez Cabeza de Vaca, who was second in command of the Narvaez Expedition, was shipwrecked and stranded in the area of present-day Galveston in 1528. He left a description of the defensive works of the Coahuiltecan Yguazes, a people with whom he lived for a while. He noted that to avoid attacks, they placed their huts in a dense thicket, around which they dug a trench. If in more open country, they dug their defensive ditch and placed brush in front of it to screen themselves as they shot their arrows (Newcomb 1978, 47).

Robert Lowie (1954, 106) described a defensive structure built by the Omaha upon learning that an attack from a combined Dakota and Ponca force was expected. They surrounded the village with a 4-foot-high embankment, on top of which they interlaced their tipi poles. Over that basic breastwork they threw their buffalo-hide tipi covers, in which they cut loopholes. Finally, they dug deep trenches within their makeshift fort to protect the women and children.

The concept of "barbed wire" defenses was utilized by the Tawakonis of Texas when they were attacked by a Cherokee raiding party in the early 1800s. Some of the Tawakonis moved into a thick briar patch to continue their fight. When that refuge failed, they repaired into the "great lodge" of the village, a semisubterranean earthlodge. The Cherokee raiders were unable to root them from their final sanctuary and withdrew (Hoig 1993, 128). Briars were also used by Southeastern Indians to close up the entrances to rapidly constructed palisades.

Shields

David Thompson (1916, 228) related that the Mandan "had shields of bull's hide, a safe defense against arrows and the spear, but of no use against balls." The artist George Catlin (in Paterek 1994, 123) described the shield of the Mandan chief Mah-To-To-Pah as formed from the hide of

9

a bison's neck, hardened with glue made from bison hooves, covered with a polecat's skin, and fringed with rows of eagle feathers and antelope hooves.

On the southeastern Plains, a very early Caddo reference (1714) described their going to war on horseback with a "little shield of buffalo hide, on the left arm, with which they parry arrows" (in Swanton 1942, 188). The Osage, living north of the Caddo, carried circular buffalo hide shields during the early years when they contended with the Spanish and their Indian allies.

The Osage manner of making the circular Plains shield is novel. They shaped it from the neck skin of the bison, which they stretched on a framework of green hickory. Finally the skin was sewn to the framework with buffalo sinew, the unique preparation of which added a magical element. The sinew from the left side of the bison bull's spinal column (Tzi-Sho) was entwined with that from the right side (Hunkah), the rationale being that a thick thread formed in this manner would be very strong because of the blending of the Hunkah and the Tzi-Sho energy (Mathews 1961, 162).

Early references to Wichita shields are sketchy. One account simply stated that for defense they used "the leather shield" (Bell et al. 1974, 352), while another noted that a Taovaya (tribe of the Wichita confederacy) chief carried a "shield of white buckskin" (Hoig 1993, 67).

One of the earliest accounts of tribal warfare on the Plains came in 1601 from Governor-General Don Juan de Onate, the leader of a Spanish expedition. The battle took shape in present-day southern Kansas between the Escanjaques and the Rayados. The exact identity of these groups is unknown; however, it is assumed that the Rayados were the historic Wichita and the Escanjaques, perhaps, the historic Osage. At any rate, de Onate chronicled the Escanjaques as armed with stone-headed war clubs, bows and arrows, and large leather shields. The shields apparently were proof against arrows, but at one point the Spanish opened fire with their arquebuses when a large force of Escanjaque surrounded them, and the bullets easily penetrated them.

A Ponca tradition tells of an encounter between the Padouca and themselves when the Ponca were buffalo hunting in the west-central Plains. The exact identity of the Padouca is problematic, but they were, no doubt, either Apache or Comanche. The Ponca said the Padouca protected themselves with long shields of rawhide (Fletcher and La Flesche 1972, 79).

Armor

The Pawnee made armor from a double thickness of elk hide with sand quilted between the layers. The Ponca tradition includes a Padouca attack during which some of the Padouca warriors wore breastplates of rawhide to which sand was glued (Fletcher and La Flesche 1972, 79).

Southeast of the Ponca, the Iowa protected their heads with turbans and their chests and backs with a sheet of heavy leather (Paterek 1994, 115). The turban is also associated with the warriors of the Ponca (Howard 1995, 137).

A Spanish account from 1759 describes a Taovaya war chief with a leather breastplate, carrying a shield of white buckskin and wearing a helmet of white buckskin plumed with red horsehair (Hoig 1993, 67). It is more likely that the helmet was, in fact, a heavy cap of buffalo hide. Fray Juan Agustin Morfi (1935, 84), in his *History of Texas: 1673–1779,* wrote of the Taovayas, "They carry shields, jackets, and caps made of leather, adorning the last of these with feathers and buffalo horns to resemble a helmet." He later added that the above was true for all the tribes of Texas. Newcomb (1978, 140) cited for the Tonkawa of southeast Texas the use in battle of bison-hide jackets and helmets.

Henri de Tonti, the chief chronicler of the expedition of Rene Robert de La Salle (in Cox 1922, 77), stated, "They [Caddo] make pointed saddles, wooden stirrups, and body-coverings of several skins one over the other, as a protection from arrows." The account continued, "They arm the breast of their horses with the same material, a proof that they are not very far from the Spaniards." Not only was soft body armor for mounted or pedestrian Plains warriors common for a brief period in Plains history, but likewise, horse armor was also widespread, diffusing with generalized Spanish equestrian culture. The Wichita also used bison-hide horse armor (Pritzker 1998, 2:515).

Discussion and Summary

The building of large-scale fortifications, "strongholds" complete with palisades, dry moats, defensive ditches, bastions, and in some cases interior caves (which may have been food caches) and apartments appeared full blown on the Prairie among riverine horticulturalist/hunters, who culturally affiliated with groups east of the Mississippi or within the Southeastern and Northeastern Culture Areas.

Turbans, widely used in the Southeastern Culture Area, were also found on the Plains. Generally, wherever turbans are found in the world, they relate to a context of equestrian warfare with swords. The turban is soft armor against sword and club strikes to the head. A turban of red-fox skin with an erect eagle feather in the back signified the Ponca warrior (Howard 1995, 137). Today among contemporary Indians, a dance costume may include leather and fur caps, particularly for warrior society dancers.

Even during the times of traditional warfare, the Osage wore what Mathews (1961, 162) refers to as a "fetish shield," a functionless, symbolic martial accoutrement, whose power resided in its sacred nature rather than in its ability to physically protect the fighter. Worn on the chest, it was light and relatively small so as not to interfere with the function of the real shield. The "fetish shield" was circular, cut from bison hide, and dyed bright red—the "round" and "red" symbolizing Grandfather Sun, the Supreme Being.

Warrior societies (voluntary associations of men with shared military experience, which might be seen as a combination of the National Guard, the Veterans of Foreign Wars, and the Kiwanis Club) prevailed among the Prairie tribes. However, a survey of the military societies of the Mandan, Hidatsa (Lowie 1913b), Ponca (Skinner 1915b), and Arikara (Lowie 1915) reveals scant evidence of symbolic or real armor in the costuming traditionally worn in the dances and rituals that functioned as the major expression of a particular warrior society's spirit and identity.

For example, the ritual costume of the Arikara Taro'xpa military organization included owl and eagle feathers worn in the hair, which was cut in the shape of a half-moon on each side; shell breast ornaments; and a white muslin shirt with red flannel around the sleeves, shoulder, and lower border. Two members carried lances, which were wrapped in red cloth and decorated with swan, owl, and crow feathers (Lowie 1915, 665). Iowa Mawatani society members wore buffalo robes, which were cut at the top into fringes. Amidst the fringes were tied otter skin streamers, which were decorated with beads and red feathers at the ends. The members shaved half of their head and let the hair on the other half grow long. In addition they wore hawk and owl feathers with one red eagle plume attached to the top of their head. In rituals and battles they painted their bodies in yellow and blue (Skinner 1915b, 699).

The theme of "death seeking" permeates the ritual behavior of the elite Prairie warriors in battle, as well as in their ritual actions and songs. An Arikara Taro'xpa leader in the heat of battle would plant his lance in the ground and not retreat unless another member withdrew it, thereby releasing him (Lowie 1915, 665). In battle the Ponca "Not-Afraid-To-Die" Society leaders, like the Arikara society leaders, stuck their lances in the ground and fought beside them. They were not supposed to flee. When they were inducted into the "Not-Afraid-To-Die" and had earned the right to be a lance bearer, they were told that they were expected to die in battle (Skinner 1915b, 787).

The apparent lack of regard for personal safety among the Prairie warriors is reflected in the war songs characteristic of the various warrior societies. The Stone Hammers of the Mandan, for example, sang, "I am on earth just for a little while. When there is a fight, I must die" (Lowie 1913b, 248). When a Hidatsa Little Dog member was offered the sash (a strip of buckskin which attached to the neck and trailed on the ground and through which the warrior would plant his lance to pin himself to one spot), he would momentarily refrain, then would hold out his hands and say, "I want to die. I will keep it" (Lowie 1913b, 267). The Raven society of the Hidatsa sang, "Ravens, you are afraid to die. You will not die. I am the one that wishes to die" and "No matter how many will die, let them die" (Lowie 1913b, 277).

Death-inviting behavior, characteristic of military elites on the Prairie, and ceremonial songs that stress the willingness, even the desire, to die in battle do not seem to "fit" with armor wearing and the creation of elaborate fortifications. It may be that the military organizations described by Robert Lowie represent a fairly recent innovation on the Prairie. There appears to be a relationship between the absence of armor and the existence of institutions which stress the facing of great danger in battle as desirable.

Standing Fights and Poison Arrows
The California Culture Area

2

The California Culture Area is not congruent with the present-day boundaries of California. Two-thirds of the state, mainly in the west, comprises the area bounded on the west by the Pacific coast and on the east by the Basin/Plateau and Southwest Culture Areas. Subareas on northern and southern boundaries show heavy influence from the Northwest Coast Culture Area in the former case and the Southwest Culture Area in the latter. Central California is believed to have the most distinctively "Californian" cultures. Major representative tribes include the Shasta, Karok, Achumawi, Atsugewi, Maidu, Konkow, Pomo, Wappo, Nisenan, Wintu, Patwin, Nomlaki, Yurok, Hupa, Nongatl, Wiyot, Sinkyone, Kato, Mattole, Yana, and Yuki in the northern third of the area; the Chumash, Yokuts, Mono, Miwok, Tubatulabal, Kitanemuk, Tataviam, Esselen, Salinan, and Costanoan in the central regions; and the Gabrielino, Serrano, Luiseno, Ipai, Tipai, Cupeno, and Cahuilla in the south.

A unique aspect of the California Culture Area is the tight grouping of many tribes in the northern third of the area. The population density for native northern California was 75.0 persons per 100 square kilometers. For the central region, the density was 39.0 persons per 100 square kilometers, while on the Plains it only reached 3.8 persons per 100 square kilometers (Kroeber 1939, pocket maps). Another way to appreciate the crowded nature of aboriginal northern California is to note that the range loosely defended by the Cheyenne and Arapaho of the Plains was about equal to the territory occupied by the Karok, Tolowa, Yurok, Hupa, Wiyot, Nongatl, Mattole, Whilikut, Lassik, Kato, and Wailaki of California. It is no wonder that sensitivity to trespassing and the necessity of boundary defense loomed so large in the martial awareness of the people.

Indians have populated the area for at least 10,000 years. Evidence of the Folsom complex, dating from 8,000 to 10,000 years ago, was found in the vicinity of Borax Lake and Lake Mohave. Dating to about 4,000 years ago, evidence suggesting warfare appears. Archaeologist Richard Beardsley wrote:

Use of the hand spear or casting lance is strongly indicated for Middle Horizon (ca. 4,000 years ago) patterns of warfare, as well as for hunting, by the numerous blades or large points embedded in crania or body skeletons of burials, and many more in presumably lethal position within the body cavity. Although burials without skulls, as evidence of head taking, occur in the Early and Late Horizon as well as in the Middle Horizon, the high percentage of indisputably violent deaths indicated by embedded projectile points seems distinct of the Middle Horizon at present accounting. (In Heizer and Whipple 1967, 158)

The acorn was the staple food of most of the California area, and the leaching of tannic acid allowed the use of acorn flour, which would otherwise be inedible. In the north salmon also played a major subsistence role. A wide variety of other foods could be obtained throughout California. The Nomlaki, for example, gathered seeds and tubers and hunted deer, elk, and rabbits. Coastal peoples like the Wiyot focused on salmon, deer, sea mammals, and shellfish. The Patwin of northwestern California fished and hunted deer, elk, antelope, bear, waterfowl, and turtles, as well as gathering seeds and acorns.

California tribes were loosely organized. Leaders were usually wealthy men who utilized their prestige to "suggest" direction to the people. More importantly, kinship awareness and mutual obligation determined what behavior would be followed. Chiefs facilitated village cohesion and arranged settlements that would bring a formal end to warfare. Warfare practices, as is the case everywhere, followed from the nature of sociopolitical organization. Fighting groups formed from small groups of kinsmen, and chiefs rarely became war leaders. Further, since the population of individual California tribes was relatively small, fighting groups were likewise small. Only on very rare occasions would village-wide military participation occur, and massing at the tribal level for battle took place even more infrequently.

Offensive weapons included, first and foremost, the bow and arrow. However, diverse opinions exist concerning the efficiency of those of the California area. In the accounts of Sir Francis Drake, who contacted the Coast Miwok and Pomo in 1579, Francis Fletcher, chaplain of the Drake expedition, observed that "their bows and arrows (their only weapons and almost all of their wealth) they use skillful, but yet not to do any great harm with them, being by the reason of their weakness, more fit for children than for men, sending the arrow neither far off, nor with any great force" (Heizer 1970, 108). On the other hand, P. H. Ray wrote of the bows and arrows of the Hupa, "The bows made by these people are effective for game up to fifty or seventy-five yards, and would inflict a serious wound at one hundred yards. After fifty yards the arrows will penetrate a deer from five to ten inches" (1886, 833).

However, an additional factor concerning the martial effectiveness of the California bowmen must be considered. Many of them used poisoned arrows. With such arrows, deep body penetration was unnecessary; merely breaking the enemy's skin was often sufficient. Arrow poisoning was reported among the Hupa, Maidu, Nisenan, Konkow, Gabrielino, Achumawi, Atsugewi, Shasta, Nomlaki, Patwin, Wintu, and Kato. Some groups, like the Gabrielino, designed extra-heavy bows especially for war, and the Tubatulabal shaped 36" arrows for use in fighting.

Thrusting spears, stone knives, daggers, sticks, rocks, and clubs were also wielded in battle. In addition, the Nomlaki used harpoons and a knobbed mahogany throwing stick. The Mono and Wintu fought with the sling, although most California tribes considered it little more than a toy. (In ancient times Greek slingers could pierce armor with a lead ball at over 100 feet.)

A variety of conditions stimulated the California Indians to organized violence. Murder of a kinsman naturally demanded vengeance, which was usually carried out by affected kin and their supporters in an ambush or surprise attack on an individual or small group. The belief that one group was directing sorcery at another could trigger violence, as could insult, rape, kidnapping, and arguments over women. However, the most formal types of warfare were generally elicited over issues of poaching or trespassing. The California Indians were unusually sensitive to tribal territory incursions. Every child was drilled in recognizing the particular boulder or stream that marked the boundaries of his or her people's territory. To cross the boundary invited death.

The standing-line fight, the epitome of California organized fighting, was hemmed in by many universally understood rules of engagement that were generally adhered to regardless of who was fighting whom. The six-month "war" between the Kato and the Yuki over an obsidian digging site exemplifies a formal martial engagement. The Kato attempted to mine the site, which the Yuki considered their territory. When the Yuki killed and beheaded a young Kato woman, the Kato chief amassed fighting men from neighboring villages. After agreeing that they wished a battle, they sent messengers to the Yuki inviting them to fight. It was agreed that the first to arrive at the fighting ground would set a fire so that the smoke would alert the opposing side that it was time to begin.

On the appointed day, several hundred warriors advanced in lines to within about 50 yards and loosed arrows at one another. Many observers waited on the sidelines, and when a fighter became exhausted, one of them would take his place. The chiefs of each group conferred and tallied the wounded and killed. After a few hours, the Yuki chief reported that his side had lost six, and the Kato chief counted four of his men dead or wounded. The chiefs walked between the battle lines, ordered their men to stop shooting, and announced that they would resume fighting in ten days.

The two sides met once more and fired at each other until three Kato and two Yuki had been hit, at which time the chiefs halted the fighting and announced that in ten days they would meet at another fighting ground. When the third formal battle produced five casualties, the chiefs once more stopped the fighting and agreed to end the war. One more action, however, was required before the two sides could return to their peaceful lives: Compensation was required. In any form of violence against another group, all destroyed or captured property or persons had to be returned or paid for. This custom created a dichotomous situation in which the military winners often became the economic losers.

During the negotiations over compensation, the men remained armed and from time to time danced threateningly and brandished weapons if the negotiations failed to go their way. When, however, payments were deemed acceptable to all parties, the men broke their weapons, threw them to the ground, and disarmed, then returned to their homes.

Hand-to-hand combat was not desired in California warfare, and formal battles ideally played out as the Kato-Yuki fight. Sometimes, however, one side would suddenly sweep forward and attempt to exterminate the other. In other cases, the formality of the engagement was even more stringent. Among the Chumash, for example, an arranged battle would find the enemies lined up facing each other in the typical manner. One man would step forward and fire a handful of arrows at the opposing side, who would attempt to dodge them. Then a man from the "attacked" side would return the same number of arrows (Grant 1978, 513).

Generally speaking, casualties were very light in California wars; however, this was not always the case. In 1769 the Spanish explorer Portola saw three burned Coastal Chumash villages. The Indians told him that "mountain Indians" had three months earlier attacked the villages, killing every man, woman, and child. From the Interior Chumash, Grant (1978, 534) recounts a vengeance raid of the Tejon against an Interior Chumash village that housed the killer of a Tejon woman. Four hundred Tejon warriors appeared and killed seventy villagers. Such cases were the exception.

Fortifications

As might be expected from the foregoing discussion of California Indian hunting and gathering culture, the relatively low level of complexity in sociopolitical organization, and concepts of warfare that tended to mitigate high casualty figures, massive fortifications as were seen particularly in the Prairie riverine area were unknown among the Californians. The sporadic and small-scale fighting did not warrant the time and energy needed to build something along the lines of the classic forts of the late prehistoric Mandan, for example. Nevertheless, some rare, scattered descriptions of fortification building in the California area can be found.

The Apwaruge, a subgroup of the Atsugewi of northeastern California, built several stone forts. One had a steep bluff on one side and enclosed a number of interconnected round enclosures 8 to 10 feet in diameter. Within the forts, trenches protected noncombatants. Significantly, the Apwaruge were horseless and were often attacked by mounted Paiutes, Modocs, and Klamath slave raiders. As on the Plains, fort building allowed a nonequestrian people to defend against mounted attackers.

Under the leadership of Estanislao, the Miwok were forced in 1829 to defend against the attacks of Spanish soldiers under Captains Sanchez and Vallejo. S. F. Cook wrote:

> Estanislao fortified a hill with brush breastworks and, if the word "fossas" can be so interpreted, an actual system of trenches. Against these defenses Sanchez failed completely, and Vallejo, even with a cannon, was not able to penetrate them until he resorted to a flank attack and covered his front by setting the chaparral on fire. (1943, 33)

In August 1841 the Wilkes Expedition, led by Dr. Charles Pickering, encountered a Nomlaki village in northern California, and one of the travelers offered a description of the settlement. "Perhaps the most striking statement was that 'the whole village was surrounded by a brush fence, which served for a stockade.' This is the only evidence of such a practice" (Goldschmidt 1951, 305).

Almost all northern California villages possessed a very serviceable refuge, the earthlodge, that would provide quick protection against the small-scale surprise raids typical of the area. Most of these semisubterranean earthlodges were covered with thick layers of dirt, which prevented easy burning, and many had entrances that would definitely slow down raiders. To enter a large Karok earthlodge, for example, one had to crawl through a low, narrow door and descend a plank ladder to reach the floor (Bright 1990, 183). The Lake Miwok constructed a *lamma*, a large earthlodge used for tribal ceremonies. Dirt-covered, it had a narrow tunnel entrance (Callaghan 1990, 270). The Shasta built an "assembly house" earthlodge that was 20 to 27 feet in diameter, dirt-covered, and excavated 6 to 7 feet into the ground. Such structures are reported for the Patwin, Maidu, Konkow, and Wintu.

Shields

The California tribes evinced little interest in shields, and the ones that did exist never attained the mystical and artistic importance of those found on the High Plains or in the Southwest. The California ethnological literature reveals that the Hupa, Karok, Patwin, Shasta, Wintu, Yurok, Pomo, Maidu, Konkow, Mattole, Nongatl, Sinkyone, and Lassik rarely, if ever, used them.

The Wiyot made large, rectangular, elk-hide shields (Elsasser 1990, 160). The Wailaki also used elk-hide rawhide shields (Elsasser 1990, 198), and Olmsted and Stewart (1990, 228) note them among the Achumawi. The Diegueno of southern California occasionally carried a round shield constructed from an unornamented piece of rawhide, which was similar to those carried by the Mohave and Yuma, who ranged southwest of the Diegueno (Heizer and Whipple 1967, 40). Shields were used in formal battles by the Monterey Bay Costanoans (Tello 1967, 218).

The above-mentioned shields, with the exception of the Yuman-influenced Diegueno example in southern California, stem from the northern third of California. Kroeber observed for the rest of the state, "The greater part of central California appears to have been armorless and shieldless" (1967, 41).

Armor

Though fortifications and shields achieved little prominence in California warfare, soft and hard armor was highly visible, especially among the tribes of the northern third of the area. Various writers describe the use of rod-armor and elk-hide armor; however, when those terms are used without qualification, as they often are, it is difficult to know exactly what form the armor took. The previous discussion of the rawhide armor of the Plains revealed that such armor was wrought in a variety of forms—jackets, shirts, vests, tunics, robes, and scaled cuirasses that were multilayered or quilted with hair side out or in or with the hair removed. Though many California armor citations do not go far enough, fortunately others offer comment on unique aspects of a local armor that allows us to perceive the many variations that occurred. Most of the references to elk hide indicate a heavy coat, perhaps composed of several layers, which hung loosely from the neck to below the knees. Nonetheless, some exceptions existed.

Both elk-hide and rod-armor were found among the Patwin (Johnson 1990, 350), while Garth (1990, 238) simply stated that the Atsugewi possessed hide armor. Elk-hide armor was employed by the Nongatl, Sinkyone, Lassik, and Wailaki, though only the Wailaki used both armor and heavy shields (Elsasser 1990, 198). Bright (1990, 183) acknowledged rod-armor and elk-hide armor for the Karok, as did Lapena (1990, 329) for the Wintu. The Karok also wore basketry hats to protect the head in battle (Bright 1990, 184).

A Smithsonian Institution photo taken in 1900 shows a Pomo man in rod-armor, an upper-torso cuirass formed of dowels of willow and hazel shoots closely twined together. The corselet had two layers. Within the inner layer the rods were sewn in tight horizontal layers, looking exactly like the hair-bone breastplates of the historic Plains Indians. On the outer layer, the rods were bound together vertically.

The Gabrielino, who lived in the location of present-day Los Angeles, slightly varied the rod-armor model. Instead of wooden dowels, they used reeds (Bean 1990, 546).

The Shasta armor seemed to combine both shield and soft-armor concepts:

> Both stick and elkhide armor were used. The latter seems to have been a combination shield and semi-armor. It consisted of a whole elkhide, the head part at the top. It was tied at the neck, with the tough part of the hide around the neck and shoulders, and protected the left side, leaving the right arm free. When wet, the hide was shaped over a very large platter basket. Two cords were crossed at right angles inside the round part. Thus formed, the left arm was slipped through these cords and the hide was manipulated for the protection of the wearer. A band of elkhide, painted, was worn around the head. (Kroeber 1976, 313)

Shasta rod-armor. Northern California.

Other sources indicate that the Shasta sometimes used bear hide instead of elk (Paterek 1994, 275) and employed split branches instead of dowels in their "stick" armor (Silver 1990, 218).

The Yurok wore the two basic forms of armor found in the area, plus slat-armor, and added layers of elk hide in their soft tunics (Paterek 1994, 288). They made elk-hide armor in the shape of jackets (Palmer 1929, 191). The Achumawi were highly protected compared to most of the fighters in their area. They used not only elk-hide armor and elk-hide shields but also wore thick caps of antelope rawhide (Olmsted and Stewart 1990, 228).

The Nomlaki's elk-hide armor reached from neck to ankles. Some accounts imply that they left the hair on and turned the hair side inward.

Hupa elk-skin armor. Northern California.

This armor was considered "dangerous" by the Yurok; that is, it was handled as a sacred object (Malinowski and Sheets 1998, 138).

The Hupa wore helmets of elk rawhide. Prior to battle they pinned their hair atop their heads to prevent an enemy from grabbing it and to offer cushioning against blows. On occasion a headband of rolled deerskin stuffed with grass added protection. They used rod-armor cuirasses, and they sometimes donned long, sleeveless elk-hide shirts of single or double thickness with fine gravel or sand glued to the surface with pitch for increased protection (Wallace 1949, 5).

The Wiyot combined large rectangular elk-hide shields with elk-hide armor for combat (Elsasser 1990, 160). The Northern Maidu wore elk-hide armor that reached from neck to knees. They also fashioned rod-armor from mountain mahogany as a cuirass, with a high collar that enabled the warrior to withdraw his head entirely from an approaching wave of arrows (Dixon 1905, 205). The shields of the Wailaki, noted above, mainly defended against multiple arrow attacks. They arranged the shields on their backs to free their hands for fighting. When a flight of arrows came, they simply turned their backs.

Concerning the rod- and elk-hide armor of California, Kroeber offers this final comment: "that . . . the two armor types are associated, not alternative; and that, confined to the northernmost portion of the state, they are to be understood as the marginal outpost of the extension of an idea that probably originated in the eastern hemisphere and for America centers in the culture of the North Pacific coast" (1976, 39).

Discussion and Summary

North American ethnology conventionally points to the high cultural developments on the Northwest Coast (Kwakiutl, Haida, Tlingit) as a center of the diffusion of armor technology to northern California. There is, of course, some truth in this. The Northwest Coast fascination with wealth is found also in northern California, in contrast to the rest of the area; likewise, the elaborate woodworking of the Northwest Coast is reflected in northern California and contrasts with the central and southern parts of the state. Still, the defensive technology of northern California is different in form, if not in spirit, from that of the Northwest Coast. The classical Northwest Coast warrior wore heavy, intricately carved wooden helmets, whereas the Californians seldom wore helmets, and when they did, they built them from rawhide or basketry. There is little rod-armor, so common in northern California, in the Northwest Coast area, a place where slat-armor is the norm.

The relative lack of armoring in central California is puzzling, for bellicosity was certainly present. Among the Tubatulabal, a number of bands would join together in miniwars that would last for days. The Chumash, as noted previously, experienced warfare that decimated entire villages. The Luiseno were considered dangerous and warlike by their neighbors and even possessed an initiated warrior class. The Cahuilla likewise had warrior *nets,* or chiefs.

The California material offers a hint as to armor usage that also suggests its relative rarity, that is, why it was not used by every fighter, even where it did exist. One should remember, however, the existence of cases (e.g., the early Plains Apaches) where descriptions depict all warriors as armored. Similarly, accounts from the Northwest Coast support universal usage, at least in some battles. But that is apparently not typical in most of native North America.

Garth's (1990, 238) account of Atsugewi warfare suggests a connection with a type of battlefield organization found among the Aztec. In that great civilization, cadets were often inserted into battle lines for hands-on experience in their formal education as warriors-to-be. To steady them in a fight and to offer guidance and protection, seasoned warriors would stand in the line between every ten or so young men and at the ends of the line. The Aztec king rarely if ever fought. In Atsugewi fighting, "good warriors," wearing elk-hide armor, were placed at intervals along the battle line and at the ends, and the Atsugewi chiefs never joined in the battle. Among the Sinkyone only those men designated as "war leaders" wore armor. Malinowski and Sheets (1998, 138) noted that "Armor was worn by some select individuals," and Paterek (1994, 248) states that among the Athabascans of northern California "important warriors had the protection of a slat- and rod-corselet." Warrior ranking was acknowledged by the Hupa (Hough 1895, 230). When describing a sample of Hupa armor, Hough pointed out that on the armor face were painted red lines, indicating the number of enemies slain or captives taken, and insignia of rank.

The Aztec/Atsugewi comparison could offer a glimpse into line fighting as it might have existed in California generations before contact, while at the same time explaining why early observers rarely described armor being universally used. There did not have to be that much of it; it simply had to be used in the right manner, at the right time, and in the right place. Further, it suggests why armor is related to elite status in native

North America, a perplexing question. In Europe, Africa, and Japan, armor was expensive, and only elites could afford it. North American Indian armor, however, was made from wood and string and for the most part used very basic construction principles, yet routinely it related to high male status. Perhaps elite status, and thus the wearing of armor, was established purely on longevity. Ranking in the Japanese samurai tradition, for example, was based as much on seniority as on other warrior qualities.

As in almost all areas, California-area armor comes over time to have a meaning not directly related to its original practical martial intent. True to the well-nigh universal pattern, the fetishistic or symbolic armor is typically associated with male power. At least two possibilities of this type of armor are found in the California area. The Hupa are ethnologically famous for their White Deerskin Dance. Still performed, it celebrates Hupa history, life, and wealth, particularly the wealth of men. The most important items displayed in the dance, the pelts of white deer, are held by the dancers before them on short sticks. Various tribes of the desert Southwest suspended deer pelts on short sticks as "curtain-shields." Such soft shielding would absorb the impact of an arrow or cause it to fall to the ground.

Another example of the transformation of defensive weaponry to ritual status, Bear Shamanism was found in a number of northern California societies. Among the Lake Miwok a novice would prove his potential by stopping a large rock that was rolling downhill. When initiated, the men donned bear skins and armor breastplates. In this warrior dress the Bear Shaman could travel great distances at superhuman speed and achieve invulnerability. The male Bear Shamans were considered dangerous while ritually empowered and might kill anyone who obstructed their passage. Women of the Lake Miwok could become Bear Shamans, but they used their superhuman speed to bring food from long distances rather than for warriorlike behavior (Callaghan 1990, 269).

A low casualty rate stands as one of the characteristics of California warfare. A few exceptions are noted above, but generally the observation is accurate. The kinship-based social system meant that small groups of kinsmen, as opposed to larger tribal-level entities, comprised raiding groups. The requirement to pay compensation meant that killing and destruction were generally held to a minimum by aggressors. The widespread use of armor, helmets, and shields, especially in northern California, curtailed death and injury, as did the formalized nature of arranged battles. Thomas McCorkle (1990, 694ff.), in his study of intergroup conflict in the California area, estimated that the Yurok, for example, averaged about two to thirteen casualties in formal battles; the Pomo ten to twenty-five; and the Yokuts, Monache, and Tubatulabal between three and seven. The custom among certain northern California groups of an extensive period of ritual purification for those who had killed in battle prevented excessive deaths. Garth writes that an Apwaruge (Atsugewi subgroup) slayer underwent a month-long period of isolation during which he ate alone, remained continent, used special utensils (including a head scratcher), avoided meat and hunting and fishing, and even discarded his bow and arrows (Garth 1990, 239). Similar behavior is reported among the Wiyot by Albert Elsasser (1990, 16ff.).

The built-in cultural mechanisms that maintain a high level of warrior awareness but which act to limit the numbers killed are similar to the coup system on the Plains. In most Plains versions of coup ranking, killing an enemy rated very low on the scale of war honors. Likewise, among the Californians, no special status accrued to a man who had merely killed many enemies in battle.

3

The Horse Warriors
The High Plains Culture Area

The High Plains area comprises about 1.5 million square miles of relatively flat, open country. Its northern boundary extends into central Alberta and Saskatchewan, where the plains/prairie habitat gives way to subarctic forests. The Rocky Mountains form the western boundary; the western edges of the tall grass prairie, the eastern; and the Rio Grande, the southern. These boundaries circumscribed the major concentration range of the bison herds that once blackened the Plains for miles. The nomadic tribes within these boundaries depended upon the bison for subsistence and the horse for transportation, bison hunting, and warfare. The historic Indians of the High Plains include the Arapaho, Sarsi, Assiniboine, Blackfoot, Plains Cree, Cheyenne, Crow, Gros Ventre, Kiowa, Plains Ojibwa, Plains Apache (aka Kiowa Apache), Sioux, Wind River Shoshone, and Comanche.

Some of the earliest evidence of the presence of humans in the New World is found on the western Plains. The Dent site in Colorado (9000 to 10,000 B.C.) revealed twelve Columbian mammoths that had been brought down by local Indian hunters. Dated to 8000 to 9000 B.C., the Lindenmeier site, also in Colorado, evidenced the hunting of the now extinct ancient bison, a creature that was half again as tall as the modern bison, with long, straight horns instead of the shorter, curving horns found on modern bison. By 6000 B.C., as witnessed through sites in Idaho, Wyoming, and Montana, Indian hunters could kill a hundred bison in one outing by using fire or manpower to drive them into box canyons, impounding traps, or sand dunes or over cliffs.

The first European to contact Indians of the Plains, the Spanish explorer Coronado led an expedition from Santa Fe northeastward in search of a fabled lost city of gold between 1540 and 1542. Ten days out of Santa Fe his chroniclers described meeting the "Querechos," possibly Plains Apaches. Without guns or horses, they transported their possessions by trains of dogs that numbered in the hundreds, carrying backpacks of between 30 and 50 pounds and dragging tipi poles.

One hundred forty years later, the Pueblo Indians revolted against the Spanish and drove them from New Spain, at the same time releasing hundreds of Spanish horses to the Indians. In another hundred years the horse had diffused over the entire Plains area, and in the mid-eighteenth century, guns spread through trade from Canada to the Indians of the Plains. The advent of the gun and horse redefined the Plains by facilitating more efficient hunting and military activity. Indians who lived on the fringe of the area poured in from the northeast, the north, the east, the southeast, and the west. In the context of the late prehistoric and early historic occupation of the Plains, the earliest Indian defensive technology—armor, shields, and fortifications—was found.

Though weapons and defenses changed over time because of the introduction of the horse and gun, the most common weapon, even in the early days of the gun on the Plains, was the bow and arrow. Mixed reviews were offered on its efficacy; on the one hand, it was described as a fearsome weapon, but other accounts downplayed its martial effectiveness.

A not uncommon name on the Plains was Two Buffalo, a designation granted to one who killed two bison with one arrow, the second bison usually being the calf of the female, who placed her body between the mounted hunter and her offspring. The shot that pierced the adult animal did not—could not—penetrate bone, shoulder muscle, and gristle, but rather entered the front "armpit" of the bison, passed through the lungs unimpeded by rib bones, and exited the "armpit" on the other side with sufficient energy to mortally wound the calf. This formidable shot required perfect timing, a great deal of luck, and a powerful bow.

The Spaniards showed much respect for the bows and arrows of the Indians they encountered in New Spain. Even with their metal armor, helmets, and shields, they soon learned, for example, not to charge into a massed flight of arrows launched by Apache warriors.

The war club ran a close second to the bow and arrow in Plains warfare. In the prehorse days, war clubs and large leather shields were brought into play for hand-to-hand combat after a preliminary "softening up" of the enemy by a flight of arrows or "darts" from spear-throwers. The older, relatively short war clubs were armed with a stone head and used with a hacking or slashing motion. The war club of later usage, designed for fighting from horseback, proved a much more powerful weapon and one of the reasons that helmets became so widespread among Plains warriors, particularly the Blackfoot, Shoshone, Crow, and Assiniboine, as well as more southerly Plains tribes. The handle of the modified war club measured 3 feet or more in length and was of a relatively small diameter. Likewise, the stone head was not particularly large but often ground to a point at both ends. Whirled in a circular motion to build up centrifugal force, the weapon was then aimed at the enemy and could crush the skull of a man or knock down a horse.

A similar weapon, perhaps the basis for the long-handled war club, was found on the northeastern Plains in the mid-1700s. Rocks were attached to thick strings about 3½ feet long, whirled to gather force, and directed at the head of the enemy. Such weapons used the same principles as the *bola perdida* of the mounted Tehuelche Indians of Patagonia and various "weighted chain" and "weighted rope" weapons found in Asia.

Lances, knives, ropes, and occasionally slings complete the repertoire of the Plains warrior. Lances were sometimes very long, sometimes short, sometimes armed with stone, sometimes with iron. Some were used from horseback; some were thrown like javelins. Warriors likewise threw rocks at each other, as well as fire. Some war stories described launching wasp nests into enemy refuges. However, the most common plan of battle, as noted above, prepared the enemy with a flight of arrows or rocks while the attackers hid behind shields, then pressed the attack home with war clubs until the enemy was sufficiently stunned to receive the coup de grace with a knife or a club. The fighting techniques brought into play were simple but effective. The Blackfoot warrior Weasel Tail told Wissler (1910, 164): "If an enemy tries to stab you with a knife, hit him on the arm or wrist and make him drop it. Then hit him over the head with your club."

The favorite knife of the northern Plains warriors was a broad, double-edged weapon obtained from traders. The Indians called it a "stabber," or "beaver tail knife," and many Blackfoot warriors used it for hand-to-hand combat. The fighter grasped the knife so that the blade protruded from the heel of his hand, thus allowing him to strike overhand to the throat or clavicle, as well as slice backhand to the face, ribs, or stomach. It served as an ideal weapon for finishing off a defeated foe and for scalping (Ewers 1958, 202).

Frank R. Secoy (1992 [1953]), in his classic *Changing Military Patterns of the Great Plains Indians,* differentiated the changing military techniques on the Plains in terms of three basic time segments: the prehorse/pregun period (before 1680), the posthorse/pregun period (ca. 1680 to the mid- or late 1700s), and the posthorse/postgun period (after the mid- or late 1700s).

In the prehorse/pregun period, Plains battles were fought on foot in well-organized units. Most typically, adversaries drew up in lines and performed complex infantry maneuvers. During this period large, heavy shields and armor were probably widely utilized. As archaeological remains bear witness, it was a time of heavy casualties and the obliteration of enemy settlements.

Secoy's second phase, the posthorse/pregun period, saw the Plains Indians adopting Spanish military horse culture. The armor became lighter and the shields and bows smaller to more easily accommodate mounted warfare. Cavalry tactics superseded those of the infantry fighter, and sheer numbers no longer determined the outcome in warfare. An outnumbered foe could ride from the battle and live to fight another day. In the posthorse/postgun period, the increasingly potent gun signaled the end to armor as it had in Europe.

Fortifications

Roaming the Plains from the headwaters of the Missouri and Milk Rivers and north into Alberta and Saskatchewan, the nomadic tribes known collectively as the Blackfeet held sway for several centuries. Key to the life of the Blackfeet was access to the enormous herds of bison that roamed the high plains from northern Mexico to the forests of Canada.

The three Blackfeet tribes—Kainah (Blood), Piegan (Torn Robes), and Siksika (Blackfooted People)—speak an Algonquin language and originated in the Northeast, the heartland of the Algonquin speakers. They migrated onto the northern Plains in the early 1700s and by the late eighteenth century had acquired guns in trade with the Cree and Assiniboine to the north and horses from various allies to the west and south.

No evidence exists that the prehistoric Blackfeet erected defenses to match the massive palisaded fortifications constructed by ancestors of the historic Mandan and Arikara of the Middle Missouri area, although they were no doubt aware of them. Their distinctive fortification was the war lodge. This defensive structure, technically a refuge as opposed to a stronghold, was built in heavily timbered areas where it could not be easily seen, preferably on an elevated site near a river or stream and adjacent to a well-known war trail. These lodges were used repeatedly through the years and repaired from time to time, and new ones were constructed as the need arose. Blackfeet war leaders, in particular, were well versed on the location of such lodges, since they served as defenses when their raiders were pursued by enemies.

Typically located within a one- or two-day march of enemy territory, the war lodges were built from deadfalls and windfalls. Very little finishing work was done on the logs and branches to better camouflage the structure. If such work was required, the Blackfeet found that their large scalping knives fulfilled the need.

The basic pattern of the war lodge was an extension, and perhaps more ancient version, of the hide-covered tipi that all Plains Indians used for shelter. Three or four logs or thick branches about 12 feet long were leaned together at the top to form the core structure, a very crude tipi base with an inside height of about 7 feet. Next, light limbs and logs were set close together against the pole foundation. This basic framework was covered with large slabs of cottonwood bark arranged in an overlapping fashion to provide waterproofing. More poles and logs were added as needed to secure the slabs of bark. A low, covered extension that jutted 10 feet or more from the door formed the entrance. The final touch created an additional breastwork of stones and logs around the exterior base of the lodge to an elevation of 2 or 3 feet. The finished structure, at a casual glance, looked like a pile of dead brush and downed tree limbs. It was a formidable enough refuge, however, that pursuing enemies approached it with great caution.

The Blackfeet war lodge could be put together in about two hours by ten men. A second version of the war lodge was rectangular in shape, although constructed in the same slapdash manner as the more conventional round floor plan, but otherwise retaining the appearance of a random pile of downed trees.

The Blackfeet also built brush and wood structures that functioned more as hiding places than refuges capable of providing some level of defense capability. One was a simple lean-to with the addition of bark slabs and, if time provided, a breastwork at the base. A second version was a dome of willow poles—as would be constructed for a sweat lodge—augmented with bark and breastwork if possible.

John Ewers (1944, 190), in "The Blackfoot War Lodge: Its Construction and Use," commented that the war lodge was found throughout the northwestern Plains area and was clearly documented for the Plains Cree, Crow, Sioux, Gros Ventre, Assiniboine, Cheyenne, Arapaho, and Arikara.

On July 15, 1806, Lewis and Clark described a large version of the war lodge as they traveled along a tributary of the Yellowstone River in western Montana:

> In one of the low bottoms of the river was an Indian fort, which seems to have been built during the last summer. It was built in the form of a circle,

about fifty feet in diameter, five feet high, and formed of logs, lapping over each other, and covered on the outside with bark set up on end, the entrance also was guarded by a work on each side of it, facing the river. These entrenchments, the squaw informs us, are frequently made by the Minnetarees and other Indians at war with the Shoshonees, when pursued by their enemies on horseback. (In Bushnell 1922, 34)

The wandering prince, Maximilian of Weid, exploring in the upper Missouri Valley on July 12 in the summer of 1833, wrote:

Just at the place where our vessel lay were four old Indian huts, of some war or hunting party composed of trunks and boughs of trees piled together in a square in which some of our party made a fire to cook their meat. (1843, 212–213)

Six days later, he made another entry in his journal:

On this day at noon, we reached, on the south bank, an Indian fort. . . . it is a kind of breastwork, which Indian war parties construct in haste of dry trunks of trees. . . . This fort consisted of a fence and several angles, enclosing a rather small space, with the open side towards the river. In the center of the space was a conical hut composed of wood. (Maximilian 1843, 216)

Captain Bonneville gave the following account of the construction and use of the Blackfeet war lodge in the early 1800s. A Blackfeet hunting party came under attack by a group of Flathead, Nez Perce, and white trappers led by Captain Milton Sublette.

The Indians immediately threw themselves into the edge of a swamp, among willows and cotton-wood trees, interwoven with vines. Here they began to fortify themselves; the women digging a trench, and throwing up a breastwork of logs and branches, deeply hid in the bosom of the wood, while the warriors skirmished at the edge to keep the trappers at bay. (Irving 1961, 58)

When Captain Sublette ordered the combined Indian and white force to attack the war lodge, "all hung back in awe of the dismal horrors of the place, and the danger of attacking such desperadoes in their savage den." The Flathead and Nez Perce described the war lodge to Sublette as "almost impenetrable, and full of frightful danger." When Bonneville finally crept within sight of the Blackfeet position, he noted, "It was a mere breastwork of logs and branches, with blankets, buffalo robes, and the leathern covers of lodges, extended around the top as a screen" (Irving 1961, 58).

The preceding accounts mentioned breastwork construction and entrenching at sites generally favored by the Blackfeet for a defensive stand when suddenly faced with overwhelming enemy numbers. Ewers noted that when Blackfeet raiders were pursued and confronted by a superior force, and in the absence of a thicket in which to prepare war lodges, they would dig foxholes or erect "rude stone forts" (1944, 191).

Paul Kane, an artist who traveled among the northern Plains tribes in the 1800s, told of the last stand of the Blackfeet war leader Big Horn and his raiders, who,

> seeing their inferiority to their enemies, attempted flight; but finding escape impossible, they instantly dug holes sufficiently deep to entrench themselves, from which they kept up a constant fire with guns and arrows, and for nearly twelve hours held at bay this large war party, bringing down every man who ventured within shot, until their ammunition and arrows were entirely exhausted. (1925, 284)

Ewers, in "Primitive American Commandos," made the following comment with respect to all Plains Indians:

> If caught on the open plains, a long distance from timber, the smaller party quickly dug fox-holes two or three feet deep with their knives, strengthening them with piles of stones if obtainable on the ground near the holes. Enemies were usually slow to attack such a prepared position. (1943, 124)

Entrenching was noted by de Onate in his historic confrontation with the Escanjaques in Kansas in 1601. After the Spanish had fired their arquebuses and an artillery piece, the Indians retired behind some rocks where they, according to one of de Onate's men, entrenched themselves (Terrell 1975, 108).

A novel form of entrenching was practiced by the northern Plains Sioux. When attackers approached and the Indians had no time to erect breastworks or flee, they would excavate the floors of their tipis, creating a shallow trench and protective earthen berm by placing the excavated soil around the edge of the circular trench. They could see beneath the edges of their tipis and shot under and through them at the enemy. The tipi, of course, created a visual blind to the attackers. This technique was practiced as late as the Sioux wars in Minnesota in 1862 (Bushnell 1922, 97). Entrenching, breastwork construction, and fighting from foxholes were defensive techniques found among almost all North American Indian groups.

South of the Blackfeet, the Cheyenne hunted bison and fought with their perennial foes the Crow, Pawnee, Shoshone, Plains Apache, Comanche, and Kiowa. They moved onto the Plains from the northeast in the mid-1700s after acquiring horses, but the expanding Siouans pressured them to move farther south. In 1804 Lewis and Clark reported the Cheyenne hunting in the Black Hills region of South Dakota.

The Cheyenne, having lived for a time along the Middle Missouri, were, no doubt, like the Blackfeet, aware of the fortification methods of the Mandan, Arikara, and Hidatsa as well as the typical repertoire of entrenching and breastwork building found almost everywhere in North America. As noted above, the Cheyenne also built war lodges.

Several accounts describe Cheyenne warriors rapidly constructing defenses against pursuing enemies. In 1837 a party of forty-eight Cheyenne left their camp on the Arkansas River to raid for horses. While they were scouting a large encampment of Comanche, Kiowa, and Plains Apache, mounted warriors from the village saw the Cheyenne and came after them. Since the raiders were on foot, the usual custom when horse raiding, they could not flee. Instead, they located themselves at the head of a ravine, utilized part of the steep embankment for defense, and constructed a stone breastwork. The warriors from the camp could not dislodge them. Instead, they employed the common offensive strategy for such situations: They kept up pressure, forcing the Cheyenne to expend arrows and bullets until they exhausted their ammunition, at which point all were killed (Hoig 1993, 111).

Some years later in 1855, a party of nine Cheyenne set out on foot to raid the Shoshone for horses. Discovered, they ran until they found a defensive position that suited them. There, under cover of a blizzard, they hastily constructed a stone breastwork about 4 feet high. When the Shoshone did not appear, one of the party left to scout and discovered that they had built their little fort at the base of a hill, a dangerous position. While half of the warriors remained in position, three searched until they found a better location nearby. They summoned the others, and together they built a second stone breastwork beneath a ledge.

When the weather cleared, the Shoshone attacked, and, unsuccessful with a frontal assault on the Cheyenne position, they climbed onto the ledge under which the Cheyenne were barricaded and attempted several methods to extricate them from their refuge. First they tried to topple the breastwork with long poles. When that tactic failed, they struck at the Cheyenne with the poles, which the Cheyenne simply grabbed and pulled into the breastwork. Then the Shoshone built a fire to drop onto the Cheyenne position to smoke them out. The Cheyenne used the poles they had taken from the Shoshone to push the fire away. Next the Shoshone shot at fragile-looking spots along the rock wall. In response the Cheyenne moved rocks to the attacked position.

Fighting from a refuge only works if reinforcements appear, if the attacked can retreat under cover of night or storm, or if the attackers withdraw. In the ill-fated horse-raiding expedition against the Comanche and Kiowa mentioned above, none of those events transpired, and the defenders all died. In the raid of 1855, however, after killing six of the raiders and losing three of their own, the Shoshone withdrew. This story is well known among the northern Cheyenne, for after the Cheyenne and Shoshone made peace, survivors of the fight discussed, reconstructed, and retold it many times.

The Cheyenne for a number of years were enemies of the Kiowa. Newcomb wrote, "Kiowas are known to have thrown up earthen breastworks for defense, and this apparently novel tactic was successful in repelling attack on at least two occasions" (1978, 210). South of the Cheyenne and Arapaho range, a Spanish expedition under Juan de Ulibarri entered a heavily fortified Apache settlement in western Kansas in 1706 (Hoig 1993, 54).

Shields

Plains Indian warriors are typically associated with small, round, feather-bedecked shields—"targets" in the language of armor—which seem to have evolved along with the horse culture in the early eighteenth century. Prior to the horse, Plains fighters carried much larger and heavier shields. The Hudson Bay Company trader David Thompson recounted a story about a battle in the early 1700s between the Piegan and the Shoshone, told to him in the winter of 1787–1788 by a Cree man named Saukamappe, who was living with the Piegan people. Both sides lined up facing each other, crouching behind their large shields, which were about 3 feet wide. From behind this protection they shot arrows at each other. The elderly Cree told Thompson that the bison-hide shields could not be penetrated even by iron-tipped arrows.

After the introduction of the horse, the Blackfeet shield changed to the typical small, round one of the historic Plains Indians. Significantly, the Spanish military, the ultimate source of the Plains Indians' horses and most of their horse culture, carried oval shields made of three or four thicknesses of rawhide.

The posthorse Blackfeet shields, resembling the Spanish shields of the time more than the earlier Blackfeet shields described by Saukamappe, were bison hide and on the average about 20 inches in diameter and a little less than an inch thick. Some were two or more ply. They were "dished," rather than flat, to a depth of about 3 inches (Wissler 1910, 162).

The Cheyenne constructed such shields, as did the Assiniboine, Arapaho, and Lakota. The Arapaho also made large, round shields (Paterek 1994, 90). The Crow shields were a little larger, and those of the historic Comanche often reached 23 to 24 inches in diameter.

The Blackfeet fashioned their shields from the thick rawhide of the neck or breast of the bison. Bison was the most commonly used material, although some tribes, such as the Dakota, used horsehide. The Blackfeet dehaired the bison hide and soaked it in boiling water. It was then shaped and weighted over an ovoid mound of dirt, which gave it its unique dish-shaped profile. As it dried, it hardened. Sometimes they hung it over a low fire to accelerate the hardening. After trimming it, they added a handgrip inside. Finally, it was painted and decorated.

Such a shield, according to Ewers, "was sturdy enough to stop an arrow and to deaden or deflect the force of a ball from a muzzle-loading flint-lock" (1980, 203). Also expensive, it cost at least one horse. Poor men who could not afford such a weapon carried a buffalo robe with the hair still attached, wrapped several times around their left arm to serve as a shield.

A large part of the expense of a war shield came from the blessing ritual, during which the appropriate shaman or priest invoked the Great Spirit to empower the shield and protect its bearer in battle. The American Fur Company once attempted to introduce polished metal shields among the Blackfeet, but the tribal religious leaders blocked them because it would have cost them an important source of income (Ewers 1980, 203). The Blackfeet warrior believed that the ultimate power of the shield rested in the sacred "medicine" paintings on the shield and the blessing of the shaman/priest. Though the American Fur Company's metal shields would have been technically more efficient, the Blackfeet philosophy of the shield forbade it. A number of examples in North American Indian literature show weaponry being rejected not on its military merits, but because it did not fit the prevailing philosophy of the users.

Robert H. Lowie wrote of the Crow:

Circular shields of buffalo hide formed the only defensive weapon. Their value rested largely on their religious associations, for they were revealed in visions. A shield was not supposed directly to touch the ground; its owner unwrapped it with circumspectness due to any sacred bundle; and like other medicines each shield had its individual taboos. (1935, 86)

Paterek added, "The Crow made many shields, for themselves as well as for trade, for they were highly valued" (1994, 11).

The earliest contact on the southern Plains between Indians and Europeans was recorded, as was noted earlier, by the expedition of General Francisco Vasquez de Coronado, who in 1541 met a number of Indian peoples as he sought the fabled City of Gold. Though he saw no intertribal combat, he did note the "buffalo-hide shield" as part of the martial repertoire of the three groups he contacted.

Operating out of the southwestern Plains in the eighteenth century, the Lipan Apache carried bows and arrows and steel-tipped lances, which they fashioned from Spanish sabres. Newcomb, in his account of the Indians of Texas, writes, "For protection they carried oval shields about three feet by two feet, made from thick, bull bison hides. Arrows and even rifle bullets glanced off these shields unless the hit was dead center" (1978, 118).

In 1847 John C. Cremony met in northern Mexico with a Comanche war chief named Janamata, or "Red Buffalo," and about a hundred of his warriors. He described the outfit worn by Janamata.

His arms consisted of a bow and quiver full of arrows, a long lance, a long sharp knife, worn in the top of his moccasin boot, and a very good Colt's revolver. A strong shield of triple buffalo hide, ornamented with brass studs, hung from his saddle bow, and his dress was composed of buckskin and buffalo hide well tanned and flexible but wholly free from ornament. (Cremony 1868, 15)

The Comanche version of the Plains horseman's shield was constructed in a unique manner. They first selected the shoulder hide of a bison bull— the thickest part in their estimation—heated or steamed it, and scraped it to remove the hair. These operations contracted and thickened the hide. Next they pounded and rubbed it with a smooth stone to flatten any wrinkles. What they did next, however, varied from typical Plains shield making.

One or more layers of circular pieces cut from it were then stretched flesh side out over each side of a circular wooden hoop, two feet or more in diameter, and sewed together around the edge of the hoop with rawhide thongs passed through eyelets punched around the edges of the layers of hide. The space between the layers, usually one inch thick, was packed with feathers, hair, or paper to stop the force of arrows, bullets, or blows from other weapons. (Wallace and Hoebel 1952, 106)

Charles Goodnight found the pages of a complete history of Rome stuffed in a shield captured from a Comanche warrior (Haley 1928, 63); and Wallace and Hoebel (1952, 106–107) commented that before the method of Comanche shield making was widely known, Anglo-American pioneers were always puzzled by the Comanche fascination with their books.

An interesting spontaneous use of the shielding concept, in this instance a kind of "rolling shield," was observed by Bonneville (Irving 1961, 129) in a fight between the Nez Perce and Blackfeet. A Nez Perce warrior had taken up a position behind a fallen log to keep the Blackfeet at bay. One of the Blackfeet warriors eventually selected a suitable log, lay behind it, and rolled it close enough to the Nez Perce to attack when the opportunity presented itself. This tactic anticipated the use in modern warfare of tanks as rolling shields for infantrymen.

Armor

Plains Indian armor is universally of the soft variety, though "soft" is a relative term. The Wind River Shoshone, perennial enemies of the Blackfeet, referred to them as "hard-clothes people," a reference to the armor the Blackfeet wore in battle. Wissler's (1910, 163) Blackfeet respondents in the early 1900s spoke of their traditions of wearing buckskin shirts of two or more layers as protection against stone and bone arrow points. One elder informed him that the Blackfeet once used long shirts, constructed of three layers of buckskin, that reached below the knees.

One of the earliest references to Blackfeet armor came from Matthew Cocking, who traveled from Hudson Bay into the Blackfeet country in 1772–1773. "They are all well mounted on light, spirited animals; their weapons, bows and arrows: several have on jackets of moose leather, six fold, quilted and without sleeves" (in Burpee 1908, 233). Cocking was apprised that these six-ply moosehide jackets were also used by the Shoshone, Gros Ventre, and Sarsi, as well as the Siksika, Kainah, and Piegan.

David Thompson described a skirmish between the Piegan and a Salish group in 1787. The Piegan confronted the Salish with "their war coats of leather hanging loose before them" (Thompson 1916, 424). This description seems to be more like that of the war shirts supplied by Wissler's informants than Cocking's description of Blackfeet moosehide jackets. Perhaps the Blackfeet had both. Ewers (1980, 205) noted that wearing body armor of several thicknesses of leather was virtually Plains-wide in the eighteenth century.

East of the Blackfeet, the Assiniboine wore sleeveless moose leather war jackets of six or more ply, and white wolfskin caps protected their heads in battle (Koch 1977, 96). In early times, Lakota tradition told of warriors wearing heavy buckskin shirts as a type of light armor (Paterek 1994, 139). In 1775 Peter Pond reported that the Yankton Dakota warriors, both mounted and afoot, wore a "garment like an outside vest with sleeves that come down to their elbows made of soft skins and several thicknesses that will turn an arrow at a distance" (in Ewers 1980, 204).

Heavy rawhide armor is attributed to the Kiowa (Paterek 1994, 119) and is described, though not identified as such, in Cremony's (1868, 15) description of the Comanche war chief Janamata, with whom Cremony met in 1847. His description of Janamata's outfit is telling. "His dress was composed of buckskin and buffalo hide well tanned and flexible, but wholly free from ornament." The reference to buffalo-hide clothing and lack of ornamentation suggests a battle outfit. Aside from the buffalo-hide shields, lances, and bows and arrows the Comanche carried into battle, they also used buffalo horn headdresses (helmets) and high buffalo-hide boots (Pritzker 1998, 46).

The Plains Indians experienced horse armoring at the very outset of their exposure to the horse. To return to the battle in Kansas in 1601 in which the Spanish engaged the Escanjaque warriors, de Onate ordered his men to armor their horses as an estimated two-thousand-man force of warriors flanked his troops.

The Kiowa (Paterek 1994, 119) used bison-hide horse armor, and so, too, the Comanche. A French administrator wrote to the French territorial minister on September 25, 1751, that a raiding party of Comanche had attacked an Osage settlement with spears and that their horses were "caparisoned" (Secoy 1951, 532).

The problematic term "Padouca" arose about this time. A long-running debate about the identity of these people has ensued ever since. The key to understanding the problem is the word identifying them in the Santee

Sioux language—Pa-hdo-ka—which means "to pierce or run through" or "piercers." This term applied to southern Plains enemies who attacked the Santee in the style of heavy cavalry. Both the Apache and the Comanche in the mid-eighteenth century were "piercers"; that is, they wore leather armor, rode armored horses, and attacked with long lances tipped with sabers stolen or traded from the Spanish. Ironically, the Padouca (Apache/Comanche) attacked the Santee in the same fashion that the Spanish had so successfully attacked them—mounted, armored, and wielding long, steel-bladed lances.

Padouca horse armor was described in some detail in the Ponca account noted in Chapter 1:

> To protect their horses from arrows they made a covering for their horses' breasts and sides, to prevent an arrow taking effect at ordinary range. This covering was made of thick rawhide cut in round pieces and made to overlap like the scales of a fish. Over the surface was sand held on by glue. This covering made the Ponca arrows glance off and do no damage. (Fletcher and La Flesche 1972, 79)

In 1731 Governor Bustillo y Zevallos, with 157 Spaniards and 60 mission Indians, engaged an army of several hundred Apache. The Spanish reported that the Apache armored themselves with leather breastplates (Hoig 1993, 84). Bourgmont (in Ewers 1980, 204) remarked in 1724 that the Padouca (the Apache in this case) went to war dressed in "specially tanned" buffalo skins to protect themselves from arrows and added that they also hung these skins over their war horses. Hoig observed:

> The Apaches, having procured horses from the Spanish, also adopted Spanish warring techniques. They began making protective armor of tough, overlapping leather for both themselves and their horses, imitative of the Spanish mail. They also took the Spaniards' cutlasses, tied them on ends of poles to make lances, and manufactured darts called *chuzas*. Their saddles, high-pommeled and high-cantled in the style of the Spanish cavalryman, were designed for support in fighting from horseback. (1993, 33)

Discussion and Summary

As would be expected, Plains defensive technology changed as martial technology in general changed—the introduction of the horse and gun being the major factors. Further, as populations on the Plains grew larger and more complexly interwoven, they became more sensitive to territorial trespass, more focused on control of trade, and more intent on protecting their bison-hunting range. These priorities were exacerbated by the great number of intruders who entered the Plains during the post-horse/pregun and /postgun period.

The equestrian nomads of the High Plains built several kinds of refuges—war lodges, entrenchments, breastworks—but not strongholds equivalent to those erected by the prehistoric and early-historic Mandan and Arikara. The Plains nomads' defensive technology compared more to that of groups to the north and west of the Plains.

As Plains armor grew obsolete in the face of advances in firearms technology, it often retained an aura of symbolic power and was worn both ceremonially and as an indicator of male rank, status, and warrior credentials. Some historic Plains male costuming can be understood as paraphernalia whose nature points to earlier forms of armored warfare.

Elaborate headdresses common on the Plains suggest a military function in a number of ways. They are a kind of helmet. Rarely worn in horse raiding and more common in revenge raiding or defensive battles, headdresses presented the warrior as larger and blurred the precise outline of the head, the major target for the war club. In some cases the headdresses were formed around caps of rawhide, which, with elaborate feather additions, provided a cushioning to blows. In many cases these buffalo-skin caps had horns still attached.

After the rise of gun culture, the Crow war club had no function as a battlefield weapon but was retained in an exceptionally heavy version as a ceremonial item (Lowie 1935, 86). Likewise, the multilayer buckskin or buffalo war shirts of the Crow were, after the gun, worn as ceremonial dress (Paterek 1994, 110). Heavy, bulky shirts that reach to just above the knee—the basic pattern of the "soft armor" war shirt—are seen in many photographs of North American Indian men taken in the late 1800s and early 1900s.

Particularly among northern Plains tribes, "trailers" (long pieces of buckskin or cloth to which additional eagle feathers were attached) were added to eagle-feather headdresses. Often, the trailer of a standing warrior wearing an eagle-feather headdress would reach the ground and in some cases would be several feet longer than that. The number of eagle feathers used for such a headdress reflected the wealth and prowess of the wearer. The headdress was seen as a sacred object because of the intrinsic regard for the eagle. Elaborate eagle-feather headdresses were generally treated much as a medicine bundle.

The possible origin of the trailer headdress as a type of shielding is suggested by an item of protective equipment called a *horo,* worn by the ancient warriors of Japan. A piece of cloth about 6 feet in length, the *horo* was attached to the back of a mounted warrior and, when filled with air, would be lifted by the wind to flow behind him as he rode. The *horo* protected the rider against arrows shot at his back, as did the trailer headdress, which flowed behind the galloping horseman. Like the eagle-feather headdress of the Plains warriors, the *horo* was believed to have mystical powers to ward off evil spirits. Ancient Japanese military traditions, in fact, recommended the wearing of the *horo* on the battlefield, because if a warrior was killed, the enemy would understand, recognizing the *horo,* that the dead warrior was not a common person and so would treat his corpse well (Ratti and Westbrook 1973, 220).

Another item of "traditional" clothing among historic Plains Indians, the so-called "hair-pipe breastplate," appeared to derive its form from early types of armor—a natural conclusion particularly among those familiar with examples of American Indian rod-armor widespread both in the Northeast Culture Area and west of the Rocky Mountains. Rod-armor is constructed of many wooden dowels sewn together. When hair-pipe "bones" are added into the costume, the suspicion that it is some kind of armor is all but confirmed. But the assumption is basically ill-founded, as hair-pipes are modern inventions obtained from white traders and manufacturers.

The tubular bead has a long history. Perhaps it was inspired by the use of animal bones in necklaces. Sites going back several thousand years in the East reveal necklaces of bird bones, rolled native copper, and longitudinally drilled conch columella. British traders noted, in the early historic period, the wearing of long conch columella beads among the Chickasaw and Choctaw of Mississippi and the Creek of Georgia.

The first use of the term "hair-pipe" in the Indian trade was recorded in 1767 and referred to silver tubular beads traded to Indians in the Ohio Valley. These beads were expensive, and in response to the traders' search to find a cheaper equivalent, John W. Campbell, founder of the Campbell wampum business in New Jersey, originated the commercial hair-pipes that appeared all over the Plains after 1800. He manufactured his hair-bones from the West Indian conch, which were brought from West Indian ports as ballast to New York docks, where Campbell bought them in lots of five and ten thousand. The Northwest Company was the first trading

Low Dog, an Oglala Sioux, wearing hair-pipe breastplate and gorget. Courtesy Denver Public Library, Western History Department.

company known to offer hair-pipes to the Plains Indians of the upper Missouri River.

The Comanche invented the hair-pipe breastplate about 1854, and its popularity spread rapidly. Photographs taken in 1868 show Kiowa, Comanche, Plains Apache, Cheyenne, and Arapaho men wearing it. By 1872 photographs of northern Plains Indians in which the hair-pipe breastplate was worn appeared. Such neck ornamentation, made of dentalium shells, was used by the Dakota at a somewhat earlier date.

These breastplates and gorgets cannot be regarded as armor, no matter how formidable they look, for the simple reason that they are too fragile and too expensive. As John Ewers, who wrote the definitive study "Hair Pipes in Plains Indian Adornment," pointed out, "In the period of general economic depression among the Plains Indians following the extermination of the buffalo, during which they subsisted largely upon government rations, possession of an elaborate hair-pipe breastplate or necklace was a coveted symbol of greater-than-average prosperity among these proud people" (1957, 64). Exorbitant expense typifies symbolic armor no matter where it is found in the world.

Finally, the Comanche inventors of the hair-pipe breastplate stemmed from Shoshone stock west of the Rocky Mountains, where rod-armor was common. The pattern and method of creating the hair-pipe breastplate of the Plains resemble those of the rod-armor corselets found among more western tribes. Further, on the Plains the hair-pipe breastplate was almost universally associated with males, warriors, high status, and wealth, as was rod-armor west of the Rockies in the ancient homeland of the Comanche.

Armor might be expected to appear in the rituals and traditional costumes of the "warrior societies" found in all Plains tribes. Each possessed a number of voluntary associations, or clubs, whose members shared military experience, sometimes fought together as a unit, and saw their major function as providing protection and service to their people. A survey of the military societies of the Crow and the Oglala division of the Teton-Dakota (Wissler, 1916), however, reveals little evidence of armor as symbol, "fetish," or real weapon.

One of the rare warrior societies that shows evidence of armor is the Tatanka Wapahun, the "Chief's Society" or "Wearers of the Buffalo Headdress" society, of the Oglala Sioux. Members painted their bodies and their lances white, carried shields, and, as their name implies, wore a headdress made of the head and neck skin of the bison. In public rituals they danced in imitation of the buffalo. As has been noted earlier, some Plains groups wore buffalo bonnets as helmets. Tatanka Wapahun members wore the buffalo headdress during dances and when they went to war (Wissler 1912, 37). Still, in the great majority of cases, the Plains warrior societies that were observed by modern researchers or remembered by elderly informants show little or no evidence of the use of armor.

Another curious fact about the warrior societies and their relationship to armor, or the lack thereof, is the recurrent theme of death-seeking behavior among their members, particularly their most highly ranked members. The Crow said that the members of the Fox Society were *ce'kuk,* "doomed to die." As with the leaders of the Taro'xpa and the "Not-Afraid-To-Die," Fox Society leaders planted their lances in battle and pledged to die if they had to. Elite members of the Crow Big Dog Society were obliged to walk up to the enemy in battle and never to retreat. "They . . . were fairly certain to be killed" (Lowie 1913a, 176). The Big Dogs, as in the case of a Crow raiding party being pursued, were to dismount and stand before the oncoming enemy to buy their comrades more time to escape. This type of behavior is found among all Plains tribes.

The apparent lack of regard for personal safety among the Plains warriors is reflected in the war songs of the various warrior societies. A Cheyenne elder in Oklahoma once sang a war song for me, the words of which were "Feel free to die. All that remains on the earth are stones." A famous Lakota warrior adage says, "Today is a good day to die." The Crow warriors of the Fox Society sang, "Listen, you Foxes. I want to die" (Lowie 1913a, 158). The Kiowa warrior chanted, "Now I am gone. I am going to leave you. I will not run anymore" (Lowie 1916, 846).

This mere sampling of seemingly foolhardy behavior in battle (planting of the lance, pinning themselves to the ground with sashes) and the death-haunted songs of the warrior societies indicate that the ethos of the Plains warriors in historic times greatly militated against the wearing of armor. How could a warrior sing, "I am the one who wishes to die" and strap on a six-ply moose rawhide vest, war shirt, and helmet? The sources of a philosophy that would place the bravest of young men in dire danger would be interesting to trace. The prehorse/pregun Plains people were clearly not "wishing to die," hence the armor and the massive fortification building. The attitude concerning defense of life carried over into historic times with the contradictory attitude of the warrior societies' members, who on the one hand sought death, while at the same time honored the custom that to lose a single man in battle negated any possibility for celebrating victory even if the overall purpose of a raid was accomplished (Lowie 1954, 105).

The art of a people often provides insight into matters of ancient costume, technology, or decoration. In the discussion of the history of armor in Europe, for example, descriptions of ancient warriors on centuries-old tapestries and paintings mix with the literature of historical accounts. The early Plains people drew, chiseled, and painted rocks and hides; and one of the earliest images they depicted was the shield. This image is dispersed throughout the Plains, although most examples are found on the northern Plains. Sometimes a freestanding shield is depicted, and in many cases, its design shows great detail. In other rock art, a head peers over the top and feet show from the bottom of a large shield. Occasionally, these large-shield figures hold a weapon, usually a club or spear, in one hand. Rarely, a shield is shown in the hands of a mounted warrior. The rock art of the Plains agrees with the descriptions of early Plains shields as being large enough to cover the entire body. Apparently, shield drawings on rock faded out shortly after the appearance of the horse. Small, round shields are rarely depicted (Gebhard 1965, 721ff.).

4 The Castle Builders
The Northeast Culture Area

The Northeast Culture Area includes the Great Lakes and adjacent territory, New England, and the Atlantic seaboard south approximately to Virginia. It is bounded on the north by the subarctic forests of Canada, on the west by the Prairie, on the east by the Atlantic Ocean, and on the south by a line which runs due west from Virginia to the eastern edge of the Prairie region.

The world of the Northeastern Indians was one of unremitting forest cover, rivers, streams, and lakes. Evidence from the Meadowcroft Rock Shelter near Avella in western Pennsylvania suggests that humans have occupied this area for 16,000 to 19,000 years. About 1000 A.D., an economic revolution transpired as most of the Northeastern Indians turned to a life heavily oriented toward the growing of corn, beans, and squash—the "Three Sisters," as they were sometimes called. Populations increased, and early evidence of warfare correlates with the development of a horticultural way of life.

The French explorer Jacques Cartier entered the area in 1534, and before that Basque fishermen worked the north Atlantic coast. In 1580 English ships sailed the coast of Maine, and in 1600 the Seneca, Mohawk, Cayuga, Oneida, and Onondaga in western New York state formed a confederation called the Iroquois, or the Five Nations. These tribes exerted an influence that reached from their home territory as far north as Quebec, as far south as Virginia, and from the Eastern seaboard to the Prairie. The early history of the Dutch, French, and English in the New World became intricately interwoven with the actions of the Iroquois. Other important tribes of the area included the Ojibwa, Illinois, Shawnee, Miami, Erie, Winnebago, Kickapoo, Fox, Sauk, Menomini, Potawatomi, Huron, Susquehanna, Delaware, Montauk, Wappinger, Abnaki, Wampanoag, Nauset, Nipmuc, Massachusett, Narragansett, Mahican, Penobscot, Passamaquoddy, Pamlico, Chesapeake, and Nanticoke.

The life of Northeastern women centered on the management of gardens and the gathering of wild foods. Over thirty different wild fruits and about fifty kinds of roots, nuts, seeds, and leaves added importantly to the diet. The women made the clothing, pottery, and various types of utensils used in cooking, mat making, and gardening, and they instigated raiding through a custom called a "mourning war." A woman who mourned the loss of a kinsman would ask her husband to avenge her grief by attacking the enemy. The power of women in Iroquois society is noteworthy. The Iroquois were matrilineal, which means that family names, clan membership, and property were bequeathed through women, not men, and matrilocal, meaning that at marriage the husband went to live in the wife's home environment, or on land owned by the wife's clan. Men did the heavy labor, hunted, fished, trapped, grew some tobacco, participated in politics and religious ceremonials, and made war. It was as warriors that they sought prestige in the eyes of their people.

Father Joseph François Lafitau (1681–1746), one of the first to describe Northeastern people in some detail, wrote that their major offensive weapons included the bow and arrow, the war club, and the thrusting spear, the war club being the preferred close-in weapon. "The *casse-tete,* or ball-headed war club, takes the place of a sword or club. It is made of a tree root, or some other very hard wood, two or two and a half feet long, squared on the sides, and widened or rounded to the width of a fist at its end" (Lafitau 1977, 115). The local bows, according to Lafitau, "are made of red cedar, or of another species of wood, very hard and further stiffened in fire. They are straight and almost of the height of a man" (Lafitau 1977, 115).

Because native copper from the Lake Superior region was traded within the broad trade networks of the Northeast area, copper arrowheads were in common use at the time of contact. "Some of their arrows were of elegant construction and tipped with copper and, when shot with power would pass through the body of a deer as certainly as the bullet from the rifle" (Ruttenber 1872, 26).

Fire arrows were shot against enemy forts and human adversaries, and poisoned arrows were deployed in warfare. Micmac arrows "were 'poisoned' with a preparation made from bark, root, and a bush, the identity of which was not known (or was not revealed in 1911)" (Wallis and Wallis 1955, 33). Edmund Carpenter and Royal Hassrick (1947, 52), in "Some Notes on Arrow Poisoning among the Tribes of the Eastern Woodlands," reported that the Erie, Cayuga, Seneca, Oneida, and Onondaga used poisoned arrows.

Guns quickly replaced traditional weapons in the Northeast. Samuel de

Champlain in 1609 introduced the Mohawks to firearms, killing and scattering them with the then unknown weapon at the Battle of Lake Champlain. By the end of the century, Northeast Indians were well supplied with muskets but retained the bow and arrow as a stealth weapon.

Northeastern Indian battlefield tactics were far from simplistic. Fighters attacked enemy forts with fire and with mining to collapse palisades. They were capable of laying siege, which they did in the 1700s to such strongly garrisoned fortifications as Detroit and Fort Pitt. "The siege of the places where they [Iroquois] encounter resistance is again a proof that they have learned the rules of military art, where ruse and industry go on an equal footing with the most intrepid force and valour" (Lafitau 1977, 14). Armstrong Starkey, in *European and Native American Warfare, 1675–1815,* stated:

> One scholar who has studied the battlefield tactics of late-eighteenth-century northeastern Indians finds them more sophisticated than those of their European opponents. Indian warriors did not simply hide behind trees, but exploited available cover to conduct moving fire on the enemy. Indians were trained to outflank their opponents and usually quickly enveloped them in a horseshoe formation. On the other hand, they seldom completely surrounded the enemy, perhaps preferring to allow them to withdraw rather than to force a desperate struggle with high casualties on both sides. Indians also understood how to conduct orderly advances and retreats "blackbird fashion," in which warriors with loaded weapons covered those whose guns required recharging. . . . In short, eighteenth-century Indian tactics resembled those of modern infantry more than did those of their European adversaries. (1998, 22)

Regardless of the tactical and strategic skills of the Northeastern Indians, the "line battle" and exchange of arrows that marked ancient warfare on the Plains and in California areas also occurred in the Northeast. "In traditional [Mohawk] warfare, large groups met face-to-face and fired a few arrows after a period of jeering, then engaged in another period of hand-to-hand combat" (Pritzker 1998, 2:631). About the Iroquois in general, Lafitau commented on the "line battle," or "duel," as he called it:

> On occasions of this sort, their small number permits them to draw together, so to speak, body to body, and fight as in a duel, as the heroes of the Iliad and Aeneid did. Quite often they know each other and speak to each other. They ask each other news, harangue each other and do not beat

each other up without first paying each other compliments, as Virgil had Aeneas do. (1977, 143)

Single-champion combat as a means of settling an issue that verged on triggering war between massed hostile groups was described in the *Jesuit Relations: 1610–1613:*

> Sometimes they decide their wars by single combat. Two bands, one of the so-called Montagnais, the other of Iroquois, had met a few years ago in readiness for battle. The leaders had advanced and were already designating the positions for the formation of the lines of attack, when it is said that one thus addressed the other: "Let us spare the blood of our followers; nay, rather let us spare our own blood. Let us settle the matter with our bare hands, and he who overcomes the other shall be the victor." The proposition was accepted, and the two joined battle. The Montagnais, by means of a combination of strategy and skill with courage, so wearied the Iroquois that he finally hurled the latter to the ground, bound him, and triumphantly carried him off upon his back. (Thwaites 1959a, 269)

Fortifications

Fortified villages appear very early in Northeastern history. The late prehistoric Owasco Culture in central New York, parts of Vermont, and eastern Pennsylvania built villages surrounded by stockades on defensible hilltop sites between 1000 and 1300 A.D. By 1300 a recognizable Iroquois Culture had spread into New York. "Warfare seems to have been common at that time, as the villages are palisaded and located on hills or steep stream banks where defense was easier" (Jennings 1989, 249).

Between 1350 and 1600 the Old Iroquois Culture, centered in the lower Great Lakes region and New York, constructed, on hilltops, villages that were sometimes enclosed by a low earthen wall upon or in which was constructed a wooden stockade. The Whittlesey Culture in northwestern Ohio between 1400 and 1650 protected their villages with a stockade of upright posts or earthen walls and upright posts combined. From 1300 to 1650 the Aztalan Culture in Wisconsin surrounded their settlements with palisades of upright logs covered with clay and grass. Bastions were placed at intervals along the stockade wall (Martin, Quimby, and Collier 1947).

During his voyages to the Northeast between 1604 and 1618, Samuel de Champlain encountered a small village in July 1605 at the mouth of the Saco River in York County, Maine. "The savages dwell permanently in this place, and have a large cabin surrounded by palisades made of rather large trees placed by the side of each other, in which they take refuge when their enemies make war upon them" (Grant 1907, 63). Champlain found fortified villages everywhere he went. "I set out on the fourteenth of August with ten of my companions. I visited five of the more important villages, which were enclosed with palisades of wood" (Grant 1907, 284).

He experienced the military effectiveness of Indian fortifications in 1615 when he accompanied a party of Huron, Algonquin, and Montagnais in an attack against an Oneida fortification. "In the distance Champlain saw the enemy's stockade and his discerning eye noted its great superiority over the fortified Huron towns which he had so much admired" (Parker 1918, 170). Four concentric 30-foot palisades of large tree trunks supported galleried ramparts from which defenders shot arrows and threw stones. The Oneida had even constructed a gutter system, which directed water to quench fires set by the attackers at the base of the palisade walls (Steele 1994, 6).

When the Huron, Algonquin, and Montagnais failed to breach the Oneida defenses, Champlain attempted two European tactics: the use of mantelets and a cavalier. The first, large wooden shields or screens, allowed the attackers to approach the walls in relative safety to undermine the stockade or set it on fire. The cavalier, a movable tower, rose somewhat higher than the defenders' bastions, and from it musket fire could prevent the defenders from occupying their towers. Neither worked against the Oneida defenders. Finally, Champlain, bearing several arrow wounds, was carried away by his Indian allies when they concluded that even with the once invincible Champlain and his "thunder poles," victory was not to be had.

Understandably, the early explorers referred to Northeast Indian strongholds as "castles." Bushnell describes a seventeenth-century Iroquois castle in the following passage:

For the erection of these castles, or strongholds, they usually select a situation on the side of a steep high hill, near a stream or river, which is difficult of access, except from the water, and inaccessible on every other side, with a level plain on the crown of a hill, which they enclose with a strong stockade work in a singular manner. First they lay along on the ground large logs of wood, and frequently smaller logs upon the lower logs, which serve for the foundation of the work. Then they place strong oak palisades in the ground on both sides of the foundation, the upper ends of which cross each other and are joined together. In the upper cross of the palisades they then place the bodies of trees, which makes the work strong and firm. . . . Be-

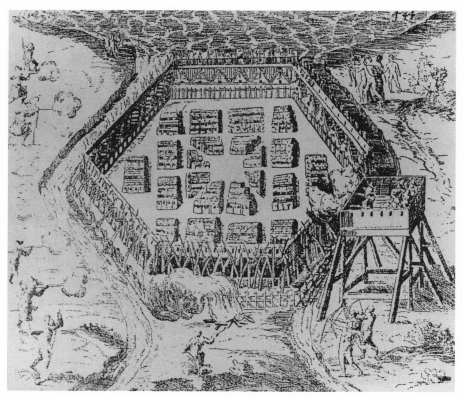

Attack against Iroquois fort.

sides their strongholds, they have villages and towns which are enclosed. Their castles and large towns they seldom leave altogether. (1919, 49)

Lafitau (1977, 16) wrote extensively about Iroquois fortified sites, which were always located with regard to defense. The Iroquois preferred a location where a stream or river looped in such a fashion that it could be utilized as a natural moat. If such a condition was not practicable, they built a dry moat.

The villages most exposed to the enemy are fortified by a palisade 15 to 20 feet high, composed of a triple row of posts, those in the middle planted straight and perpendicularly, the others crossed and interlaced like sawbucks, reinforced throughout by heavy, thick bark to the height of ten or twelve feet. All along the inside of this palisade, the Indians place a kind of gallery or circular walk made of trees laid horizontally, all joining the palisade and placed on great forked posts of wood stuck into the earth. At regular intervals, there are redoubts or watch towers, which, in war time, are filled with stones as a defense against scaling and with water to put out fire. They climb up there (to the battlements) by steps cut into the trunks of trees which serve them as ladders. The palisade also has openings cut in it by way of battlements. The nature of the terrain determines the shape of their enclosures. These are sometimes polygons, but the greatest number are of round or spherical shape. . . . The palisade has only one exit, through a narrow door set in on a slant, closing with cross bar through which people have to pass sideways. (Lafitau 1977, 16)

In 1634 Arent Van Curler visited an Oneida castle.

We marched boldly to the castle, where the savages opened to let us pass, and so we marched through them by the gate, which was 3½ feet wide, and at the top were standing three big wooden images of cut wood, like men, and with them I saw three scalps fluttering in the wind, that they had taken from their foes as a token of the truth of their victory. This castle has two gates, one on the east and one on the west side. On the east side a lock of hair was also hanging; but this gate was 1½ feet smaller than the other one. This castle is situated on a very high hill, and was surrounded by two rows of palisades. (Beauchamp 1905, 112)

One might wonder how people using only stone tools could fell the many hundreds of trees needed for the two and three rows of palisades typical of the larger Northeastern forts. David Cusick offered this explanation:

At first they set fire against several trees as required to make a fort, and the stone axes are used to rub off the coals, as to burn quicker; when the trees burn down they put fire to it about three paces apart and burn it down in half a day; the logs are collected to a place where they set up round according to the bigness of the fort, and the earth is heaped on both sides. (In Beauchamp 1905, 113)

A Mohawk fort in 1665 offers insight into the preparation of strongholds for long sieges. A French chronicler wrote that the stronghold featured a triple palisade, the walls of which stood 20 feet in height and were flanked by four bastions. Inside the fort were stocked "prodigious quantities of provisions and an abundant supply of water in bark tanks" (Beauchamp 1905, 115).

The Iroquois, of course, were not the only Northeasterners who built fortified villages. In 1689 Pere Sebastien Rasles visited an Abnaki village near Quebec, an enclosure of closely set posts which surrounded the tightly spaced houses of the defenders. When Henry Hudson, in 1609, sailed up the river that would bear his name, he encountered such groups as the Esopus and the Munsee, both of whom surrounded their villages with palisades (Bushnell 1919, 29).

Edmund O'Callaghan provided two descriptions of Esopus forts:

> The fort is defended by three rows of palisades and the houses in the fort encircled by thick cleft palisades with port holes in them, and covered with bark of trees; . . . (1850, 49)

A second Esopus fort was described during its construction:

> The fort was a perfect square with one row of palisades set all round being about fifteen feet above, and three feet under ground. They had already completed two angles of stout palisades, all of them almost as thick as a man's body, having two rows of port holes, one above the other; and they were busy at the third angle. These angles were constructed so solid and strong as not to be excelled by Christians. (O'Callaghan 1850, 73)

The Huron fortresses, as noted above, greatly impressed Champlain. Their stronghold of Hochelaga, which once stood on the site of Montreal, was visited by Jacques Cartier during his second expedition in 1535.

> The city of Hochelaga is round, compassed about with timber, with three courses of rampaires, one within another framed like a sharpe spire, but laide acrosse above. The middlemost of them is made and built as a direct line, but perpendicular. The rampaires are framed and fashioned with pieces of timber, layd along the ground, very well and cunningly joyned togither after their fashion. This enclosure is in height about two rods. It hath but one gate or entrie thereat, which is but with piles, stakes, and barres. Over it, and also in many places in the wall, there be places to runne along and ladders to get up, all full of stones, for the defence of it. (O'Callaghan 1850, 55)

Cartier offered some comment on the battle dress of the people of Hochelaga. They "are evil people, who goe all armed even to their fingers' ends. Also they shewed us the manner of their armour, they are made of cordes and wood, finely and cunningly wrought together" (O'Callaghan 1850, 128).

Similar in basic structure, Huron and Iroquois fortifications epitomized "castle" building among Northeastern Indians; however, they were not impregnable to attack by Indian enemies. In 1648 a Seneca war party destroyed the strongly fortified Huron town of Teanaostaiae. Of its 2,000 inhabitants, 300 were killed and 700 taken captive. A year later, a combined group of Seneca and Mohawk defeated the Huron fortress at Taenhatentaron (Steele 1994, 70–71).

When the English arrived in Massachusetts Bay, they found a temporary peace between the Massachusetts Indians and their southerly neighbors the Wampanoag and the Narragansett, but early accounts described naval warfare between the two groups involving forty to fifty canoes. The Massachusetts also lived ostensibly at peace with their northern neighbors the Pawtucket. However, all of these groups had from time to time fought each other, and the possibility that it could happen again led to the construction of a number of fortified villages in the area. In 1621 the Massachusetts commanded two forts—in each case a circular palisade about 40 or 50 feet in diameter surrounded by a breast-high trench. Log palisade forts belonging to the Pequot dotted the Connecticut shore, and the Pawtucket manned three fortified villages near the present-day city of Franklin, New Hampshire, to defend against the Mohegan and the Mohawk.

The forts in this area were somewhat less grand than the castles of the Iroquois. Typically, a palisade of tree trunks 10 feet high and sunk about 3 feet into the ground surrounded a few acres of land. Loopholes allowed marksmen to fire from inside. Two narrow entry doors were heavily guarded. Large quantities of food were buried at these sites, which suggests the need to withstand sieges (Russell 1980, 188).

Jesuit accounts from 1670 confirmed that the Mascouten and the Miami lived in palisaded villages a three-day march from Green Bay, Wisconsin. At the same time, the Kickapoo occupied fortified villages several miles from the territory of the Mascouten and Miami.

During King Philip's War in 1675, the Narragansett were forced into a last-stand defense in their stronghold on a four-acre island in a vast swamp. The United Colonies had raised almost a thousand troops—mostly volunteers from Massachusetts and Connecticut—to send against the Narragansett, and they were joined by 150 Mohegan and Pequot warriors. When the attack came on December 19, 1675, the Narragansett were desperately adding the finishing touches to their main stronghold. A captured Narragansett had betrayed their secret location. Bare trees denied the Narragansett forest cover; and the usually mucky, impenetrable swamp was frozen over. The Narragansett fort was encircled by a double row of palisades, complete with firing platforms, blockhouses for flanking fire, and surrounding massive *abattis,* obstacles formed by felled trees with sharpened branches facing the enemy. Beyond the *abattis* a deep flooded ditch could be crossed only by a single log bridge (Hodge 1969 [1913], 53). The colonial militia captured the stronghold for a brief time but was driven out. Finally, the attackers set the hundreds of shelters within the structure on fire. In the smoke and confusion, the surviving Narragansetts slipped away. The United Colonies casualties were 70 dead and about 150 wounded. Of the Narragansett, at least 48 warriors were wounded and 97 killed (Steele 1994, 102).

In the western reaches of the Northeast area, fortified villages are recorded for many groups. The Peoria were met by a French army officer in 1756 along the Illinois River. "The village of the Peoria is situated on the banks of a little river, and fortified after the American fashion, that is, surrounded with great poles and posts" (Bushnell 1919, 40). The Peoria's enemies, the Sauk and Fox, built fortified sites and in 1732 operated from fortified settlements along the Fox River in Illinois.

The Potawatomi of Illinois in the early 1800s built a stronghold on the Kankakee River. They leveled the trees around the fort and erected both a stockade with loopholes for musket fire and, at strategic locations within the walls, five long blockhouses. They situated their stronghold on a hilltop with a large swamp to the rear and the river in front (Temple 1958, 140).

Not only could the Northeastern Indians build strongly fortified sites, but they were also well versed in the rapid construction of breastwork defenses. Much Iroquois information is available on this subject. Champlain, traveling with the Iroquois, observed the camps they prepared while moving in contested terrain:

> Proceeding about three leagues farther on, we made a halt, in order to rest the coming night. They all at once set to work, some cut wood, and others to obtain the bark of trees for covering their cabins, for the sake of sheltering themselves, others to fell large trees for constructing a barricade on the river-bank around their cabins, which they do so quickly that in less than two hours so much is accomplished that five hundred of their enemies would find it very difficult to dislodge them without killing large numbers. They make no barricade on the river-bank where their canoes are drawn up, in order that they may be able to embark, if occasion requires. (Grant 1907, 157–158)

Sometime later, Champlain and his Indian allies encountered another group of Iroquois, and again the Iroquois rapidly constructed a formidable breastwork.

> They had come to fight. We both began to utter loud cries, all getting their arms in readiness. We withdrew out on the water, and the Iroquois went on shore, where they drew up all their canoes close to each other and began to fell trees with poor axes, which they acquire in war sometimes, using also others of stone. Thus they barricaded themselves very well. (Grant 1907, 163)

Entrenching defense is also mentioned for the Northeast. In 1712, for example, the French and their Indian allies attacked a thousand men, women, and children of the Mascouten and Fox, who withdrew onto an island, dug trenches, and repelled several attacks. Again in 1730 the Fox and Mascouten used entrenching for a quick reaction to attack and later added a breastwork to the rim created from the earth raised by digging the trenches (Gibson 1963, 11, 20).

Abler (1970, 25) cautions us to remember that not all Northeastern towns were fortified. Only six of the eighteen Huron towns Champlain contacted were hardened. Fortified towns tended to be principal towns, or settlements on a frontier with an enemy. Still, in the early seventeenth century, even if a Northeastern town was not encircled in rows of stockade, it was inevitably placed on a defensible hilltop site.

Shields

The types of shields of the Indians of the Northeast varied; however, as with those of the California area, they showed little in the way of painted decoration or magical talismans.

Joseph Lafitau commented on the shields of the Iroquois:

> Their shields were of willow and bark, covered with one or many skins. Some are of very thick skin. They were of all sizes and shapes. (1977, 115)

Samuel de Champlain, traveling in Canada, wrote that the Indians carried "a round shield of dressed leather made from an animal like the buffalo" (Grant 1907, 282). He specifically commented on the use of "bucklers," small, round shields carried by the Montagnais and the Algonquins as they prepared to attack an Iroquois position in 1610. The Indians of the Hudson River valley, when contacted by Henry Hudson, "protected themselves with a square shield of tough leather" (Ruttenber 1872, 25).

The Wampanoag warriors of Cape Cod used shields made of bark slabs (Steele 1994, 84). The Huron warrior carried one of two types—one a small, round rawhide shield and the other of bark and almost large enough to cover a man's body. The Miami's shields were made of buffalo rawhide. Long rawhide shields are reported for the Potawatomi, Illinois, and Ottawa (Pritzker 1998, 2:659, 648, 606). The Lenape in Pennsylvania and Delaware preferred large wooden or moose rawhide shields (Pritzker 1998, 2:672).

An account in *The Jesuit Relations and Allied Documents* (1659–1661) showed how the Iroquois in a fight with the French rapidly constructed large shields.

> On the shore there was a large rock that could be used as a means of defense by those who should first seize it. The enemy, well aware of this, took each two or three pieces of wood which they joined together and bore in front of them as mantelets, thus sheltering themselves from the hot fire constantly leveled at them by the French. But the latter could not prevent them from seizing this advantageous position. (Thwaites 1959b, 213)

Another citation in the *Jesuit Relations* depicted the Iroquois rapidly employing the concept of shielding even in the absence of their conventional battle shields. In this instance they were attacking an Erie fort. After a number of charges were repulsed, they hit upon a novel tactic.

> They took counsel to use their canoes as bucklers; they carried them before them, and by favor of this shelter behold them at the foot of the entrenchment. But it is needful to climb the great stakes, or the trees of which it is built. They set up their same canoes, and make use of them as ladders to mount upon this great palisade. (Thwaites 1959b, 93)

As with armor, Northeastern shields became obsolete in the seventeenth century as soon as modern firearms entered the arsenal.

Armor

Hard armor of wood was found throughout the Northeast area in early times, although soft armor—rawhide corselets, long tunics, war shirts—is rarely mentioned. Lafitau offered this description of Iroquois armor:

> Their breastplates were also a fabric of wood or little reed wands, cut in proportional lengths, clasped against each other, twined and woven very

Armored Huron warrior.

neatly with little cords made of antelope or deerskin. They had thigh and arm guards of the same material. These breast-plates were made to resist arrows with bone or stone heads but would have been no protection against iron arrowheads. (1977, 115–116)

Lafitau was describing rod-armor for the Iroquois, and using it for the thighs and arms is relatively unique.

For the Huron, both rod-armor and slat-armor were mentioned (Pritz-ker 1998, 2:684). Two drawings from the era of early contact show ambiguity concerning the nature of their armor, and patterns depicted on one of the suits suggest a third possibility—the use of wicker armor.

Pierre Charlevoix had the following comment on Iroquois armor:

When they attacked an entrenchment, they covered their whole body with small, light boards. Some have a sort of cuirass or breastplate of small, pliable rings, very neatly worked. They had even formed a kind of mail for their arms and thighs made of the same material. (1966, 649)

He also made the questionable assertion that the Mohawks "wear seahorse skins and bark of trees made by their art as impenetrable as steel, wearing a headpiece of the same" (Charlevoix 1966, 649).

Concerning Huron armor, Elisabeth Tooker, in her Smithsonian Institution publication "An Ethnography of the Huron Indians," wrote:

They also wore a sort of armor and cuirass, which they called *aquientor,* on their back, legs, and other parts of the body for protection against arrows. Although it proved protection against arrows tipped with stone points, it was ineffectual against those with iron points. The cuirasses were made of white rods cut the same length and pressed against one another, very tightly sewn and interlaced with little cords. (1964, 30)

Helmets are not referenced for the Huron, but the Iroquois sometimes wore them (Lafitau 1977, 115).

Several New York pipes and carved heads have helmets. They seem made of a series of hoops, gradually becoming smaller and sometimes with a knob at the top. They were woven of twine. Another kind was cylindric, with some animal's head in front and a cover for the neck behind. (Beauchamp 1905, 128)

The Lenape, who lived south of the Iroquois, used wooden helmets and carried large shields in lieu of armor (Pritzker 1998, 2:612).

Russell, speaking of early accounts of the Indians of New England, described the use of a breastplate: "If his tribe is at war, he would very likely wear over his heart a shield of two or three thicknesses of untanned dry rawhide which the sharpest arrow could not pierce" (1980, 191). Slat-armor is specifically mentioned for the Massachusetts, and in the far northwestern reaches of the Northeast Culture Area, the Ojibwa wore slatt- and rod-armor with greaves, or shin protection, made of the same material (Paterek 1994, 63).

For the most part, the small window in time through which we can observe Indian armor, before it disappeared in the face of the gun, is murky in terms of specifics. The time of Indian armor was so long ago and vanished so quickly that we are left with sparse information on a fascinating time. However, the event which turned the Iroquois away from armor forever is well known.

Samuel de Champlain, with his Algonquin and Montagnais allies, encountered a large raiding party of Iroquois on the lake that now bears his name. The Iroquois immediately beached their canoes and built a breastwork while Champlain and his cohorts remained in their canoes out of arrow range. Apparently, the Iroquois expected a formal fight and dispatched an emissary to ask if the Algonquin and Montagnais wished to engage in combat. Receiving an affirmative reply, the representatives concluded that they would wait until sunrise to begin so that everybody could see better.

Through the night both sides sang war songs and shouted insults. "When the day had come, the Iroquois went out of their fort to the number of nearly two hundred men walking slowly in battle order, with a Spartan gravity and composure with which Lord Champlain was well pleased" (Lafitau 1977, 142). Leading the Iroquois march were three armored chiefs, wearing long plumes. When the two parties approached within arrow distance, Champlain stepped forward with a gun. Surprised, the Iroquois momentarily ceased their advance, but recovering quickly, they continued until Champlain fired his arquebus. Two chiefs dropped dead, and a third was wounded. Champlain later wrote:

> The Iroquois were greatly astonished that two men had been so quickly killed, although they were equipped with armor woven from cotton thread, and with wood which was proof against their arrows. This caused great alarm among them. As I was loading again, one of my companions fired a shot from the woods, which astonished them anew to such a degree that, seeing their chiefs dead, they lost courage, and took to flight, abandoning their camp and fort, and fleeing into the woods, whither I pursued them, killing still more of them. (Grant 1907, 165)

Their armor had failed them. The Iroquois stripped it off and threw it to the ground so that they could better flee. The Algonquins and Montagnais carried it away as war trophies. After their fight with Champlain, the Iroquois rarely wore armor again. Graymont concluded:

> They therefore abandoned their useless armor and changed their style of attack. Instead of the massed charges of armored warriors on the battlefield, which had been their favored practice, they adopted a more individualistic

style of warfare in which warriors fired while concealed behind trees and rocks. (1988, 59)

Discussion and Summary

By the early 1600s, the Northeastern Indians had learned that their shields and armor stood obsolete against the gun. Interestingly enough, armor continued to be used a century and more later on the Plains and over two centuries more in the California area. But in the Northeast it disappeared so rapidly that only a few Europeans even saw it, and examples are extremely rare in Northeast museums.

The most reported form of armoring in the Northeast was the rod-armor cuirass, but helmets and arm and leg protection were rare. Likewise, there is scant mention of soft armor, war shirts, rawhide breastplates, leather tunics, or war coats, perhaps because of the relative unavailability of the bison to the Northeast Indians at the time of contact, although moose could have been used.

The stockades and various kinds of fortifications, relative to the examples on the Missouri River, seem very sophisticated, but dry or wet moat construction in the Northeastern area was relatively scarce.

A rare example of the symbolic use of defensive technology was found at the site of Onneyuttehage, the fortified town at which the Dutch first made contact with the Oneida in 1634. The town contained sixty-six houses and was enclosed in a double-palisaded wall 767 paces in circumference. Outside the palisade the citizens buried their dead, surrounding each grave with a purely symbolic miniature stockade (Grumet 1995, 381).

Some relationships between the religious beliefs of a people, particularly those ideas relating to the afterlife, and the manner in which their warriors comport themselves in battle obviously exist. It would be reflective of one's theoretical bent to say whether the belief system gives rise to the battlefield behavior or the battlefield behavior becomes rationalized by the belief system. At any rate, it is noteworthy that the Iroquois, who at contact wore complete body armor (helmet, cuirass, greaves, and cuisses), carried large shields, and built massive forts, should have the religious belief that portrayed death as a dark prospect for the warrior. Their traditional ideas about death suggest they would not lightly consider martyrdom, whereas the historic High Plains warriors seemed to seek death in battle or at least were motivated to flirt with it closely.

Richter wrote in "War and Culture: The Iroquois Experience":

Iroquois beliefs made death in battle a frightful prospect. Slain warriors, like all who died violent deaths, were said to be excluded from the village of the dead, doomed to spend a roving eternity seeking vengeance. As a result, their bodies were not interred in village cemeteries, lest their angry souls disturb the repose of others. Both in burial and in the afterlife, a warrior who fell in combat faced separation from his family and friends. (1983, 535–536)

The Importance of Influential Neighbors
The Plateau/Basin Culture Area

In terms of physical boundaries and cultural entities, a precise delineation of the Plateau/Basin Culture Area (roughly located in the west-central United States) appears to be impossible. Kroeber, in his classic treatment of North American culture areas, wrote, "California has generally been reckoned a distinct area ever since American culture began to be classified geographically; but the Great Basin has been bandied about" (1939, 49). He surveyed the several ways American ethnologists have attempted to make sense of this area. The modern approach goes more lightly. The physical environment of the Great Basin reflects similarities and differences with the Plateau, and northern Plateau cultures differ strikingly from southern Great Basin people. However, in the northern areas of the Basin and the southern areas of the Plateau, a certain cultural blending can be seen.

Generally speaking, the Great Basin might be construed as that area lying between the Rocky Mountains and the Sierra Nevada and within the states of Colorado, Utah, and Nevada. Although the Basin is generally an arid land, the mountains running north and south through the area offer varied environments at higher elevations, providing a variety of foodstuffs. Resources, though adequate, were scattered and could only support small groups, who moved constantly to harvest the seasonally available food supply. Some of the populations grounded in the Great Basin—most notably the Shoshone—rose to great influence by adapting various Plains culture traits based on an equestrian lifeway. The Great Basin–oriented Bannock, Paiutes, Ghoshutes, and Utes fared somewhat less spectacularly.

North of the Great Basin lies the Columbia Plateau, which features three powerful rivers offering a seemingly limitless supply of food through the runs of salmon that ascend them annually. The Plateau Culture Area combines the Columbia Plateau, the Snake River Plain, and the Fraser Plateau in southern British Columbia. The cultures of the Plateau reflect their own local genius, histories, and adaptations, plus heavy influences from the Plains Culture Area on the east and the Northwest Coast Culture Area on the west. Tribes of the southern Plateau region include the Klamath, Northern Shoshone, Umpqua, Tutuni, Coquille, Upper Chinook, Nez Perce, and Modoc, while the northern Plateau supported the Kutenai, Flathead, Cayuse, Umatilla, Walla Walla, Sanpoil, Okanagon, Klatsop, Spokane, Couer D'Alene, Kalispel, and Shuswap.

Subsistence practices varied north and south and east and west through the Plateau/Basin area. In the south small-scale gathering and hunting of small game prevailed except for those Basin tribes who had begun to tap a bison-hunting way of life. In the Plateau the western tribes placed great emphasis on salmon, while the eastern tribes turned toward bison hunting on the plains.

Archaeological evidence in the Plateau area dates to 10,500 years ago, and most sites of that antiquity are found where, in historic times, Indians established salmon-fishing centers. In the Great Basin the oldest materials date to about 9,000 years ago and indicate that the Indians in the area followed a dispersed gathering way of life that would continue well into historic times. One of many puzzles that has been revealed by archaeological investigation is that the Indians did not make great use of piñon nuts before 5,000 years ago, although they used them extensively after that time.

The weaponry of the Plateau/Basin area holds few surprises. Traditionally, the bow and arrow, war club, thrusting spear, and dagger defined the offensive weapons of all tribes. Since obsidian (volcanic glass) was readily available, most arrows, spears, and knives featured razor-sharp obsidian blades, which had the nasty tendency to shatter on impact and pierce the body with numerous slivers. Lewis and Clark were not impressed with the bows of the Plateau. "These weapons are not, however, very powerful, for many of the elk we kill have been wounded with them; and, although the barb with the small end of the arrows remain, yet the flesh closes, and the animal suffers no permanent injury" (in Biddle 1962, 361). However, not all observers agreed. P. H. Ray, writing on the bows and arrows of the Klamath, remarked, "The bows made by these people are effective for game up to fifty or seventy-five yards. After fifty yards the arrow will penetrate a deer from five to ten inches" (1886, 833).

Though the penetration of the Plateau/Basin bows may be in question, they still proved dangerous because of arrow poisons, which were used by the Northern Shoshone, Nez Perce, Klamath, Modoc, Klatsop, and Interior Salish.

Several writers refer to the use of poison. To Wyeth, the arrows seemed to have been dipped in some dark-colored fluid, which had dried on them. Clark was told that the arrows were dipped into a compound made of pulverized ants, and the spleen of an animal. The mixture was placed in the sun and allowed to decay. "The result was such a deadly poison that if the arrow broke the skin in touching a person, it was sure to produce death." Another source mentions the use of rattlesnake poison both for the chase and in war. (Lowie 1909, 192)

Arrows were doctored to enhance their effectiveness by the Upper Umpqua through magical arrow charms purchased from men who had "arrow Medicine" obtained in dreams or vision quests (Pritzker 1998, 1:303).

The style of making war varied from the Great Basin to the northern Plateau. The causes were standard: to right a wrong, to defend honor, to seek booty, to take slaves, to steal horses, to achieve glory, to defend territory, or to open new territory. The people of the central and western Basin practiced little warfare; did not don armor, helmets, or shields; and did not engage in large-scale fortification building. However, this changes with the tribes grounded in the eastern areas of the Basin. The Wind River Shoshone, or Eastern Shoshone, for example, adopted a Plains style of warfare with the acquisition of the horse. They wore armor and carried small, round shields of bison hide. As on the Plains, great ceremony surrounded the construction of a shield. The Wind River Shoshone often sent war parties in excess of three hundred fighters against their enemies. Shamans accompanied these raids to divine the course of future fighting and to heal wounded men and horses. As with the historic Plains warrior behavior, Wind River Shoshone men occasionally committed what amounted to suicide in their attempts to demonstrate extreme forms of bravery and utter contempt for death.

Only slight variations on the above themes appeared among peoples like the Klamath and Modoc. They fought for the same reasons that spurred the Shoshone, and they, too, donned armor and shields. Their kin-based feuding was acted out in ambush and raids. When fighting among neighbors, they often resorted to the formal "line battle." Like the northern California peoples, they sought compensation after formal fights in the form of wealth, food, weapons, slaves, or clothing. (These customs were also practiced by the Umpqua, Tutuni, and Coquille.)

As with the Shoshone, shamans attended the warriors, but in the case of the Klamath and Modoc, women performed active roles in battles. They often assumed responsibility for the capture of children and the killing of the elderly who attempted to resist a raiding party.

Fortifications

The large-scale strongholds common in many parts of North America are rarely found in the Basin or the Plateau region. The natives' defensive technology resembles that of the High Plains and California. For tribes like the Lower Chinook, crude log and bark stockades are occasionally mentioned, but for the interior Plateau/Basin, breastwork construction and some entrenching are normally the extent of defensive building efforts. Kaj Birket-Smith and Frederica De Laguna (1938, 376), however, did report the use of palisades by the Lillooet.

A rare description of a Ute fortification was written by E. M. Harmon, a pioneer in the Grand County area of Colorado:

> On the crest of a timbered knoll sloping down to the Fraser River a short distance from the town of Granby, there is what apparently must have been a fort at some time. The side of the knoll away from the river is supported by a ledge of sandstone, forming a perpendicular wall or cliff some fifty or sixty feet in height, from the top of which a crescent-shaped barricade, composed of rocks and rotted logs, enclosed a cleared space of less than half an acre in extent. (1945, 167)

The breastwork had been erected in the early 1800s by a Ute hunting party that suddenly found itself in the way of forty Cheyenne and Arapaho raiders. The tale was told to a friend of Mr. Harmon's in the late 1800s by a Ute subchief named Antelope.

Ordinarily, the Ute would have withdrawn from such a large raiding party, but the women and children with them would have hampered a retreat, so they made a stand. Men, women, and children working together built a 4-to-5-foot-high breastwork on a strong defensive position in about two hours.

The raiders studied the refuge while discussing a plan of attack. Since their horses were useless against the steep Ute position, they dismounted and surrounded the breastwork, taking cover behind available rocks and trees. In lieu of a mass charge at the position, they approached and fired individually, a no-win strategy resulting in a stalemate. The situation finally was resolved in favor of the Utes when an unmarried Ute man slipped away in the night to a nearby Ute village for help. The next morning, when the Cheyenne and Arapaho raiders found one of their horse guards with his throat cut and a horse missing, they accepted the inevitable and retreated.

The Flathead, living in the northeasternmost reaches of the Plateau country immediately on the western borders of the Blackfeet, employed a variety of defensive techniques. They constructed a number of wood and stone fortifications at easily defendable positions in their territory, into which they could retire when pursued by enemies. They selected camping sites near streams and coves where rock and trees could be utilized as construction material. Further, like their enemies the Blackfeet, when pursued, the Flathead fled into timber thickets or dug trenches to ward off attack (Fahey 1974, 19).

Fur trader David Thompson reported another Flathead defensive action when in 1810 they were attacked by a large force of Piegans (McGinnis 1990, 32–33). The Flathead pulled down their tipis and formed them into a breastwork, even using some of their horses as part of the barricade.

Ewers, when writing about the war lodges of the northwestern Plains area, noted that the Salish built what he referred to as "rectangular, house-like forts" (1944, 186).

The method of digging trenches inside a lodge, which was noted for the Sioux in Chapter 3, was also found in the Plateau area. In the following, a Blackfeet party surprised a small camp of Nez Perce, who

> showed themselves as brave and skillful in war as they had been mild and long-suffering in peace. Their first care was to dig holes inside of their lodges; thus ensconced, they fought desperately, laying several of the enemy dead upon the ground; while they, though some of them were wounded, lost not a single warrior. (Irving 1961, 129)

Shields

The Great Basin can be quickly eliminated when considering widespread or complex use of shields or armor. Some shield use is reported for the Ute (Callaway 1990, 350). Historically, armor is unknown in the region, but archaeological evidence (Paterek 1994, 191) of large, decorated shields in the Fremont Complex in Utah exists (A.D. 550–1450).

The Sioux called the Eastern Shoshone "Big Shields" because of the body-covering shields used by the prehorse Shoshone. They claimed that the Shoshone would form an unbroken wall by crouching behind their shields (Paterek 1994, 196), which were manufactured with much ritual and prayer from the rawhide of a young buffalo bull. Such shields are also reported for the Northern Shoshone (Pritzker 1998, 1:334). After the acquisition of the horse, the Shoshone abandoned their large shields and adopted the small, round ones that were easier to wield from horseback.

The Nez Perce made the transition from the larger body shields of the preequestrian era to the round Plains style of the horse period. They stretched green elk hides over a hoop frame and trimmed them, when dry, to about 14 inches in diameter (Spinden 1974, 227). Like all Plateau/Basin peoples who adopted the Plains shield, they incorporated various quasi-religious behaviors. Ritual surrounded the manufacture of the shield: It was blessed by a holy man or woman; when not in use, it was mounted on a tripod so as not to touch the ground; and it faced west, a sacred direction. The Flathead also carried a Plains-style shield made of several layers of buffalo rawhide (Paterek 1994, 220).

Large rawhide shields were used by the Walla Walla, Umatilla, and Cayuse in early times and gradually abandoned for the target of the Plains as the horse became more common (Cox 1922, 194). The shields of the Interior Salish (Lillooet, Thompson River Indians, Okanagon, Shuswap) covered the whole body and were composed of splinters of wood like stays and enclosed with hemp twine (Paterek 1994, 222).

The shields of the Okanagon are described below.

Shields of varied shape and construction were used in warfare to parry arrows and spear thrusts. One type was circular (about three feet in diameter) and convex. It was made of rawhide from the neck of an elk, deer, or horse, or when obtainable from buffalo or grizzly bear hide . . . stretched and sewn over a hoop of blue wood, to which a cross of wood was bound. David Isaac, of northern affiliation, reported that both of the cross-sticks bowed outward so that the shield was convex. The shield was held by the horizontal cross-stick or by a cross-piece of buckskin. Round shields of wood were reported by Suszen as the common type, but no details were obtained. Square shields were made of hide or sticks. The hide shields were often bent along the vertical axis so as to present a prow-shaped front which would more easily deflect arrows. The square slat shields were made of sticks "braided" closely together in a checker weave. . . . Shields were used mainly as parrying instruments, and held in the left hand by a man armed with a club. (Post and Commons 1938, 55)

The Lillooet rolled marmot skins thickly around their left arm in lieu of more conventional types of shields (Spier 1928, 358). The shields of the Thompson Indians were described in 1900 by James Teit, a member of the Jesup North Pacific Expedition.

[Shields] . . . were made of wood, and covered with the hide of some large animal, such as the elk, buffalo, or bear; or they consisted of two or three thicknesses of hide only. They were small, circular and flat in shape, being probably not over two feet in diameter, ornamented with elk-teeth, hair, and feathers, generally the last-named. The large copper kettles which the Indians bought from the Hudson Bay Company were beaten out, polished, and made into small, circular shields. Another kind of shield consisted of a large, almost square piece of stiff elk-hide, sometimes double, long enough to cover most of the body, being from four to five feet in length, and three to four feet in width. It was fastened around the neck or shoulder with a thong and two loops were attached for the thumbs of both hands, by which means it was hoisted around to protect any part of the body. (Teit 1900b, 265–266)

Armor

As has been noted, armor was historically unknown in the Great Basin but found universally on the Plateau. Lewis and Clark produced one of the earliest descriptions of Plateau armor when speaking of the Eastern Shoshone: "They have a kind of armor, something like a coat of mail, united by means of a mixture of glue and sand. With this they cover their own bodies and those of their horses, and find it impervious to the arrow" (in Hough 1895, 646). Shoshone armor was often quilted (McGinnis 1990, 6), and Robert Lowie, when writing on the Northern Shoshone, stated: "The armor consisted of many folds of dressed antelope skin, united with glue and sand. This served to protect the bodies of both men and horses" (1909, 193). The quilting on the Shoshone armor held the mixture of sand and glue in place within the layers of the armor (Paterek 1994, 196).

The Nez Perce used not only a shield but also a helmet and armor. The elk rawhide helmet rose above the crown of the head about 10 inches, and a flap hung behind to protect the neck. They formed a sleeveless tunic from elk hide which hung to just above the knees (Spinden 1974, 228). Slat-armor, although used by tribes of the lower Columbia and the Northwest Coast, seems to have been unknown to the Nez Perce.

The Clatsop of interior Oregon fashioned armor as tunics of layered elk hide. They sometimes attached slats within the layers for extra strength. In some Clatsop areas, warriors sewed strings of deer hooves over the front and back of armor tunics for added protection. In addition, they decorated their armor, as they did their rawhide helmets (Paterek 1994, 322).

The Klamath and Modoc wore elk-hide armor of two or more layers as a sleeveless jacket or vest, as well as slat-armor (Pritzker 1998, 1:366). Slat-armor in the form of a cuirass featured many small rectangular pieces of wood that were pierced and sewn tightly together, sometimes overlapping. Slats made a better overall covering than bound rods, or rod-armor, because they provided more coverage and fewer open articulation zones between the slats or rods through which an arrow, knife, or spear blade might enter. Slat-armor was the type worn by the classic Northwest Coast tribes, who dwelt to the north of the Klamath. The Lillooet, Thompson Indians, Colville, and Okanagon wore rod-, slat-, and elk-hide armor, as did the Walla Walla, Umatilla, Umpqua, Tutuni, Kalispel, Shuswap, and Kutenai.

Of the Thompson Indian armor, Teit writes:

A coat of mail was sometimes made in the form of a cuirass. It consisted of four boards an inch and a half thick, two for the front and two for the back, which reached from the collar-bone to the hip-bone. These boards were laced together with buckskin and the whole covered with thick elk-hide. A vest of armor was made of narrow strips of wood from half an inch to an inch in thickness, and went entirely around the body. The strips of wood were placed vertically, and laced together with bark strings. This vest reached from the collar-bone to the hip-bone, and was held over the shoulders by means of thongs. Such vests of armor were generally covered with one or two thicknesses of elk-skin, with a cut fringe around the bottom, and painted with animal and geometrical designs, according to the dreams of the owner. Another kind of armor was in the form of a tunic of elk-hide, that reached about half way to the knee. The sleeves came to the elbows. Before being used, it was soaked in water, and was then said to be perfectly arrow proof. (1900b, 265)

Teit had this to say about the armor of the Lillooet.

Armor consisted of vests made of boards or rods, and of sleeveless tunics of double elk-skin reaching to the knee. Some of the last-named were painted with animal designs in red and white. The vests were of vine-maple wood, and were generally covered with an ordinary shirt, or a single elk-skin tunic. (1900a, 234)

The Okanagon used several kinds of armor (Post and Commons 1938, 55). A single piece of large animal rawhide, reaching below the hips, was worn like a poncho. The sides were laced together, then soaked in water, shaped, and allowed to dry stiff. In another style two pieces of thick rawhide were laced up the sides. Designed for protection of the neck and shoulders, this tunic was often worn under the poncho type of soft armor. They also used several plies of moose hide for a tunic that reached to the hips. The Okanagon employed rod-armor of blue wood twined together with hemp cord, which reached from the armpits to slightly above the hips. They wore no helmets but augmented their armor with one of several kinds of shields. As with most groups, the majority of combatants went into battle wearing only a breechclout and body paint.

Discussion and Summary

Traditional defensive technology in the Great Basin is relatively nonexistent as compared to other regions. The extremely sparse, scattered, and highly mobile populations (fostered no doubt by the uniquely difficult eco-niche afforded hunters and gatherers in the Great Basin) were not prone to elaboration in fortification building, body armoring, or any other aspect of material culture (with a few notable exceptions such as basketry). These tribes built refuges at best. Where they existed, defensive works probably achieved no higher level than entrenching and breastwork construction.

The Plateau provides a different picture. Because of the salmon and bison, Plateau people gathered in large groups and perceived the need to defend favored fishing and hunting sites, as well as access to those sites. Likewise, the overall sensitivity to border maintenance is attested to by the "line battles" and subsequent compensation. The universal presence of armor in the area, including the use of large body shields, faded as the horse and gun and subsequent Plains cultural influences affected the economy and warfare patterns of the Plateau. Armor was abandoned and shields abruptly transformed to the small, round shape like those of the Plains. Photographs of Plateau tribes taken in the late 1800s show Plains-style tipi encampments and men with fringed buckskin shirts, hair-bone breastplates, eagle-feather headdresses (which the Plateau tribes claim they invented), and small, round shields.

6 Warriors with Glittering Shields
The Southwest Culture Area

The Southwest Culture Area includes New Mexico, Arizona, the southern halves of Utah and Colorado, and small portions of southeastern California and Nevada. It is an area of sharp contrasts. The Rocky Mountains push into its center, producing high, cool valleys and numerous deep canyons. At the foot of the mountains begins the high desert, through which several important rivers, fed by mountain snows, flow. In the west the lower reaches of the Colorado River and the Gila River and in the east the Rio Grande provide habitable sites along their meanders in an otherwise forbidding landscape.

The Southwest holds a greater variety of Indian cultures than can be found in any other part of North America. The Pueblo groups include the Hopi, Zuni, Tiwa, Keres, Jemez, and Tewa. The Navaho in the central part of the area reflect a combination of Pueblo and Apachean traits, reworked in a distinctively "Navaho" fashion. The Apache are represented by the Mescalero, Chiricahua, White Mountain, San Carlos, Cibecue, and Tonto. The Navaho and Apache—the Dine who entered the Southwest barely a hundred years before the Spanish arrived—are Athabascan speakers. In the deserts and river valleys and deltas to the west live the Pima, Papago, Yuma, Maricopa, Havasupai, Mohave, Yavapai, and others.

The Indians of the Southwest followed a combination of hunting, gathering, and horticulture, with varying emphasis from area to area. The Pueblo peoples were the most committed horticulturalists of the Southwest, while the Apache were probably the least. The Navaho combined the hunting and gathering of the Apache with the horticulture of the Pueblo and later the animal husbandry introduced by the Spanish. Groups like the Pima and Mohave practiced horticulture but were more dependent on hunting and gathering than the Pueblo peoples.

While the Navaho and Apache are comparatively modern citizens of the Southwest, evidence of the earliest inhabitants dates to over 20,000 years ago. Because the ancestral Pueblo and later prehistoric Pueblo populations built impressive structures and left millions of ceramic artifacts, their history is better known than, for example, that of the Yuman farmers of the lower Colorado River.

Archaeological evidence indicates that up to about 900 A.D. the Southwestern Indians were basically hunters and gatherers with some small reliance on cultigens. During the first few centuries A.D., corn horticulture became increasingly important. People gathered in larger living groups and built pit houses with sizable storage caches for corn. Around 800–900 A.D. pit houses gave way to larger above-ground habitations. After 900 A.D. big masonry, multistoried pueblos with kivas (ritual chambers) and blocks of rooms appeared. These structures were first described by the Spanish explorers and today can be seen in the Southwest, still housing viable Indian populations.

Evidence of warfare appears in the archaeological record from 1 A.D. to 900 A.D., during which time hunting and gathering shifted toward horticulture and small nomadic groups grew to larger sedentary groups. Some fortification building occurred, but it was relatively minor. From 900 to 1200, warfare declined but picked up again about 1250. From this point forward, the defensive technology of the Southwestern groups evolved rapidly from a relatively simple base.

Steven LeBlanc offered a provocative, if peripheral, observation on the rise of Southwestern warfare:

> The increase in warfare in the Southwest, beginning in the 1200s, was not unique to this region. It was a continent-wide phenomenon. There was an increase in warfare in the Northwest Coast area, as seen in an increase in fortifications dating to around this time. There is also considerable evidence from the plains and the central United States for increased warfare in general. Also, shifts in settlement patterns and site layouts similar to those seen in the Southwest are known for the Northeast. And, palisaded villages and the development of no-man's-lands also occurred. . . . The close parallels with Europe involve not only changes in population—a period of low growth followed by growth and then decline—but also an architectural happening. The great Chaco sites were being built at the same time the great Gothic cathedrals were under construction. Furthermore, on both continents, the subsequent fourteenth century was calamitous. . . . Warfare increased at the same time elsewhere on the continent; the great site of Cahokia, near St. Louis, Missouri—location of the biggest prehistoric site and the largest pyramid north of Mexico—flourished at the same time as the Chaco and Gothic architectural events. (1999, 40)

The basic weapon in the Southwest, as elsewhere in North America, was the bow and arrow, and as with previous cases the bows of the Southwest are viewed favorably by some early observers and dismissed by others. In 1770 a Spanish military man described the weaponry of the Yuma. "They rarely have a quiver. Few have as many as five bad arrows, and their bows are worse" (Forbes 1965, 79).

The efforts of the Southwestern Indians to create arrow points that were difficult to remove, to contaminate them to cause an infected wound, and to use poisoned arrows suggest that the bows and arrows of the Southwesterners were not intrinsically lethal weapons (Forbes 1965, 95). Arrow poisoning was used by the Navaho, Havasupai, and the various Apache and Pueblo groups.

Haley, writing on the Apache, stated:

> Although visually unimpressive, the Apache self-bow drove their cane or hardwood arrows with surprising force, reasonably effective to a range of 150 yards and quite steadily accurate at 100 yards and less. Arrows striking a tree at short distance frequently drove into the wood until they were not removable—sometimes over halfway; deer shot at short range were usually run through and the arrows recovered beyond. (1981, 45)

Spanish accounts detailing the penetrating power of sinew-backed bows, which came into general use in the Southwest after 1300 A.D., are noteworthy. Arrows shot by such bows could penetrate Spanish armor and pin a man to his horse (Haley 1981, 98). A simple self-bow could propel an arrow at 35 meters per second, while a dart from an atlatl, or throwing stick, moved at only 21 meters per second. A sinew-backed bow, however, could throw an arrow at 43 meters per second.

One of the truly impressive feats of archery is firing accurately and quickly from a galloping horse. The Japanese martial art Yabusame, or "Three Target Shooting," is entirely devoted to this skill. In the early 1800s, George Catlin observed Apache warriors competing at their version of Yabusame, except they were shooting at ten targets.

> For this day's sport, which is repeated many times in the year, a ground is chosen on the prairie, level and good for running, and in a semicircle are made ten successive circular targets in the ground by cutting away the turf, and making a sort of "bull's-eye" in the center, covered with pipe-clay, which is white. Prizes are shot for, and judges are appointed to award them. Each warrior, mounted, in his war costume and war paint, and shoulders

naked, and shield upon his back, takes ten arrows in his left hand with his bow, as if going into battle, and galloping their horse around in a circle of a mile or so, under full whip to get them at the highest speed, thus pass in succession the ten targets and give their arrows as they pass. The rapidity with which their arrows are placed upon the string and sent is a mystery to the bystander, and must be seen to be believed. No repeating arms ever yet constructed are so rapid, nor any arm, at that little distance, more fatal. (Catlin 1868, 191–192)

Other typical weapons of the Southwest included lances (a specialty of the equestrian Apache), stone-headed war clubs, knives, daggers, slings, atlatls, and fending sticks. The latter were generally used with the atlatl for knocking down arrows. Two types of swords were employed prior to Spanish contact. Shortly before 1100, a two-handed wooden sword was developed in the Southwest. Though some might consider it to be little more than a toy, the greatest swordsman in Japanese history, Miyamoto Musashi, used only a wooden sword in his heyday, defeating the number-two swordsman in an epic duel with a sword he whittled from a boat oar. The second type of sword, constructed from a stick about 3 feet long, was inset with obsidian blades to create a continuous cutting edge, which, according to an early Spanish observer, "would split a man asunder" (Goddard 1931, 10). The Spanish military observed the Aztec at the same time making swords in this fashion capable of decapitating a horse.

The most humble weapon of the Southwest, particularly of the Pueblo peoples, was the rock, which when hurled down from pueblo roofs, proved quite effective. Coronado's first military encounter with the Pueblo Indians almost cost him his life when he was knocked from his horse by a rock.

The people of the whole district had collected there. . . . These folks waited for the army, drawn up by divisions in front of the village. When they refused to have peace on the terms the interpreter extended to them, but appeared defiant, the "Santiago" [battle cry] was given and they were at once put to flight. The Spaniards then attacked the village, which was taken with not a little difficulty since they held the narrow and crooked entrance. During the attack they knocked the general down with a large stone, and would have killed him but for Don Garcia de Lopez de Cardenas and Hernando de Alvarado, who threw themselves above him and drew him away receiving the blows of the stones, which were not few. (Castañeda 1966, 23–24)

The above military reaction of the pueblo dwellers points to a formal concept of warfare. They abandoned the safety of their walls and lined up "by divisions" to confront the Spaniards. When the cavalry charged, they retreated into the pueblo to continue the fight. This pattern of fighting is common across all of North America wherever fortifications are found. From the Chickasaw to the Huron and from the Mandan to the Zuni, records indicate that a highly disciplined body of fighters would leave the confines of their fort to engage attackers, withdrawing only if the tide turned against them.

A battle between the Yuma and the Maricopa in 1842 presents another example of a formal battle and, in this case, the preliminaries to establishing battle lines. The Yuma force was led by two chiefs, one carrying a white feathered staff, the other a black one. One of the staff bearers, a man considered the bravest and best of all, also carried a shield and walked slightly in front of his brother staff bearer. The two war chiefs were followed by club- and spear-carrying warriors, who preceded the largest group, the archers, who fired volleys over the heads of their frontline troops as they approached the enemy. If mounted warriors had been present, they would have carried lances and taken positions on the flanks of the attacking force. Forbes wrote:

> In the autumn . . . the Yumas again came to attack the Maricopa village, but did not attempt to surprise it. They formed in line of battle opposite the line of Maricopas, who were equally courageous. The war chiefs stood between the lines. Each man was armed with a club only. The Yuma chief said to his opponent: "I am ready to have you strike me first if you can." The Maricopa chief answered: "It is for me to let you try your club on me, because you want to kill me, and you have traveled far to satisfy your heart." In the personal combat that ensued the Yuma was killed, the sharp end of his opponent's club piercing his side. The fight became general, each attacking the man opposite him in line. (1965, 76)

Another example of personal combat, or "champion fighting," comes from a fight between the Jocomes Apache and Sobaipuris in Arizona in the early historic period. Though several hundred warriors came to battle, the issue was resolved by a formal combat between ten men from each side (Spicer 1962, 127).

> This description provides a good model for the Puebloan fighting that occurred several centuries earlier during the 1300s. It is easy to envision a few

particularly large and strong Pueblo warriors, with three-foot shields, leading fighting men from a village. Every warrior on both sides would know each leader's reputation as a fighter and could identify them as the sun glistened off the selenite designs on their shields. (LeBlanc 1999, 111)

As everywhere in North America, raids and ambushes were far more common than formal line battles and champion duels. Regardless of the form of battle, the various fighting styles were energized by a passionate belief that warfare expressed spiritual power as well as serving as a means of acquiring it. This notion, in some form, was held by almost all the Southwestern peoples. Success in warfare for the Yuma was the concrete expression of spiritual strength because warfare for them possessed a strong mystical value as the means whereby the spiritual power of the entire tribe was enhanced and at the same time demonstrated (Forbes 1965, 74).

A Spanish naval officer interviewed a Yuma warrior in 1540 about warfare. "Hee answered that they had warre and that on very great, and upon exceeding small occasions: for when they had no cause to make warre, they assembled together, and some of them sayd, let us goe to make warre in such a place, and then all of them set forward with their weapons" (Dobyns et al. 1957, 46).

For the Yuma, the act of fighting was as important as winning, if not more so. In 1848, in another contest with the Maricopa, the Yuma were forced to retreat but remembered the battle with pride because their women joined the fight at the side of their husbands and brothers (Forbes 1965, 74–75). Types of warfare, weaponry, manner of fighting, and attitudes about warfare were shared by all the Yuman tribes of the lower Colorado River, as well as many of their enemies.

Fortifications

Malcolm F. Farmer (1957), in "A Suggested Typology of Defensive Systems of the Southwest," concluded that the Southwest exhibited six basic types of "defensive systems": (1) palisade, (2) tower, (3) fort, (4) hill slope retreat, (5) fortified village, and (6) guard village. The palisade system involved a wall around an entire village or walls around one or more houses. Though usually upright logs, the wall was sometimes stone. Towers were constructed of stone and, though possibly used for ceremonial events, served mainly as defensive refuges. They were located within a village or in some isolated area, often atop large (sometimes house-sized) boulders or points of rock. Often the arrangement provided a clear line of sight to the next tower, which could be several miles away. Forts were single, large structures, usually featuring stout walls, built on easily defended locations such as a hill or mesa. Hill slope retreats comprised one or more walls that functioned as a breastwork, or temporary refuge, at a time of attack and, as the name implies, were aligned on hills or hill slopes. Fortified villages not only featured many of the previously mentioned systems but also augmented them by a design that satisfied ease of defense and that might include walls, palisades, retreat areas, towers, fortifications, and locations on elevated or other kinds of easily defended sites. Guard villages, a type of garrison, housed those who served as defenders of a group of related villages.

One of the earliest known Southwestern forms of fortification dates from between 700 and 900 A.D. In northwestern New Mexico, an upright log palisade, through which brush was intertwined, encircled single houses or groups of houses. These sites could be quite large. One around the Knobby Knee site (Colorado) exceeded 30 meters in diameter and comprised about five hundred large logs. This type of fortification appears to have diminished after 900 A.D., yet as late as 1799, José Cortez wrote that the Kohuanas and Halyikwamais, who lived south of the Yuma, had built palisades around their small villages (Forbes 1965, 59).

LeBlanc considers palisades to be a class of walls that could also include freestanding walls of adobe or stone or the outer walls of inward-facing rooms. Building a site so that the structures themselves form a defensible wall is another type of protective feature, one which provided the most widespread method of settlement defense in the Southwest. Often the walls of rooms created an unbroken perimeter, accomplished by constructing massive blocks of rooms with no exterior doorways. Typically, the outer walls rose two stories, ensuring a very effective barrier (Forbes 1965, 56–57).

This masonry-apartment-complex/fortification became more widespread after 1000 A.D., and some reached incredible size and complexity. In 1541 Coronado sent Captain Hernando de Alvarado with twenty men to scout the village of Acoma, a rock fortress called Hakukia by the Zuni. Castañeda described what the Spaniards found when they arrived:

> The village was very strong, because it was up on a rock out of reach having steep sides in every direction, and so high that it was a very good musket that could throw a ball as high. There was only one entrance by a stair-

way built by hand which began at the top of a slope which is around the foot of the rock. There was a broad stairway for about 200 steps, then a stretch of about 100 narrower steps, and at the top they had to go up about three times as high as a man by means of holes in the rock, in which they put the points of their feet, holding on at the same time by their hands. There was a wall of large and small stones at the top, which they could roll down without showing themselves, so that no army could possibly be strong enough to capture the village. On the top they had room to sow and store a large amount of corn, and cisterns to collect snow and water. (1966, 39)

Interestingly, Castañeda observed that when the Spaniards appeared, the Acoma warriors left their impressive fortress and formed battle lines to face them. Only when their lines were imperiled did they withdraw into their sky fortress.

Attackers not familiar with the pattern found Acoma's mazelike streets difficult to navigate. A network of tunnels connected various kivas and houses throughout the pueblo. Around the base of the mesa on which Acoma sat, foxholes and trenches, as well as numerous deep holes designed to break the legs of Spanish horses, deterred intruders. In 1541 Coronado's captains referred to Acoma as "the greatest stronghold in the world," and in 1581 members of the Chamuscado-Rodriguez expedition named it "the best stronghold in existence even among Christians" (Knaut 1995, 38).

Castañeda also described Matsaki, another impressive fort.

This is the only village that has houses with seven stories. In this village certain houses are used as fortresses; they are higher than the others and set up above them like towers, and there are embrasures and loopholes in them for defending the roofs of the different stories, because like the other villages, they do not have streets, and the flat roofs are all of a height and are used in common. The roofs have to be reached first and these upper houses are the means of defending them. (1966, 45)

The formidable Pecos pueblo was situated in the Rio Grande Basin athwart a major war trail of nomadic invaders.

To survive, its people built houses that towered four stories above the ground and merged them so that sentinels could traverse the rooftops of all without descending. At the second-story level, eaves formed a balcony-like lane that encircled the entire pueblo. Below the eaves, no opening pierced the adobe walls, for all entrances and exits were made by means of portable ladders. Surrounding the settlement was a low stone wall that secured a large courtyard and a spring that provided the town with an emergency water supply. These protective measures were evidently quite effective because there is no archaeological evidence that Pecos was ever taken by enemies. (Kenner 1969, 6–7)

The historical record supports this last statement. Castañeda observed upon arriving there that "the people of this town pride themselves because no one has been able to subjugate them" (in Kenner 1969, 7).

The Navaho in 1818 made use of a mesa top with sides too steep for a horse or mule to climb. They built a breastwork of large stones on the summit, which ascended 1,800 feet above the desert floor, to defend against the forces of Colonel Don Facundo Melgares. Melgares besieged them for over forty days but to no avail. They had brought food with them, and a spring on the mesa provided a permanent water supply (McNitt 1972, 65).   Towers as defensive structures date from the early centuries A.D. up to about 1300. Best developed in the northern areas of the Southwest, they are most elaborately displayed in the Mesa Verde and McElmo areas of southwestern Colorado. The tower complex at the Hovenweep Monument provides excellent examples from the same general time span as Mesa Verde and shows placement in a defensive plan. The five towers extend in a straight line for 15 miles in a line-of-site arrangement. Technically known as a "strategic system," the martial structures connect to defend a large area better than single towers could. Albert Schulman, in "Pre-Columbian Towers in the Southwest," provided the following precise description of the Hovenweep complex:

Towers may be found on boulders, mesa edges, or canyon tops, usually near other ruins.

FORMS: Circular, rectangular, or rectangular with round corners.

SIZE: Present height varies from 8 to 10 feet; thickness is 2 feet; and width varies from between 15 and 26 feet.

CONSTRUCTION: The towers are generally of better construction than the other buildings. Building materials consist of sandstone blocks of irregular size and shape, fastened in place with mud and mortar. On the outside wall, these blocks are often smoothed. Walls are usually of two layers and average 2 feet in thickness. The towers are usually two-storied and may be surmounted by a parapet. They may be fitted with a number of slit windows.

CONCLUSION: The defense motif is strong in the Hovenweep architecture. The buildings of the Hovenweep are designed and situated virtually always with a view toward strategic position and defense. (1950, 292)

While towers seem most developed in the northern reaches of the Southwest, the southern zones featured the *trincheras,* a hill slope retreat of low stone walls. Though most of these constructions occur in central and southern Arizona, the *trincheras* is also associated with the eighteenth-century Navaho in northwestern New Mexico. Some of the earliest examples in northern Mexico date to before 200 A.D. This kind of construction included as many as a hundred low stone walls that either encircled a hill completely or appeared only on a section of it, with a stone breastwork found on the associated hilltop. In historic times the Utes of southern Colorado constructed such refuges. In the Southwest the majority of *trincheras* date from about 500 to 1150 (Farmer 1957, 254–255).

Shields

The Southwest fascination with shields equaled that of the Plains warriors and exceeded theirs in producing a greater variety of designs. One of the earliest types, the fending stick, was used with atlatls, or spear throwers. Held in the left hand, it deflected atlatl darts. When the simple self-bow came into use, the fending stick was displaced because of the difficulty of knocking away the smaller, faster arrows at close range. Sometime about 1100 a two-handed wooden sword, carefully crafted from oak, entered the Southwest. It was quickly superseded by the one-handed sword in conjunction with a larger wicker shield, which was in turn nullified a few centuries later by the superior firepower of the sinew-backed bow (LeBlanc 1999, 97).

Prehistoric shields have been excavated from burials at the Mesa Verde, Mummy Cave, and Aztec sites. All are basketry. Wright noted:

The coil of the basket is a bundle of three willow rods laced together with yucca in a simple, non-interlocking stitch to form a circular plaque roughly three feet in diameter. The center is bowed outward slightly to leave room for the hand behind the hard wood grip. The shield is supported by this short hand grip, lashed with yucca across the inner convexity. . . . The outer surface of the Aztec shield has been painted. The central portion is blue-green with a thin rim of red. The outer margin of the shield was covered with pitch and sprinkled with powdered selenite for sparkle. (1976, 4)

It is doubtful that basketry shields could have deflected arrows shot from sinew-backed bows, which could pierce Spanish chain mail. Against stones, clubs, and wooden swords, however, they would have proven both light and effective. After 1300, the time of the introduction of the sinew-backed bow, shields were made of thick elk, bison, and horse rawhide.

> In the period just prior to the coming of the Spaniards, there were at least three distinct shield traditions: basketry, netting and hide. Of these three, the basketry and netted shield do not survive into historic times except as miniature ritual objects. Examples of hide shields have not been found in other than the historic era, though they must predate this period. (Wright 1976, 7)

Zuni expert Frank Cushing wrote, "The Pueblo tribes carried round shields of basketry, heavily and closely netted cotton, or of thick rawhide, symbolically painted" (in Hough 1895, 628). Paterek's comment on the Pima reflects Cushing's "shields of closely netted cotton": "Shields were made of a heavy fabric painted black with white spokes, a design that was supposed to have power over the enemy when rotated" (1994, 176).

The Mohave used two types of shields, both round and about 2 feet in diameter. Constructed of deer- or horsehide, they mainly protected the heart. For one, rawhide was stretched over a rim of mesquite or screwbean wood. The other had no wooden rim but was fashioned by sewing two thicknesses of rawhide together. In both cases a leather thong affixed to the inside served as a handle. The Mohave painted them either all red or all black (Stewart 1947, 265).

Navaho shields were originally buckskin and probably used mainly to parry arrows shot from a self-bow. In time, however, the Navaho, like other Southwesterners, manufactured their shields from horse or bison rawhide. W. W. Hill (1936, 11), in "Navaho Warfare," described the Navaho with a Plains-style shield. He stated that they utilized hide from the hip of a bison or horse, and occasionally in two layers. The green hide was shaped over "a knoll about the size of an ant hill" and trimmed to 18 inches in diameter when dried. Usually the finished shield had an interior handle and decorations on the surface and the rim. Sometimes it was creased down the middle and could be folded when not in use, although what appeared to be a folded shield to some early observers may have been a more conventional shield tied in such a manner as to preserve its curvature. In some cases thick rawhide thongs laced the edges for more strength. Also enhancing the strength, the Navaho bent a branch into a circular shape and tied the shield to it by adding interior crosspieces.

The Navaho typically painted their shields black with a white design in the center. As a final magical augmentation, they attached a small bag of "squirrel pollen." The pollen was poured on a Rio Grande ground squirrel and shaken off, placed in a small bag, and tied to the shield. They believed that this would render the warrior invisible. Hough described another type of Navaho shield: "The Navaho made shields of cedar rods twined together with cord which may be connected with the cord armor of the Athapascans" (1895, 628).

A folded shield of small laths was reported for the Ceris and Chicoratos of New Mexico. It was closely interwoven with cords in such a manner that, when not required for use, it could be closed like a fan and carried under the arm.

An account (Spier 1928, 356ff.) dating from the mid-1800s, of a Yavapai raid on a Havasupai camp in the Grand Canyon, offered information on the defensive techniques of both groups. Buckskins were used in at least two ways as shields during this fight. The Havasupai draped a deer pelt over a short stick (sometimes a bow) and held it before them as a "curtain-shield" and closed on their enemies with a hatchet in their right hand. At one point in the account, the Yavapai were trapped and out of arrows. They quickly built a breastwork and hurled stones down at the Havasupai, who parried the stones with buckskins hanging from their left arm, yet another curtain-shield technique. A number of times, runners were sent back to the Havasupai camp for more deerskins, as the ones in use lost their effectiveness after absorbing rocks and arrows for a number of hours. At several points the account mentioned that the men walking behind their curtain-shields approached to within a few feet of the enemy. The curtain-shield was described for the Havasupai, Walapai, Hualapai, and Yavapai.

The eastern Apache used round shields, in style like those of the Plains but in some cases a little larger. When fighting on foot with a shield, they were trained to crouch low and extend the shield before them so that they almost disappeared from view as they approached the enemy.

Armor

Many types of armor were used in the Southwest. The Hopi went into battle wearing moccasins, a white kilt, sash, and several layers of deerskin wrapped around their torsos or, in lieu of the body wrapping, a suit of basketry armor (Paterek 1994, 16). Breastplates of rib bones were found in some Pueblo archaeological sites (Paterek 1994, 179). Pueblo Indians used leather jackets as battle coats (Goddard 1931, 106), and they also wore cuirasses of either elk or bison skin or padded cotton and yucca (Hough 1895, 647).

The leather wrapping around the middle of the body, noted above for the Hopi, was also employed by Mohave warriors, but instead of leather, they braided vines of black-eyed peas and wrapped them around their stomachs for protection (Stewart 1947, 265). Other tribes in the Mohave area covered their stomachs with horsehide wraps.

A Navaho warrior selected the thickest buckskin he could find for his war shirt. This garment, often as many as four layers thick, fit tightly around the neck, and the sleeves reached almost to the elbow. To secure the layers after they had been cut to size, the Navaho rubbed a glue made from a cactus leaf into the layers and pressed them together until the glue set, then quilted the entire surface to maintain the shirt's shape. The four-ply armor was used in offensive actions. Warriors fighting from horseback wore a much heavier eight-ply leather shirt, which reached the knees and split in the front and back so that the horse could be straddled (Hill 1936, 9).

The Apache reflected the general armor-making techniques of their linguistic brethren the Navaho, except that the various Apache groups seemed more influenced by Spanish battle dress. In the process of acquiring horses from the Spanish, they adopted the dress and fighting techniques of their enemy. They already had a leather armor tradition that provided a cuirass equal to the leather upper-body protection worn by the Spaniards; however, they slightly modified their more ancient version with a cuirass of overlapping leather scales, more along the line of the best-made Spanish garment. They borrowed the concept of armoring their horses with rawhide sheets and scaled armor, as well as donning helmets of rawhide. They affixed Spanish cutlasses to the ends of their lance shafts to make a Spanish-style pike, or lance.

Armor was widely dispersed throughout Apache society. In 1731 Governor Bustillo y Zevallos, with over two hundred men, met an equal number of Apache in a battle near San Antonio. All the Apache were wearing "leather breastplates." And on January 2, 1758, twenty-two Apache appeared and expressed a desire to talk with the commander of a small garrison in northern Mexico. Hoig wrote, "The fact that these men were sporting six leather military jackets, five short swords, and lances made a deep impression on the Spaniards" (1993, 26).

Groups that wore armor as well as groups that did not used helmets and various kinds of head protection. The Navaho had two kinds of hats for battle—one type made from the head pelts of badgers, wildcats, skunks, or mountain lions, and the other from two layers of deerhide. Both were equipped with chin straps (Hill 1936, 9). The Yuma's skin helmets were discontinued sometime after 1540 (Forbes 1965, 101). The Pima used turbans in battle, as did the Jicarilla and Mescalero Apache (Paterek 1994, 160).

Discussion and Summary

Several possible external influences affected armoring and fortification traditions in the Southwest. The Spanish effect is clear, especially with the Apache. They borrowed the Spanish style of body armor and horse armor and the employment of lances, shields, and cavalry warfare, building on their more ancient traditions of leather and rawhide armor. The quilted armor found in northern Mexico, called *escupile* by the Aztec, strongly influenced the Southwest. The use of curtain-shields is rare and seems dispersed in the western reaches of the Southwest area and into California.

The styles of warfare found in the Southwest—ambush, raid, formal battles, defensive struggles, etc.—are universal in native North America, though the fortifications are highly distinctive. Breastworks and entrenching are found everywhere, but multistoried pueblos, often in amazingly effective defensive positions, as well as towers and *trincheras,* stand as distinctively Southwestern in design.

Southwestern armament and martial behavior infiltrated the religious life of the area. The Navaho connected success in warfare with certain complex rituals known as Ways. They considered the territory of the enemy and the ghosts of slain enemies evil and implemented ritual acts to defeat this evil. The three most important Ways of going to war included the Monster Slayer Way, the Enemy Way, and the Yei Hastin Way; and raiding involved the Blessing Way, Bear Way, Big Snake Way, Turtle Way, and Frog Way. The Mountain Chant Way, for example, specifically mentioned suits of armor constructed of several layers of leather (Matthews 1883–1884, 73). The leader of the war party had to be knowledgeable of the prayers and observances of the several Ways of going to war (Hill 1936, 6).

Two of the most important Zuni gods are the Warrior Twins. They were armed, as were the warriors of old, with long bows and black stone-tipped cane arrows carried in long-tailed catamount-skin quivers; with slings and death-dealing stones carried in fiber pockets, spear throwers, and blood drinking broad knives of gray stone in fur pouches with short face-pulping war clubs thrust aslant in their girdles. And shields of cotton plaited with yucca upon their backs. About their bodies they wore a casing of scorched raw-hide, horn-like in harness, while upon their heads were helmets like the neck-hide of the elks from which they came. (LeBlanc 1999, 47)

Finally, as with High Plains shield art, painting shields on kiva masonry or scratching or painting them on rocks became widespread in the Southwest in the mid-thirteenth century. After 1325 war-related figures, along with other rock-art motifs, were displayed both on rocks near villages and in the open country some distance away, so that they became part of the Pueblo terrain and definition of Pueblo space (Schaafsma 2000, 33).

7

Land of the Cold Snow Forests
The Subarctic Culture Area

The interiors of Alaska and Canada shape the Subarctic Culture Area. This land of dense forests, rivers and streams, bogs, lakes, and punishing cold best suited small, mobile bands who pooled their meager resources from hunting, trapping, gathering, and fishing. Some of the Subarctic groups occupied territory that gave them access to migrating herds of bison and caribou, while rivers that ran with salmon several times a year favored others. Hunting targets for most bands included squirrel, rabbit, fox, beaver, porcupine, moose, deer, and bear. The many bodies of water teemed with whitefish, salmon, pickerel, trout, perch, and sturgeon. Game birds drawn to the lakes and marshes were harvested in their season.

The groups that roamed the subarctic forests comprised Algonquin speakers in the east and Athabascans in the west. Little culturally differentiated the two. Major tribes of the Subarctic area include the Koyukon, Tanana, Tanaina, Kutchin, Han, Nabesna, Tutchone, Hare, Kaska, Tahltan, Slavey, Beaver, Carrier, Chilcotin, Cree, Chipewyan, Dogrib, and Yellowknife. And, since most evidence points to Siberia as the major source of the American Indians, it is not surprising that the western subarctic would hold some of the more ancient archaeological finds in the New World, including projectile points dating back almost 20,000 years in Saskatchewan.

Warfare, admittedly of a very low level, occurred frequently in the Subarctic because of the harshness of life and was characterized by raids, ambush, and brawls in lieu of formal battles. Resources had to be protected, with each group struggling to maintain a reputation that would hold potential invaders at bay. The Kutchin, for example, lived at the edge of Inuit territory and often engaged them militarily. The Kutchin recounted to Slobodin (1960, 78) three incidents that spurred them to attack. In the first, a contest of the hunting magic of an Inuit and a Kutchin escalated to the point that each enlisted friends and relatives to join the struggle. Another fight started when an Inuit man claimed a Kutchin had cheated him while trading; the rape of a Kutchin girl precipitated the third.

The Kutchin, like most subarctic groups, preferred to fight during good weather. They particularly favored war in the spring just before the ice broke up in the lakes and rivers, since they felt confident they could move faster than the Inuit under those conditions. During the winter the Kutchin were dispersed, trying to survive in weather that could hover at twenty below zero for months at a time.

A Kutchin raiding party might number two or three dozen men. Led by a band headman or a man known for his prowess as a war leader, the raid would be instigated by someone with a grievance. He or she notified the potential war leader, who, in turn, selected three subleaders. The family instigating the fight presented the leader with a wolverine pelt, which he cut into strips and gave to each man, who wrapped one around his head. This act signified his willingness to partake in the action, as well as connecting him to the wolverine, one of the most ferocious animals of the subarctic forests.

Kutchin attacks on an enemy camp followed a predictable pattern, up to a point. The war leader indicated a tent for each man, or group of men, to attack at a given signal. The men surrounded the sleeping camp. When the signal came, they rushed the target tent, knocked it down, and brought clubs to bear against the inhabitants, who struggled to free themselves. Those who ran were shot with bows and arrows. The Kutchin, like most area groups, killed men, women, and children in these raids. At the time of the attack, bodies of the victims were disjointed in an act of sympathetic magic to reduce the speed and agility of the enemy. Also, some ceremonial cannibalism occurred (Slobodin 1960, 84). If their adversaries lived in a log house instead of tents, the Kutchin blocked the exits, poured oil over the structure, and set it on fire (Vanstone 1974, 50).

The Tanana occupied the western borders of the Kutchin. Called "Rat People" by their neighbors, they were constantly involved in fighting, "like muskrats during mating season." They fought mainly to avenge the death of, or injury to, a relative, particularly a member of one's clan. Tanana wars featured surprise night attacks with a greatly superior force and the indiscriminate killing of men, women, and children. This vendetta-like nature of warfare was common among the Athabascans, particularly the Tahltan, Callbreath, Carrier, and other groups west of the Rocky Mountains. Since revenge for an injury constituted another injury that, in turn, had to be avenged, the Indians tried to wipe out the entire family and close relatives of the aggressor, even if this necessitated visiting several different camps. Since war was based on revenge and revenge usually meant death, prisoners were not taken (McKennan 1959, 96).

In eastern Canada the Micmac engaged in formal battles that both sides agreed to begin and end under certain conditions—when the sun set or when a certain number of men on each side had been killed, for example (Wallis and Wallis 1955, 217). Still, as with most northerners, basic Micmac warfare was ambush and raids largely centered around issues of vengeance.

The weaponry of Subarctic warriors included bows and arrows, of course. They did not manufacture special arrows for war, as some groups did, but utilized their hunting arrows. Only the Micmac used arrow poison (Wallis and Wallis 1955, 33). The Kutchin warrior's favorite weapon was a two-and-a-half- to three-foot club made of a caribou antler from which the second tines had been cut. The antler was boiled to soften it and straightened or bent into a shape desired by a particular fighter (Slobodin 1960, 82). The Kutchin used lances, and like most Subarctic bands they favored a particularly heavy version for killing bears, moose, caribou, and men. Two kinds of knives were made for hand-to-hand combat, a style of fighting much more typical here than in many native American areas: one, a two-edged copper dagger characteristic of the Alaskan Athabascans; the other, a rare double-ended knife, with a caribou antler handle in the middle and copper blades on either end, used by wealthy senior warriors (McKennan 1959, 37).

The Tanana employed the typical array of Subarctic weaponry—bows and arrows, knives, spears, and clubs. They made a specialized adze from antler that looked like a pickax (Vanstone 1974, 51), an excellent weapon for piercing armor. The Sekani added to the general Subarctic weapons repertoire a moose jaw club and a bayonet affixed to the end of their bows (Denniston 1990, 436).

Fortifications

Very little can be said about fortification building in the Subarctic. Only on the northern fringes of the Northeast Culture Area and along the northern edges of the Great Lakes are found the palisade sites so typical of the heartland of the Northeast Area. The Ottawa, living north of Lake Huron, occasionally surrounded their villages with palisades (Pritzker 1998, 2:648), and along the south bank of the Miramichi River, the Micmac dug defensive entrenchments (Wallis and Wallis 1955, 217). The bands of the northern forests no doubt employed breastwork building, but there is little mention of it. Early accounts often indicated the use of natural cover and elevations when the situation warranted it.

Shields

The Subarctic people employed a number of shield styles; however, like groups other than those of the Plains and Southwest, theirs were functional as opposed to mystical defenses. Since the Subarctic bands had easy access to heavy-pelted animals—moose, bison, and caribou—it is no surprise that shields come from their hides. The Anishinabe designed shields from several layers of moose rawhide, as did groups like the Ottawa (Pritzker 1998, 2:648), Montagnais/Naskapi, and Chippewa (Paterek 1994, 48).

Various kinds of wooden shields were prevalent. The Sekani covered oblong wooden shields with pitch and pebbles (Denniston 1990, 436). The Slavey sewed willow twigs tightly together (Pritzker 1998, 2:735). The Kaska wove together two or three planks of birch, each about 3 feet long, and added thick layers of grease to the surface (Honigmann 1954, 94). The Carrier Indians manufactured wooden slat shields, oval in shape (Paterek 1994, 352).

A missionary in lower Canada in 1633 described a shield as well as the manner in which it was used in battle:

> He bore with him a very large buckler, very long and very wide; it covered all my body easily, and went from my feet up to my chest. They raise it and cover themselves entirely with it. It was made of a single piece of very light cedar; I do not know how they can smooth so large and wide a board with their knives; it was a little bent or curved in order the better to cover the body, and in order that the strokes of arrows or of blows coming to split it should not carry away the piece, he had sewed it above and below with cord of skin: they do not carry these shields on the arm; they pass the cord which sustains them over the right shoulder, protecting the left side; and when they have aimed their blow they have only to draw back the right side to cover themselves. (In Beauchamp 1905, 127)

Armor

Rod- and slat-armor, breastplates, and multi-ply rawhide jackets and tunics are found in the Subarctic Culture Area, and attaching sand and pebbles to shields and armor with pitch is more highly developed by far than in any other area.

The Carrier Indians constructed armor from several layers of moose rawhide, or from wooden slats, to which they fastened pebbles for added protection. This kind of cuirass armor was widespread in the central and eastern Subarctic. The Ahtna warriors' armor consisted of wooden rods or of rabbit or beaver skins pitched and coated with sand and gravel (De Laguna and McClellen 1990, 652). The Montagnais/Naskapi adopted slat-armor from the Iroquois, while the Tahltan wore tunics of mountain goat hides, and the Slavey, cuirasses of willow twigs (Paterek 1994, 368, 374, 371).

Writing about the western Dine in general, Morice commented, "While on the warpath they also wore a kind of armor or cuirass consisting of dried sticks of the same kind of wood, *Amelanchier alnifolia,* arranged in parallel order and kept together with babiche lines interlaced in several places" (1889, 140). Vanstone observed of the western Dine, "Slat armor similar to that found among the Eskimo and along the Pacific Coast was used most prominently by the western Athapaskan groups in Alaska" (1974, 51).

Morice offered the following description of early Dine armor:

Another sort of armor, indigenous to the Dene nation, was the *peoesta.* . . . This had the form of a sleeveless tunic falling to the knees, so that it afforded protection to the whole body save the head. . . . The armor of cuirass was of moose skin, which, when sewed according to the proper pattern, was soaked in water, then repeatedly rubbed on the sandy shore of a stream or lake and dried with the sand and small pebbles adhering thereto, after which it was thoroughly coated with a species of very tenacious glue, the principal ingredient of which was boiled isinglass obtained from the sturgeon. Being again, before drying, subjected to a thorough rubbing over, it received a new coating of the aforesaid glue. When this process had been repeated three or four times, it formed an armor perfectly invulnerable to arrows over the part which was protected. (1889, 140)

Concerning Dine armor, Hough wrote:

The skin coats were always made in one piece folded over, sewed above the shoulders, leaving an orifice for the head and with a hole cut out of the left side for the left arm, the right side of the garment remaining open. The skin was often doubled, and more frequently the coat was reinforced with pieces of thick hide. Sometimes shoulder guards were added. (1895, 641)

Pierre de Charlevoix encountered armor north of Niagara Falls:

When they attacked any entrenchment, they covered their whole body with small light boards. Some have a sort of cuirass, or breastplate, of small pliable rings very neatly worked. They had even formerly a kind of mail for the arms and thighs made of the same materials. (1966 [1744], 337)

The armor of the Kaska of Fort Laird in 1866 is described in Honigmann's "Ethnography and Acculturation of the Fort Nelson Slave": "From their neck down to their thighs, they wear a mat of willow switches; it covers the whole front and guards against arrows as it is closely matted for that purpose" (1946, 99). Those Kaska who lived between the Slave and the Tahltan made sleeveless bear-hide coats that reached to the knees, hair side out (Honigmann 1946, 93).

In the latter 1770s, an account of the Cree stated that they wore "coats of mail, made of many folds of dressed leather, which are impenetrable to the force of arrows" (Ewers 1980, 204).

The Tanana coated bear-hide armor with a layer of pitch and sand. McKenna (1959, 97) suggested that they may have obtained it through a trade network. The Upper Tanana claimed that they had never used armor; however, they had a name for it, *ditcin-ek,* or "stick shirt," and believed that their culture hero, Tsa-o-sha, had worn it.

Slat-armor, as well as that made from large-game rawhide, is reported for the Western Kutchin (Slobodin 1960, 83), Cree (Sutton 2000, 93), Chilcotin (Pritzker 1998, 2:705), and Chippewa (Paterek 1994, 48).

The final three types of armoring are quite rare and singular to the Subarctic area. J. Alden Mason wrote in "Notes on the Indians of the Great Slave Lake Area," "I was informed that armor was made of plates of copper buckled together for use in warfare with the Eskimo" (1946, 168). The Chandalar Kutchin warriors' breastplate, called *ekain,* was fashioned from the shovel antler of a caribou (McKennan 1959, 37), and the Micmac hung an oblong piece of hard wood, suspended by a thong around the neck, under their rawhide war jackets as a breastplate (Wallis and Wallis 1955, 33).

Helmets are described for a number of Subarctic bands. Indians in Ontario at the time of contact wore ones of cedar or basswood. Those of the Thaltan were of mountain goat rawhide (Paterek 1994, 374), whereas the Kaska donned a caribou-hide helmet, hair side out, which was lined with birch bark (Honigmann 1954, 93).

Discussion and Summary

Authorities suggest that slat-armor predominated in the western areas of the Subarctic and rod-armor in the east. Slat-armor in the west is generally associated with the Northwest Coast tribes, who, in turn, were greatly influenced by such groups as the Chukchee and other Siberian peoples, who traded with the Indians and Aleut and manufactured metal slat-armor.

Hough wrote:

> The slat type of wooden armor seems to be central among the Koluschans in the north, while the rod type runs southward and is central among the Tinne of British Columbia. The slat armor has some resemblance to the Eskimo coat, and might be regarded as the working out of the plate-armor idea in a region where wood is abundant and twined weaving common. ["Koluschans" was the Russian designation for the Northwest Coast Indians, and "Tinne" is an early spelling of "Dine."] (1895, 636)

The predominant shield of the Subarctic Culture Area has several layers of moose, elk, bear, bison, or deer rawhide, although wooden styles were also used. Covering pitch and glue with sand and pebbles is more highly developed in the Subarctic than elsewhere, and the one mention of copper slat-armor echoes the models from the Chukchee-Indian trade. Employing the shovel antler from the moose as a breastplate is unique to the area.

The ritual isolation of men who killed in battle was a widespread custom in this area. The Chilcotin (Lane 1990, 408) practiced this behavior, as did the Ahtna (De Laguna and McClellen 1990, 652). In the former case, the man simply withdrew for an unspecified period from all members of his band except his wife. In the latter case, a more elaborate ritual behavior was practiced. The warrior was considered to be somewhat unbalanced at this time; he wanted to be alone, and he found sleep difficult. He could not hunt or fish because it was thought that his impurity would poison the food. He wore strings around his hands, wrists, knees, and ankles, symbolizing the attempt to control his wildness. The Ahtna warrior remained in this condition for approximately one hundred days.

The Salmon Kings
The Northwest Coast Culture Area

8

The Northwest Coast Culture Area extends from northern California to the south coast of Alaska. Population is centered along the coastal strand and islands that characterize the region. Extensions of the culture area run inland through the forests and along the bays and fjords to the north-south mountain spine that borders the east. This area encompasses the coasts of northern California, Oregon, Washington, British Columbia, and Alaska, as well as Vancouver Island, the Alexander Archipelago, and the Queen Charlotte Islands. The Northwest Coast Culture Area lies 1,300 to 1,400 miles from north to south in a straight line, but because of the great intricacy of the islands and coastline, a true shoreline measurement would probably double this figure.

Thirty-nine languages were spoken on the Northwest Coast with a number of sociopolitical groups comprising each linguistic group. The Tlingit, for example, were organized into three regional tribal groupings, which in turn comprised sixteen smaller groups, or villages.

At the height of the region's traditional development, the Northwest Coast societies represented the richest hunting-and-gathering cultures on earth. They lived in a territory abundant in fresh- and saltwater fish, shell-fish, big game, aquatic fowl, wild plant foods, and sea mammals, with salmon being the staple. Most food could be acquired during the summer and autumn months, allowing much leisure time in the spring and winter when elaborate ceremonials were performed, and arts and crafts—particularly painting and wood carving—were developed to a high degree. The societies of the region were organized into complex systems of rank, clan, and class based on the manipulation of wealth. Hereditary crests similar to the European coats-of-arms identified individual families. The area's cedar plank houses often exceeded 20 by 60 feet, and canoes reached 60 feet in length.

The main tribes in the northern area were the Tsimshian, Haida, and Tlingit. In the central area the Nuu-chal-nulth (Nootka) and the Kwakwaka'wakw (Kwakiutl) held sway on Vancouver Island and portions of the adjacent British Columbia mainland. On the British Columbia coast north of the Kwakwaka'wakw, the Heiltsuk (Bella Bella), Nuxalk (Bella Coola), and Haisla lived. South from the Nuu-chal-nulth, the Salish-speaking tribes (Makah, Quileute, Tillamook, Alsens) and others were found.

Recent archaeological findings (Ames and Maschner 1999, 88ff.) indicate that humans have been living in the Northwest Coast area for at least 11,000 years. It is likely that earlier materials exist but cannot be accessed because numerous sea level changes have inundated the coast over thousands of years.

Between 4400 and 1800 B.C., changes in temperature and sea level made more feasible the gathering of marine mollusks as a resource, and settlements in the vicinity of this resource grew more stable. Shellfish debris over many centuries formed middens that could cover thousands of square meters and rise to a height of several meters.

By 1800 B.C., the sea level stabilized at modern levels. Likewise, the forests assumed a contemporary profile with the appearance of vast stands of western red and yellow cedar, woods crucial to traditional manufacturing techniques. From 1800 B.C. to about 300 A.D., the Northwest Coast people built their characteristic large plank houses, intensified reliance on salmon, established themselves into large permanent villages, ranked themselves socially by wealth, evolved a distinctive art style, constructed large seagoing canoes, and engaged in warfare.

The earliest evidence of violence on the Northwest Coast dates to between 4400 and 1800 B.C., the Early Pacific Period. A male skeleton with a bone point embedded in his spine, found at Namu, dates to 2200 B.C. At a site in the same era at Prince Rupert Harbor, several bodies appear to have been bound and decapitated. Twenty-one percent of the skeletal remains of the latter Early Pacific Period displayed trauma from interpersonal violence (Ames and Maschner 1999, 209). In the Late Pacific Period, which dates from 200–500 A.D. to 1850, the most persuasive evidence of expanding warfare is the many fortifications, trench embankments, and hilltop villages discovered throughout the region.

Northwest Coast Indians warred for a variety of reasons. They sought revenge for affronts against their populations by other groups (murder, rape, assault, theft) and for what they felt to be insults against their honor, status, and the prerequisites of such ranked positions; they raided for slaves; they fought over women; they struggled to acquire, as well as defend, valuable food sources; they battled to defend territory and also to win it; and they fought for control of trade and trading routes.

An oft-noted confrontation stemming from sensitivity to offended honor was observed in December of 1860 by Lieutenant Commander Golovnin, a Russian naval officer who was visiting Sitka, the Russian capital of southeast Alaska. He was overlooking the Tlingit village that adjoined the fortified capital when Indians poured out of one of the larger houses, shouting and running in all directions. They soon regrouped, dressed in armor and fully armed. To the lieutenant's astonishment, they began to fight, and before the Russians dispersed them with several cannon rounds fired over their heads, twenty Tlingit had been wounded, two critically. The following day, when Lieutenant Golovnin interviewed the combatants, he learned that the Sitka Tlingit had outsung the Yakutat Tlingit in a potlatch ceremony—a very important event for the Tlingit in general—and not for the first time. Since the Yakutat Tlingit's honor had been offended, their response was to fight.

Wars over access to food and trade were widespread. In 1852, for example, a Chilkat Tlingit chief named Chartrich led a raiding party against a Hudson Bay Company trading post 300 miles into the interior. He destroyed the fort, which he felt was impacting the trade of the Tlingit. Numerous battles were waged over control of various rivers and streams that had unusually strong salmon or eulachon (a fish that produced an oil that was an important trade commodity) runs.

The battles of the Northwest Coast Indians—particularly those of the Haida, Tsimshian, and Nuu-chal-nulth—produced high casualty rates. The Nuu-chal-nulth attacked other Nuu-chal-nulth groups, killing all men, women, and children, to take their land and salmon fishing sites.

Helen Codere, when describing Kwakwaka'wakw warfare, wrote:

> Kwakiutl warfare was not valorous. It was waged out of feelings of grief, and shame, the desire to retaliate, or, above all, to acquire or maintain the prestige of being considered utterly terrifying. It was waged on the outnumbered and the unsuspecting, on victims rather than enemies. (1950, 98)

The Kwakwaka'wakw delivered hundreds of men to a battle, or more likely ambush, in 50- to 70-foot canoes, each carrying thirty to fifty men. The Northwest Coast people commonly battled on open water in canoes.

Technically speaking, not all raiders were warriors. Boys who showed the right personality traits (surliness, aggressiveness, hostility, insensitivity, violence) were educated as warriors. Trained in the martial arts, these young men practiced running, swimming, and diving and were taught to be cruel and treacherous and to ignore all rules of decent social behavior. Their people disliked and feared them because of their violent outbursts, which could come at any time and for the slightest provocation. They carried rocks to attack people who irritated them. Never smiling or laughing, they walked with stiff, jerky motions—which to the Kwakwaka'wakw indicated tension and anger—and never wore a shirt or robe over their right shoulder, so that they would always be ready to fight. These martial specialists were sprinkled throughout the ranks of raiders to stiffen them for the displays of ferocity that Kwakwaka'wakw warfare demanded.

Professional warriors, also found among the Coast Salish tribes, delighted in causing fear and consternation among their fellow villagers. The southern Salish tribes believed terrifying spirits, which they had been trained to seek in dreams and vision-seeking expeditions, animated these "mean men." When going into battle, such men, through songs taught to them by their war spirits, could whip themselves into a berserk frenzy. Among northern Salish tribes, warriors did not seek spiritual powers to make them wild in battle but rather considered the role as a professional position which ran in families. Fathers in family lines that did not have the prerogative to create professional warriors still sought to elicit the desire to fight well in at least one of their sons.

The military organization of the Snoqualmie, a Puget Sound chiefdom, included Fall City, a town devoted to military training, and Tolt, the administrative center. Fall City was strategically located near Tolt and was protected upriver by Snoqualmie Falls, downriver by the Tolt Fort, and on either side by the Rattlesnake Mountains. Young boys who at the age of twelve or thirteen exhibited warrior traits were sent to Fall City for martial arts training. The best of them became the elite force of the chief, and these semiprofessional soldiers conducted raids and ambushes at his direction. Rarely were their wars overly bloody or long-lived. The same formal and arranged battles that were found in the south in California occurred in the southern area of the Northwest Coast, as seen in the following description of the Indians of the Puget Sound area.

> Having once determined on hostilities, they give notice to the enemy of the day on which they intend to make the attack, and having previously engaged as auxiliaries a number of young men whom they pay for that purpose, they embark in canoes for the scene of action. Several of their women

accompany them on their expedition, and assist in working the canoes. On arriving at the enemy's village, they enter into a parley, and endeavor by negotiation to terminate the quarrel amicably. . . . Should their joint efforts fail in procuring redress, they immediately prepare for action. Should the day be far advanced, the combat was deferred by mutual consent till the following morning, and they pass the night intervening in frightening yells and making use of abusive and insulting language to each other. They generally fight from their canoes, which they take care to incline to one side presenting the higher flank to the enemy; and in this position with their bodies quite bent the battle commences. Owing to the curve of their canoes, and their impenetrable armor, it is seldom bloody. . . . The same description will apply to most of the battles on the Sound except where northern tribes are concerned, who are more warlike and ferocious. (Gibbs 1877, 190–191)

That their battles are "seldom bloody" is also attributed to the custom of ceasing the fight when warriors on both sides were killed. They then made peace, exchanged presents, and returned home. This custom worked only for the local tribes, not the more northerly raiders (e.g., Kwakwa-ka'wakw, Nuu-chal-nulth, etc.).

Dramatic evidence for the confidence and daring of the Northwest Coast warriors, particularly the Haida, can be read in records of their attacks against Spanish, Russian, British, and American trading ships. The Indians were not always successful against the muskets and cannons of their would-be victims. The first to record an attack was Captain James Hanna, one of the first maritime traders on the Northwest Coast. He had sailed from China in April 1785 in a brig of 60 tons and anchored in Nootka Sound. The Nootka traded with him for a few days before attempting to take his ship. In 1789 Haida Indians attacked the *Iphigenia* as it approached the Queen Charlotte Islands, and in April 1791 they assaulted the *Gustavas,* under Captain Thomas Barnett. In July 1792 the Indians of Kyoquot Sound unsuccessfully attacked the *Hope.*

In 1794 the Haida captured two trading vessels, the first a British ship in the Houston Stewart Channel. Little is known about this incident although the following supplies a fourth-hand account:

A large ship supposed to be English and to belong to London put into a Sound at the south end of the Queen Charlotte Islands, some time last winter with the loss of some of her masts: the natives for several days traded very peaceably with them, but from the distressful situation of the ship, several of the crew sick, and others on shore providing new masts, they took their opportunity and cut off the vessel, killing the whole crew. (Howay 1925, 297)

In 1794, in overcoming the second ship, the *Eleanora,* under Captain Metcalfe, the Haida killed all but one of the crew. The Indian raiders took only a few minutes to accomplish their victory and suffered no casualties (Howay 1925, 298). In 1799 Indians attacked the *Dragon* and the *Caroline* in Norfolk Sound, and in 1803 the Nuu-chal-nulth captured the *Boston* in Nootka Sound. In the same year the Nuu-chal-nulth assaulted two other traders.

The Northwest Coast warriors wielded a great variety of weapons. Early accounts of Tlingit weaponry documented bows and arrows tipped with shell, bone, or copper; spears; clubs; and daggers. The spear was hurled with the aid of an *atlatl,* or "spear thrower" (Knapp and Childe 1896, 37). For hand-to-hand combat, they used a dagger described as "a peculiar affair, short and one bladed, with ordinarily four edges, something like a bowie-knife, somewhat dull, but in the grasp of an infuriated savage a deadly weapon" (Knapp and Childe 1896, 37). They also liked a two-ended dagger with one end longer than the other. The weapon was grasped in the middle by a bone handle to attack an armor-wearing fighter at close range (Holm 1990, 216).

The Chehalis, one of the Southwestern Coast Salish, had a mussel-shell knife and a whalebone dagger for close-in fighting (Hajda 1990, 509); and the Kwakwaka'wakw's varied weaponry is described below.

Weapons for war were the lance, about one and one-half meters long, made of a single piece of yew wood; a club of whale bone; the stone dagger; the battle-ax; a stone club enclosed in hide, with a short handle provided with a loop by which it was suspended from the wrist; the bone dagger; and bow and arrows with barbed stone points which made dangerous wounds because they had to be pulled or cut out. They also used the sling, which was made of dressed elk skin. Ordinary stones were used with the sling. Lance and sling were said to have been the principal weapons. (Boas 1966, 105)

Arrow poisoning is rarely recorded for Northwest Coast warfare, but it may have been used by the Southern Coast Salish tribes (Suttles 1990, 495). The close proximity of the Southern Coast Salish groups to the tribes of northern California, where arrow poisoning was widely practiced, supports this suggestion. Firearms were added to the repertoire of the Kwakwaka'wakw in 1785, and by 1846 guns proliferated throughout the Northwest Coast area.

Fortifications

Fortifications—often located in defensible positions on historically known tribal boundaries—became prevalent on the Northwest Coast beginning about 200–500 A.D. In August of 1779, Vancouver visited a number of fortified sites in southeastern Alaska, observing

> the remains of no less than eight deserted villages . . . all uniformly situated on the summit of some precipice, or steep insular rock, rendered by nature almost inaccessible, and by art and great labor made a strong defense . . . These fortified places were well constructed with a strong platform of wood, laid on the most elevated part of the rock, and projecting so far from its sides as to overspread the declivity. The edge of the platform was surrounded by a barricade of raised logs of wood placed on each other. (Ames and Maschner 1999, 210)

In the same year, De la Boca y Quadra observed a Tlingit fortification, likewise situated on a rocky summit, with ladders required to mount it. In 1778 Captain James Cook wrote of a Haida hilltop fort on Graham Island, and Newcombe described several dozen such sites for the Haida (Ames and Maschner 1999, 211).

Another important eighteenth-century fort, the Tsimshian fortress at Kitwanga, was oriented to control an important "grease trail," a route from the coast to the interior along which eulachon oil was traded. Built on a steep-sided hill in the Skeena River floodplain, it covered about 1,000 square meters and was surrounded by an outward-tilted palisade. Logs with branches trimmed to sharp points hung along the top of the walls as an *abbatis,* or they could be rolled down on attackers who attempted to mine or set fire to the palisades. Inside, five large plank houses sheltered the defenders. Hidden trapdoors under the floors accessed storage pits and escape tunnels.

Many hundreds of years before the classic palisade forts of the eighteenth century, Northwest Coast people created such structures as the Kuiu Island refuge in Tebenkof Bay in southeastern Alaska. On a steep-sided island, it controlled access to the most productive salmon stream in the river. The top had been cleared, and shell middens covered the area. A number of such sites in the area, some including stone terraces, date between 1440 and 1650.

Franz Boas offered the following description of a Kwakwaka'wakw fort:

According to the statements of old men, the village was protected in time of war by a stockade with a single entrance. The stakes of the palisade were about three fathoms long and were tied together with cedar withes. On a platform erected on the inside of the palisade, high enough to give a clear view of the surrounding country, watchmen were stationed at regular intervals. Ditches, about three meters deep, with a covered underground entrance, led into houses. They were guarded by sentinels. When the village was attacked, they offered a chance of escape to the people. (1966, 105)

Boas (1966, 105) also commented on "fortified houses" located on "elevated places." If the Kwakwaka'wakw were attacked and had no time to enter the strongholds, they would mount the roofs of their houses and draw the ladders up after them (Codere 1950, 100).

At another point in his famous *Kwakiutl Ethnography,* Boas described an attempt by the Kwakiutl to overcome the fortified Bella Coola village of Talio.

At that time, the village was surrounded by a double stockade, the top being crowned by thorns. At each corner, a strong box was fastened at the top of the stockade and served as a watch tower. The Talio people had only four guns. The Kwakiutl sent out two spies, who reported that the village was well fortified, and that they would not be able to enter unless the stockade was destroyed. (1966, 111)

The fortifying of houses, as Boas noted for the Kwakiutl, was practiced by the Bella Bella, who lived on a maze of islands off the west-central coast of British Columbia. Their multifamily homes sometimes reached 105 by 15 feet. They built stockades and defensive ditches around the houses, which were elevated about 20 feet on thick timber pilings. The houses were entered by ladders, which were drawn in if the stockade and dry moat were breached.

Many tribes of the Puget Sound area fortified their houses with thick boards 12 to 15 feet tall, which were strengthened by sturdy posts and crosspieces. Loopholes for firing arrows or guns were inserted in the wall (Castile 1985, 152).

The tribes of the southern area of the Northwest Coast constructed large strongholds against infringements, especially by the northern tribes.

For protection against these attacks they have large enclosures, 400 feet long and capable of containing many families, which are constructed of pickets, made of thick planks, about 30 feet high. The pickets are firmly fixed into the ground, the spaces between them being only sufficient to point a musket through. The appearance of one of these enclosures is formidable, and they may be termed impregnable to any Indian force: for in the opinion of the officers, it would have required artillery to make a breach in them. The interior of the enclosure is divided into lodges and has all the aspects of a fortress. (Castile 1985, 152)

Three Coast Salish tribes owned forts to defend against their major enemies, the southern Kwakwaka'wakw groups. The Samish, Lummi, and Semiahmoos forts were designed by the same man around 1820–1830. The Semiahmoos fort featured stockades surrounding large plank houses, with tunnels connecting the houses and loopholes along the stockade wall. The builder created a means to light the area at night by hoisting baskets of flaming pitch above the level of the stockade. This basic plan was followed by the Lummi and Samish, except that the Samish added poisoned stakes around their fort (Suttles 1974, 378). The Sliaman, Squamish, and Seshelt, whose forts were styled after those of the Lummi, Samish, and Semiahmoos, dug escape tunnels from inside the forts to some point in the surrounding forest. Underground rooms could be entered by easily defendable tunnels (Barnett 1955, 49). The Sliaman arranged large rocks along the top of their palisades to drop on attackers.

The Coast Salish of British Columbia built "fighting houses," semisubterranean earthlodges in style but designed as fortresses. The floor was excavated 6 feet into the earth, and a sturdy roof of logs and planks was covered with earth. The entrance, a low inclined passageway, proved difficult to enter and easy to defend (Barnett 1955, 51).

Ronald L. Olson offered the following detailed description of a fort of the Quinault, a tribe of the Oregon coast:

Perhaps about 1800 the people of *kwi'nait* enclosed the village in a palisade which consisted of posts about 16 feet long set into the ground about three feet. The posts were made of 18-inch cedar and cottonwood split in half and set round side out. The posts were strengthened by lashing hemlock poles about four inches in diameter just below the tops of the posts. Several openings in the wall served as gateways. These were closed by means of doors which were barred from the inside. Around the inside of the wall a cedar plank about 18 inches wide was placed as a shooting platform. It was placed at such a height that the head and neck of a man standing on it were above the top of the posts. The plank rested on stout pegs set into holes chiseled into the posts. In times of danger sentries paced back and forth along the platform. Several other villages were also palisaded. (1936, 117)

Earthworks, as well as palisades, were found in the Northwest Coast area frequented by the Coast Salish tribes. A site on a point between Baynes Sound and Deep Bay forms an ellipse-shaped enclosure 265 paces in circumference. The embankment slope stretches 15 paces in length, rising at an angle of 50 degrees from the bottom of the borrow ditch, which served as a dry moat, to the top of a parapet. The area within was cleared to create a flat surface. About 150 feet to the north stood a similar, though smaller, structure, the two being connected by a trench (Newcombe 1931, 7).

The most northerly of the Northwest Coast tribes, the Eyak Indians of the Copper River Delta in Alaska, constructed a primitive type of fortification.

In the center of the village, according to Galushia, stood the fort or stockade, used as a refuge in time of war. It was built of upright posts instead of planks, and because of its construction was given the same name as the fish trap. There was a single door. A space inside was excavated for a depth of a few feet. Galushia does not know whether this structure was roofed, or whether a house was built inside the stockade. Food was stored in the fort. (Birket-Smith and De Laguna 1938, 43)

Sometimes a Northwest Coast tribe occupied a powerful defensive position without massive palisades, bastions, and dry moats—as in the case of the Snoqualmie, described earlier. Their administrative center, Tolt, was backed by a steep sand hill that was virtually impregnable and controlled traffic on the river. Only elite warriors knew the secret trail to its summit. At the top, a breastwork surrounded a natural pond and caches of food and weapons.

One of the most dramatic examples of Northwest Coast fortification building took place in 1804. Two years earlier the Tlingit, believing that the Russians posed a direct economic threat to their fur trade, attacked the Russian fort St. Archangel Michael at Sitka, killing all its occupants. At the time the Russian military commander and governor, Alexander Baranov, was patrolling to the south in the vicinity of Kodiak Island.

In the summer of 1804, Captain Baranov set out with four vessels, 120 Russians, 800 Aleut and Kodiak islanders, and three hundred kayaks to punish the Sitka Tlingit. They bombarded several Tlingit villages, but the

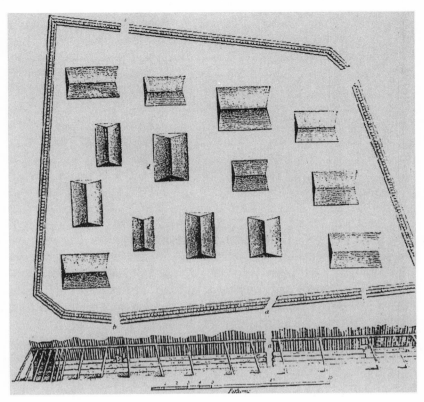

Tlingit fort at Sitka. 1804.

Indians had retired into their fort at the head of a shallow bay that Baranov's heavy warships could not navigate. When Baranov dispatched his fighters in kayaks, the Tlingit abandoned the fort, which was typical of the palisade fortifications constructed by the Indians of the area, to skirmish. The Russians found that their musket balls simply bounced off the armor worn by the Tlingit.

Baranov commenced bombarding the fort with cannon fire but, receiving no response, ordered several hundred Russian sailors and Aleut with 5 cannons and 150 guns to take it. When his assault group neared the fort, the Indians opened fire with their own cannons and muskets. All of the Russian sailors were wounded, including Baranov; the Aleut were routed; and several of the Russian ships were damaged.

The following day Baranov bombarded the fort once more but was disheartened when, after each round, he watched helplessly as the Indians ran out to collect the Russian cannon balls that had bounced off the palisade. Finally, on the night of October 7, the Indians slipped away to Chatham Strait, where they built another fort. The effectiveness of the Tlingit revolt and fear of their skill in warfare kept the Russians from any further expansion for the next fifty years (Ames and Maschner 1999, 212).

The sheer number of forts on the Northwest Coast is impressive. Archaeological (excavation), ethnographic (interview), and historical (written record) sources identify fifty-five forts among the Tsimshian, Haida, Kwakwaka'wakw, Heiltsuk (Bella Bella), Nuxalk (Bella Coola), Nuu-chal-nulth, and Salish. Franz Boas mapped twenty forts for the Kwakwaka'wakw alone, and fourteen are known for the Angoon Tlingit. Moss and Erlandson wrote:

> If the number of ethnographically documented forts for the Angoon Tlingit is representative of other *kwaans* (local groups), there may be 300 or more ethnographic forts for the Tlingit area of southeast Alaska. If other Northwest Indian groups had comparable numbers of forts, there may have been well over a thousand ethnographic forts on the Northwest Coast. (1992, 76)

Shields

Perhaps because armor was so highly developed on the Northwest Coast, shields played a relatively small role in warfare. The Kwakwaka'wakw, Haida, and Nuu-chal-nulth rarely used them; similarly, the Eyak did not rely heavily on them.

> The description of the Eyak shield is not very clear, but it seems to have been different from the ordinary round shield of the Plains. Generally speaking the shield did not play a very prominent role in the northwestern parts of the North American continent, where slat or leather armor in many cases took its place. (Birket-Smith and De Laguna 1938, 466)

Shields of "wooden splinters" were found in areas surrounding the Eyak, e.g., among the Aleut and Pacific Eskimo, as well as Indians of the Mackenzie and northern Plateau areas. The Upper Chehalis, a Coastal Salish group, constructed shields from cedar slats (Hajda 1990, 509), and the Tsimshian Indians used beaten copper (Paterek 1994, 299). The Chinook carried Plains-style circular shields of elk hide, about 18 inches in diameter (Ray 1938, 60). The Nuxalk (Bella Coola) and allied groups on the coast of British Columbia utilized heavy shields of moose rawhide.

Armor

The armor of the Northwest Coast Indians is by far the most elaborate and effective of any North American Indian group. The complexity is least noticed among the most northerly Northwest Coast groups, most elaborated among the central area peoples, and moderately developed among southern groups. The Eyak battle dress, however, was very basic; they simply wore a leather apron into battle (Birket-Smith and De Laguna 1938, 70).

The Haida, on the other hand, wore rod-and-slat armor, which included not only upper torso protection but also greaves for the thighs and lower legs. The front and back of the cuirass were slats, while rods in the side pieces allowed more flexibility. Under this armor they wore elk-hide tunics, and on their heads, heavy wooden helmets. The Russians found that arrows could not penetrate this armor, nor could a musket ball shot from moderate range, and the Spanish noted that Haida helmets were as heavy as iron.

Haida chiefs sometimes wore a twisted copper necklet very much like the neck torques of the Celts. A Haida myth tells of a noble who was turned into a salmon. When the fish was caught, the women could not sever its head because it wore one of these copper necklets. A functional connection possibly exists among the Haida copper necklet, the Celtic torque, and the gorgets of classical European armor.

> An early description of Tsimshian armor shows its complexity. Their war garments were formed of 2, 3, or more folds of the strongest hides of the land animals they were able to procure. In the center was a hole sufficient to admit the head and left arm to pass through, the mode of wearing them being over the right shoulder under the left arm. The left side of the garment is sewn up, but the right side remains open; the body is, however, tolerably well protected, and both arms are left at liberty for action. As a further security, on the part which covers the breast, they sometimes fix on the inside thin laths of wood. (Vancouver in Hough 1895, 646)

Paterek noted for the Tsimshian, "Armor was fashioned from two or three layers of tough elk-hide in a large, flat rectangle with an opening for the head; it was partially sewn together or tied at the sides" (1994, 336). Pritzker wrote that the Tsimshian wore "hide and rod armor over moosehide shirts as well as wooden helmets" (1998, 1:297).

Captain Cook presented this description of Tlingit armor:

They encase almost the entire body in a wooden or leather armor. They make a breast plate of wood, and an arrow-proof coat of thin flexible strips bound with strings like a woman's stays. They wear helmets with curiously carved visors, and a kind of jacket, or coat of mail, made of thin laths bound together with sinews which makes it quite flexible, though so close as not to admit an arrow or dart. (In Hough 1895, 637)

In 1791 Tomas de Suria, traveling along the Northwest Coast with Commanders Alejandro Malaspina and José Bustamante, encountered Tlingit warriors.

The fighting Indians wear all their arms, a breast-plate, back armor, a helmet with a visor or at least what serves that purpose. The breast and back armor are of a kind of coat of mail of board two fingers thick [wide?], joined by a thick cord which with much union and equality joins them. In this junction the thread takes an opposite direction, it being the case that even here the arrows cannot pass through, much less in the thickest part of the boards. This breast-plate is bound to the body by the back. They wear an apron of armor from the waist to the knees of the same character which must hinder their walking. Of the same material they cover the arm from the shoulder to the elbow, on the legs they use some leggings which reach to the middle of the thigh, the hair inside. They construct the helmet of various shapes; usually it is a piece of wood, very solid and thick, so much so, that when I put one on it weighed the same as if it had been of iron. They always have a great figure in front, a young eagle or a kind of parrot, and to cover the face they lower from the helmet a piece of wood which surrounds this and hangs from some pieces of leather in the middle of the head to unite with another one which comes up from the chin. They join at the nose, leaving the junction for the place through which to see. It is to be noted that before they put this armor on they put on a robe like that of a woman but heavier and thicker, with certain kinds of work. (In Wagner 1936, 158)

For the Tlingit, Olson and Olson wrote:

The most impressive form of Tlingit dress was the warrior's armor. A complete outfit required a wooden helmet, oftentimes made into an animal or crest design. Below the helmet was a neck piece or visor to protect the man's face. His chest and waist were covered with a leather jacket or tunic over which he wore wooden slat armor. The armor was so effective that

Tlingit Indian in armor. 1791.

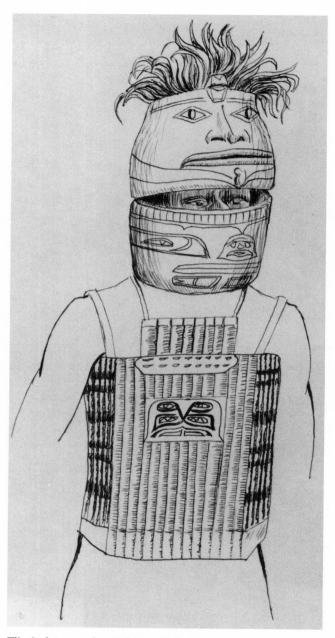

Tlingit slat-armor breastplate and helmet.

after the introduction of firearms, they simply added another layer of leather over the armor so the musket balls would not penetrate. (1991, 23)

The helmets mentioned by Cook and others "were ordinarily designed to represent the crests of the ancestors from whom the paternal grandfathers of the warriors who use them had descended" (Shotridge 1919, 44). After the demise of armor, these helmets became clan hats used for ceremonials. A Russian observed the Tlingit's helmets in 1792: "On their heads they wore large wooden hats which were fastened to the rest of their armor with thongs. . . . The Russians aimed directly at their heads, but the bullets did not penetrate the thick head covering" (in Miller 1967, 134).

The Tlingit employed armor at sea as well as on land. In an encounter at sea, the assailants paused and put on their armor before advancing. The boats were turned slightly so that the gunwales intervened between them and their enemies. Each person encased himself in a wooden or leather cuirass. Outside this he wore a kind of jacket. (Knapp and Childe 1896, 36–37)

The visors, mentioned by all observers for the Tlingit, were held in place by a loop of spruce root, attached to the interior, that the warrior held in his teeth. The leather tunics worn under the wooden armor were typically painted with clan insignia and skulls. The painted leather armor alone was donned when a fighter needed more mobility or was of a relatively minor status.

The American Museum of Natural History houses a Tlingit greave, or piece of lower leg armor. Hough presented the following detailed description of the artifact:

It is made up of 12 slightly tapering hard wood slats and 8 rods sewn together with sinew cord. The portion not covered with weaving bears a totemic painting. When curled around the leg the hollowed-out portions accommodate the instep, and knee joint. It was secured by thongs and probably with a band or a garter. The holes along the upper edge are probably for attaching the greave to the cuisard. . . . This greave leads to the inference that a similar protection was extended to the upper legs and the arms. With heavy wooden helmet, the slat coat and armor for the limbs, we have a picture of an Alaskan warrior armed cap-a-pie. (1895, 372)

The Tlingit warrior showed originality in the creation of his armor. A Russian explorer in 1805 wrote of a Tlingit warrior armed for battle wearing a buckskin strip around his neck from which hung iron plates cover-

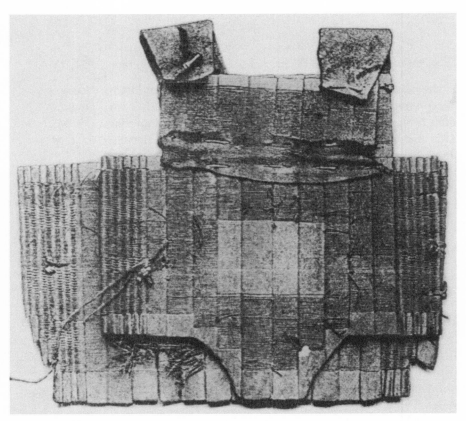

Tlingit slat-and-rod armor.

ing his breast (Hough 1895, 633). Boas collected a Tlingit leather battle jacket (late nineteenth century), which featured Chinese coins sewn to the surface to harden it. The presence of the exotic coins can be understood in terms of the fur trade. The traders brought sea otter furs from the Northwest Coast to China, where they were sold and traded for spices, which were then taken to Boston. A portion of the profit outfitted another ship bound for the fur trade on the Northwest Coast. Chinese coins collected during the journeys interested the Indians and so became part of the ongoing trade in the area.

Franz Boas tersely commented on Kwakwaka'wakw armor: "Armor *(L'pe'tsa)* was made of dressed elk skin *(ala'g'em)*. They do not remember having used helmets or armor made of rods" (1966, 105). Codere stated with regard to the same group, "Body armor made of wooden slats was part of war equipment" (1950, 99).

A more complex description of Kwakwaka'wakw armor follows:

The men wore an unusual type of armor as shown in a Curtis photograph of a Kwakiutl warrior; strands of rope were bound around the torso and over the shoulder to form a sort of breastplate. A wraparound skirt of woven, shredded cedar bark was worn beneath this. They also made armor from elk hide and from wooden slats. The warrior went barefoot and bareheaded. No shields were mentioned by sources consulted. (Paterek 1994, 315)

Captain Cook observed Nuu-chal-nulth armor:

The only dress amongst the people of Nootka, observed by us, that seems peculiarly adapted to war, is a thick leathern mantle doubled, which, from its size, appears to be the skin of an elk or buffalo, tanned. This they fasten on, in the common manner; and it is so contrived, that it may reach up, and cover the breast quite to the throat, falling, at the same time, almost to the heels. It is, sometimes, ingeniously painted in different compartments; and is not only sufficiently strong to resist arrows, but, as they informed us by signs, even spears cannot pierce it; so that it may be considered as their coat of mail, or most complete defensive armor. (In Miller 1967, 47)

Several sources indicated that painted armor was worn only by their war chiefs. Further, the long hide tunic described by Cook was occasionally reinforced by wooden rods sewn to the outside of the thick hide. As with the Kwakwaka'wakw, helmets were apparently not part of the Nuu-chal-nulth battle dress.

East of the Nuu-chal-nulth, the Nuxalk (Bella Coola) and the Heiltsuk (Bella Bella) of British Columbia used several kinds of hide-based and wood-based armor. The Heiltsuk wore tunics of multiple layers of deer hide, and the Nuxalk made slat-armor from maple and birch in lieu of leather tunics or in addition to the multi-ply leather underarmor.

Elk-hide war tunics of at least two layers were worn by the Salishan speakers of the south-central and southern regions of the Northwest Coast (Squamish, Klallam, Halkomelen, Comox, Pentlatch, Seshelt, Skagit, Sky-homish, Puyallup, and others), but reports on the presence of rod-armor or slat-armor among the southern Salish groups conflict. Pritzker (1998, 1:284) claimed that the Southwest Coast Salish had slat breastplates, while Suttles and Lane (1990, 495) contended that aside from a "hide shift," no armor was worn.

The Puget Sound Indians preferred a long hide tunic and cedar-bark, bear-grass, and leather helmets that withstood arrows as well as their armor. There is mention of a cuirass constructed of "slips of hard wood" laced together with bear grass (Castile 1985, 152). Eighteenth-century Spanish explorers in the Juan De Fuca Strait described a war garment used by the local Indians:

> We bought some of these which look like the breast doublets in Spain but are very thick. On asking them if they made use of these to protect them-selves from intemperate weather they said "no," but that for that purpose they had and wore an abundance of blankets of very coarse wool, with which most of the crew have supplied themselves, and that they only used the skins during their skirmishes or war to protect themselves from the ar-rows. They put them on double and only open on the left side. (Wagner 1936, 179)

In another encounter with the Indians in the Juan De Fuca Strait, the Spanish traded for leather cuirasses six to eight skins thick. The Indians explained that this armor was for their battles with Indians of the north coast.

On the Washington coast most warriors entered battle naked, except a few chiefs with elk hides or armor of wooden slats or whalebone (Paterek 1994, 339). Quinault armor was described as follows:

> Armor consisted of a sleeveless shirt *(gwatke'lks)* reaching to mid-thigh. It was made double, of the heaviest elk skin, and laced up the front. It is said that an arrow shot from the strongest bow would scarcely penetrate the double thickness. Rod and slat armor of wood or whalebone (baleen) was sometimes worn in addition. There were no protective devices for the head beyond the ordinary hat, or for neck, arms or legs. The shield was unknown. (Olson 1936, 118)

Quinault warriors painted skulls on their war tunics to represent the number of enemies they had killed. Multi-ply, hanging elk-skin armor was seen among the Chehalis, Quileute, Tillamook, Umpqua, Tutuni, Tolowa, and Coquille (Miller and Seaburg 1990, 583).

Armor appeared in Tlingit duels of honor. Each combatant held the end of a length of rope in his left hand and a dagger in his right. They fought until one was vanquished or dropped the rope. In these stylized battles the fighters wore heavy leather tunics under slat-armor and donned masks and helmets (Knapp and Childe 1896, 41).

As was observed with the horse armoring on the Great Plains, Indians armored the vehicles that transported them into battle. On the Northwest Coast, that vehicle was the canoe. Sailing along the coast of Washington, Captain George Vancouver encountered canoes that "were furnished with rudely cut boards set at each end about three feet above the gunwales. They were perforated and the warriors could shoot arrows through the holes without exposing themselves" (Gunther 1972, 850).

Discussion and Summary

Among the Tlingit, Haida, Tsimshian, Kwakwaka'wakw, and Bella Coola, large sheets of copper, simply referred to as "coppers," were considered items of great value and were usually owned by the highest-ranking individuals in a village. These breastplate-shaped items reached 30 to 36 inches in width and 20 to 25 inches in length. A typical example in the National Museum of Canada is 0.017 inches to 0.025 inches thick and weighs 2 pounds (Couture and Edwards 1940, 202). The size of these plates of copper varied from 7 or 8 inches to 4 feet in length. The upper part of the coppers was sometimes engraved with totemic designs of the bear, eagle, crow, or whale (Richard 1939, 34). Prior to Western contact, "coppers" were fashioned by the Indians from native copper found in Alaska and parts of Canada. After contact, Russians and British along the Northwest Coast traded in "coppers" fabricated in the West expressly for the Northwest Coast Indian trade.

Most modern scholars feel that "coppers" are merely symbolic items, a dramatic unit of measure. For example, Richard wrote, "These coppers have the same function which bank notes of high denomination have with us. The actual value of the piece of copper is small, but it is made to represent a large number of blankets and can always be sold for blankets" (1939, 34). Coppers accompanied the transmission of chieftainship and were usually placed beside the bodies of deceased chiefs to symbolize their wealth and supernatural power.

Some observers, however, point directly and indirectly to the root of the "copper" in the armoring culture of the Northwest Coast. James Colnett, who in 1787 was the first European to see "coppers," wrote: ". . . their copper breastplate which is their underarmour, nothing would induce them to part with it" (1787, 136). Richard (1939, 34) wrote that the "coppers" were at one time worn suspended from the neck like a breastplate. A custom of the Siberian shaman suggests a connection between ritual "coppers" and breastplate armor. (In succeeding chapters, the role of Siberian populations in the diffusion of armor into the Northwest Coast area will be examined in detail.) They wore numerous protective pendants of iron and copper under their coats, the items considered to be armor.

> The breastplate, the most enduring element of the ancient costume, appears to be a possible antecedent to coppers. Some investigators believed the breastplate to be very ancient and possibly Chinese in origin (mention is made in a Chinese source of such an object in 263 A.D.) and transmitted north by the Tungus. It was worn by the Tungus on the naked body inside the coat and was always tied by a strap around the neck and another at the waist. Breast pieces vary among the many Siberian peoples who wore them, but some almost duplicate the outline of coppers. Several have rib-like motifs reminiscent of Kwakiutl coppers. (Jopling 1989, 123–124)

A number of Northwest Coast Indian tribes symbolically guarded the breast with copper. Children wore copper pendants for protection, and "coppers" were often pressed to a sick child's breast to augment healing. These Indians painted the faces of mythic entities on them and hung them at chest level, and copper collars were believed to offer spiritual protection.

The connection between weaponry and religious symbolism is clearly noted by Holm's comment on Tlingit art: "Weapons and war regalia resembled shamans' implements in many ways, and perhaps the concept of utilizing supernatural power in the shaman's contest with the malevolent spirits carried over to human conflict" (Holm 1990, 614). The similarity between motifs on a shaman's mask and the warrior's helmet is also noteworthy. Perhaps a stylistic connection exists between the shaman's hat (helmet?) on the Northwest Coast and the "helmet masks" of the Zuni (Hultkrantz 1987, 116). The "helmet mask" is remarkably similar to the helmets of many Pueblo groups.

> Helmet masks encircle the head like a rounded bag over the top of the head. These masks, which completely cover the dancer's head, are made of deer or buffalo skin or simply cowhide. The mask is usually crowned by bunches of feathers; the more feathers, the more important is the *kachina* (an ancestral spirit, or rain spirit). (Hultkrantz 1987, 119)

The Zuni helmet mask that encircled the head like a "rounded bag" is echoed on the Northwest Coast. Some helmets are mentioned as being baglike masks of elk skin with holes for the eyes (Paterek 1994, 299).

The economic role of armor production was particularly important for the Chinook of the Columbia River. Their elk-hide armor was reputed to have been the finest on the Northwest Coast. In great demand, it was traded widely. One type of armor manufactured and traded by the Chinook was the *clamons*.

A heavy stiff vestment of double thickness of elk skin covered the body down to the ankles; arm holes were provided, leaving the arms free. This was quite impenetrable to arrows. On the head was worn a helmet of elk skin or perhaps heavy basketry work in cedar bark or bear grass. (Ray 1938, 60)

The *clamons* was nearly half an inch thick (Hough 1895, 640). The Chinook also made a light rod cuirass fashioned of ironwood dowels, which fit under or over the *clamons*. They generally wore one or the other, not both types of armor.

Clamons were very popular trade items. Ruby and Brown note:

Fastest-moving items in the northern market were the clamons, the protective armor so demanded by oft-warring peoples of Vancouver and the Queen Charlotte Islands and other points on the upper Northwest Coast. Chinooks had carried on a clamon trade with northern peoples for years. (1976, 61)

An early indication of the value of Chinook armor comes from the records of traders who plied the area. Captain Samuel Burling "obtained from the Chinooks sixty-three sea otter skins and twenty-seven clamons at a rate of two sea otter skins and four clamons per copper sheet" (Ruby and Brown 1976, 72). Another trader estimated that the 192 *clamons* he had acquired from the Chinook would fetch him 677 prime sea otter pelts from the Indians of the Queen Charlotte Islands. In return for the *clamons,* the Chinook received 10 pounds of powder, 4 muskets, 304 copper rods, 73 tea kettles, 16 pounds of sheet copper, 3 quart-sized copper cups, 6 copper saucepans, a pewter jug, 18 silver-hilted swords, 4 common swords, 62 iron bars, 300 pounds of musket balls, 4 yards of cloth, 8 blankets, 16 copper buckets, 7 files, 3 tin powder flasks, 2 brass Guinea kettles, and 30 dozen buttons (Ruby and Brown 1976, 72).

9

The Strongbows
The Southeast Culture Area

The northern boundary of the Southeast Culture Area extends from Delaware westward to the confluence of the Missouri and Mississippi Rivers. The western border runs from the area of St. Louis southwest to the eastern border of Oklahoma and then southward to the Gulf of Mexico. The Atlantic coast and the southern Gulf Coast form the eastern boundary. This area encompasses the present-day states of Florida, Georgia, Alabama, South Carolina, North Carolina, Virginia, Maryland, Delaware, Mississippi, Louisiana, Arkansas, Tennessee, Virginia, and West Virginia; southern portions of Ohio, Indiana, and Illinois; the southeastern quadrant of Missouri; the eastern edge of Oklahoma; and southeast Texas.

The physical environment of the Southeast Indians included the Flatwoods, an area stretching 20 to 40 miles inland from the gulf or ocean shore. It is an area of sandy hillocks and swamp dominated by conifers, scrub oak, saw palmettos, cypress, cane, and savannah grass. In the southern regions of the Southeast Area, an Interior Coastal Plain rises 200-plus feet above sea level in the area of Alabama, Arkansas, Tennessee, and Texas. In the eastern area, the Coastal Plain environment melds into the Piedmont of the Appalachian range. Such major rivers as the Missouri, Ohio, Cumberland, Tennessee, and Potomac dominate the northern reaches of the Southeast Area. The landforms of the region are designated as the Appalachian Highlands, the Interior Low Plateau, and the Ozark-Ouachita Highlands. Temperatures are moderate and rainfall plentiful over most of the region. The river drainage offered prime cultivation areas for Native Americans, while the plateaus, lowland swamps, and mountain forests supplied excellent deer, turkey, and bear hunting. Easy access to streams, rivers, ocean, and gulf provided many species of fish and shellfish for the sustenance of the inhabitants.

The Southeast proved an extremely productive environment for societies following a combined horticultural and hunting-gathering way of life—one of the richest in North America. It is no wonder that the earliest European explorers in the region discovered the area so crowded. The chronicles of the expedition of Hernando De Soto, who led an expedition from Florida to the Mississippi River from 1539 until his death on May 21, 1542, indicated major Indian towns generally within a day's march of each other. Sometimes the neighboring towns could be seen from the earthen pyramids the Spanish found in almost every village. Population growth and the requirement for land to feed such growth played a major role in Southeastern warfare.

Evidence places the earliest Indian occupation of the Southeastern Area at about 10,000 to 15,000 years ago at Warm Mineral Springs and Silver Springs in Florida, the Williamson site in Virginia, and the Quad site in Alabama, among others. At that early date, Native Americans of the Southeast focused on big-game hunting with the use of the atlatl, or spear thrower. By about 8,000 to 10,000 years ago during the Archaic Period, Indians massed into larger and more sedentary groups and exploited a wider range of plant and animal species than did their predecessors. During this time pottery and the new technology of shaping stone by polishing and grinding were developed. Sites from this period feature some truly huge refuse dumps often associated with shellfishing. For example, the Stallings Island site near Augusta, Georgia, has a shell midden 6 to 12 feet deep, 500 feet wide, and 15,000 feet long.

Three thousand years ago during the Woodland Period, Southeastern Indians first practiced horticulture and built somewhat more permanent, fortified villages. Evidence of increasing warfare—from archaeological and ethnohistorical sources—would continue into the Mississippian Period, which spanned from A.D. 700 until the time of contact, when De Soto found that most villages north of Florida were fortified and that each group encountered seemed involved in constant hostility with surrounding groups.

The inadvertent introduction of diseases by the Spanish in the sixteenth century, and the impact of their ruthless use of advanced weaponry, coupled with natural disasters like drought and weather pattern shifts, which negatively affected harvests, decimated the tribes first encountered in the Southeast. The following tribes, although some still exist in much-reduced numbers, are known today mainly by the few scholars who study the early history of the Spanish and French in the New World: Calusa, Ais, Tequesta, Timucua, Apalachee, Natchez, Tunica, Tutelo, Yuchi, Pischenoa, Mugulasha, Washa, Quinipissa, Napissa, Acolapissa, Tangipahoa, Chakchiuma, Taposa, Ibitoupa, Chawasha, Ouacha, Alabama, Okelousa, Pascagoula, Moctobe, Koroa, Yazoo, Tioux, Grigra,

Chitimacha, Atakapa, and Opelousa. After these groups had been disrupted or exterminated, those remaining reorganized into tribal entities familiar today: Chickasaw, Choctaw, Creek, Cherokee, Catawba, Powhatan, Seminole, Caddo, and Quapaw.

The great majority of Southeast Indians at the time of contact followed a way of life based on horticulture and hunting. Though vigorous most of the time, trade receded somewhat during times of the greatest threat from warfare. The Chickasaw, for example, traded slaves, buckskin, and refined bear oil for stone that could be worked into blades and points, and exotic items such as conch shell drinking cups from the Gulf, pipestone, galena, grizzly bear teeth, copper, and obsidian, some of which came from as far away as Lake Superior and the Rocky Mountains. The Natchez trade with the French focused heavily on tobacco production, while the key item in Creek trade to the British was buckskin. Regardless of the items involved, trade remained crucial to the Southeasterners and yet another reason to go to war if trade routes or associations were threatened. In the early 1700s in Mississippi and Louisiana, almost all Indian warfare in some way centered on trade problems. For decades, the chronic refrain in official documents of early-eighteenth-century New Orleans involved the French and British rivalry over trade relations with the Choctaw and Chickasaw, sworn enemies.

Since the first Europeans to encounter the Southeastern Indians were Spanish, French, and British military men, we have a richly detailed record of the Indians' weapons. The first description comes from the spring of 1540, when Spaniards of the De Soto expedition entered the ritual center of Talimeco in present-day Georgia. There on a high earthen mound sat a temple with a high-pitched, vaulted roof 100 feet long and 40 feet wide and covered with finely woven cane mats. Strings of conch shell beads and freshwater pearls hung everywhere. Most impressive, however, was what awaited the Spaniards at the door of the temple. Six pairs of lifelike wooden statues, each wielding a different weapon, flanked the entrance. The first pair held maces; the second, wooden "broadswords"; and the third, clubs of two parts connected with a swivel. The fourth pair handled battle axes; the fifth, bows and arrows; and the sixth, pikes with copper points. The account noted eight small annexes to the temple filled with weapons and shields. Over a hundred years after the Spanish, English colonists in Virginia would describe temples of the Powhatan chiefdom serving as a kind of armory, filled with weapons. Of this array, the club, in one of its many forms, and the bow and arrow were their major weapons.

The Southeastern bow averaged 50 to 60 inches in length and had a pull weight of 50 pounds. The Spaniards soon discovered that it had an accuracy- and killing-range of about 200 paces and that their arquebus and metal armor provided little protection against it. They finally abandoned most of their metal armor for quilted-cotton armor several inches thick that they had encountered in their wars with the Aztec. The Indian arrows punctured chain mail and armor with great force, and a Southeastern warrior could shoot six to seven arrows in the time required for a arquebus fighter to load and fire his weapon (Hudson 1976, 245). The Indians learned to quickly approach the Spanish gunners after they had fired, loose arrows at them, and retreat out of arquebus range before the Spaniards could shoot again. Though the Spanish had to deal with powerful bows and well-crafted arrows, there is no mention of Southeastern warriors using arrow poisons in battle.

The war club was the preferred shock weapon of the Southeast, as well as a major symbol of warfare, power, and male status (see Van Horne 1993). The Natchez war club resembled a wooden cutlass with one edge sharpened and the other dull. A 3-inch ball was carved on the tip. Many war clubs resembled a broadsword with no weight-forward device, as seen with the Natchez version. In other cases a thickening of the front part of the "blade" created the weight-forward effect. Timucuan war clubs displayed a flat, spatulated end with sharp edges.

The Powhatan used a variety of war clubs:

> Some were stout wooden batons with one or two sharp edges, which the English called "swords"; others were batons with sharp stones or imported iron set into them. The "sword" shown in Robert Beverley's account is tapered and gentle curving, with abstract engraving above the narrow, hand held end and two long feathers and a turkey and bear at the wide, club end. A baton-like "sword" was known as a *monacock*. The other warclub was a tomahawk, or hatchet with a socketed head made variously of deer antler or "a long stone sharpened at both ends." There were also "cudgels" and "clubs" and "weapons like a hammer," all of which might have been ball-headed clubs. (Rountree 1989, 124)

The Susquehanna Indians designed another variation on the war club by inserting a deer antler through a wooden handle to form a pickax type of weapon. De Soto's chroniclers described a war club used by Indians at the mouth of the Mississippi River that was set with "very sharp fish bones." Obsidian-edged "swords," capable of decapitating a horse, were encountered by the Spaniards in their wars with the Aztec. The De Soto entrada confronted a similar weapon at Cofitachequi (Georgia), but not elsewhere in its travels in the Southeast (Swanton 1946, 569).

Lances, the preferred weapon for bear and bison hunting, were found among all Southeastern groups. In most parts of North America, weapons for killing those two animals were used also to kill men. "Short lances," used for stabbing but not throwing, are reported for the Timucuan, and throwing spears, or javelins, for the Chickasaw, Cherokee, Natchez, and Alabama (Swanton 1946, 583).

Less common weapons included knives of bone, stone, and cane and the *atlatl,* or spear thrower. Such weapons were excavated from archaeological deposits at Key Marco, Florida, and at sites in Arkansas and Tennessee (Swanton 1937, 584). One of De Soto's chroniclers, Garcilaso de la Vega, described this spear thrower when groups related to the Chitimacha attacked the Spanish at the mouth of the Mississippi:

> One Spaniard was wounded by a weapon that the Castilians in the Indies call a *tiradera* (javelin), which we shall call more accurately a *bohordo* because it is shot with a stock of wood or a cord. The Spaniards had not seen this weapon in all the places they had visited in Florida until that day. (Swanton 1937, 584)

The *atlatl* has the effect of lengthening the thrower's arm, thus increasing velocity and therefore the force of the thrown spear or dart. *Atlatl* darts could pass entirely through a man wearing a coat of mail (Kniffen, Gregory, and Stokes 1987, 143).

Slings were part of the arsenal of the Southeastern warrior (Hudson 1976, 245). When Cabeza de Vaca and his companions of the Narvaez expedition passed along the Gulf Coast near Pensacola and Mobile Bays, Indians carrying slings and *atlatl* darts attacked them. They appeared to the Spaniards to be simple hunters, for they had large quantities of fish, but little if any corn, and did not carry bows and arrows. The Spanish army had experienced Indian slings in the wars against the Inca. Women herders in particular, experts with slings for defending their herds, harassed the Spanish with their stone missiles in Peru.

The Spanish encountered another Indian weapon in the latter days of the De Soto expedition when they attacked the Tula, who lived near present-day Fort Smith. Garcilaso wrote that in the waning moments of the battle, Juan Paez, captain of the crossbow troops, fought from horseback in pursuit of a Tula warrior who carried only a 6-foot staff. Paez threw his lance at the Tula, but the warrior, while running, deflected it with his quarterstaff and struck Paez in the face, knocking out most of his teeth (Hudson 1997, 321). About a week later the Tula attacked the Spanish with quarterstaves, bows and arrows, and lances.

The French artist Jacques Le Moyne de Morgues, who traveled with Rene Laudoniere to Florida in 1564, observed the Timucuan warriors:

> For greater adornment and magnificence they allow the nails on their fingers and toes to grow long and file the fingernails at the sides with a shell, so that they become very sharp. Timucuan men were adroit warriors. They used the bow and arrow and long- and short-handled clubs with great dexterity. They used their long, sharp fingernails at times to tear the skin of their victim's forehead and pull it down so that the flowing blood blinded the victim. (In Bullen 1954, 323)

The Southeastern warriors effectively manipulated Spanish weapons they found or seized from the enemy in the heat of a fight. This skill is understandable. The fundamental weapons of the Spaniards and the Indians were the same, and the principles for their efficient use—handgrip, body mechanics, etc.—were similar. Both antagonists had shields, swords, and lances. The crossbow of the Spaniards reflected the longbow of the Indians.

The following anecdote from De Soto's battles with the indomitable Tula illustrates the Indians' adroitness with the Spanish weapons. At the end of the fight the Spaniards saw a lone warrior hiding behind a tree. When they boxed him in with their horses, the Tula picked up a Spanish battle-axe dropped during the fight and engaged the Spanish who surrounded him. Juan Carranza approached the Tula but was struck so hard that his shield was split and his horse wounded seriously enough to force Carranza to withdraw. When Carranza's companion, Diego de Godoy, attacked the Tula, he suffered Carranza's fate: The warrior, grasping the axe in two hands, split his shield and severely wounded him. A third mounted Spaniard attempted to lance the Tula, but the warrior struck his horse with such a powerful blow that the horse went down, mortally wounded. Finally, one Gonzalo Silvestre deflected one of the Tula's murderous blows and struck him with a sword. Even though the Indian's left hand was severed, the warrior, gripping the axe in his right hand, continued his attack until, weak from loss of blood, he fell (Hudson 1997, 325).

The Southeastern Indians not only possessed formidable weapons, martial training, and ferocious courage, they combined these attributes in a complex and disciplined manner both offensively and defensively. One of the earliest observations of the orderly movement of warriors was Le Moyne's mid-sixteenth-century description of the massing of Indian forces under Outina as he set out to attack Potavou, a neighboring chief in northern Florida:

> When Saturioua went to war, his men preserved no order, but went along one after another, just as it happened. On the contrary, his enemy Holata Outina, whose name, as I now remember, means "king of many kings," and who was much more powerful than he as regards both wealth and number of his subjects, used to march with regular ranks, like an organized army; himself marching alone in the middle of the whole force, painted red. On the wings, or horns, of his order of march were the young men, the swiftest of whom, also painted red, acted as advance guards and scouts for reconnoitering the enemy. These are able to follow up the traces of the enemy by scent, as dogs do wild beasts, and when they come upon such traces, they immediately return to the army to report. And as we make use of trumpet and drums in our armies to promulgate orders so they have heralds who by cries of certain sorts, direct when to hold or to advance or to attack, or to perform any military duty. After sunset, they halted and are never wont to have battle. For encamping they are arranged in squads of ten each, the bravest men being put in squads by themselves. When the chief has chosen the place of encampment for the night, in open field or woods, and after he has eaten, and is established by himself, the quartermasters place ten of these squads of the bravest men in a circle around him. About ten paces outside of this circle is placed another twenty squads; at twenty yards farther, another of forty squads; and so on. *(Narrative of Le Moyne 1875, 3)*

De Soto's chroniclers left an account of Indian military formations from his confrontation with Indians at Vitachuco, in Florida. The Indian force approached the Spaniards in ranks, maintaining straight rows as they came, with their officers placed in the center of the formation for protection. At Coosa the chief met De Soto with a large force organized into squadrons of twenty men marching in orderly rows.

DePratter (1991, 45), after studying early accounts of Southeastern warfare, concludes that four major points recur. First, forces were always divided in identifiable squadrons. Second, attack and defense were achieved by the complex manipulation of these units. Third, drums, whistles, stylized shouts, and various flags and banners coordinated battlefield behavior. Finally, fire was routinely used to burn houses and palisades and to create a smoke screen to assist in attack or retreat.

The orderliness of Southeastern martial behavior is seen in the way the Indians protected their leaders. John Smith (in Swanton 1946, 689) wrote that on the day he was captured by the Powhatan chief Opechancanough and taken back to the chief's village, the Indians marched in strict order. Five bowmen were stationed in front of the chief and five behind. On his right and left walked two men, one carrying a sword and one "a peece." Smith was placed directly behind the five bowmen, who marched behind the chief, and bowmen were behind him and to his right and left. The remainder of the warriors moved in a line behind Smith, each with a handful of arrows and bows at the ready. One "sergeant" kept order in the front of the line, and another at the rear.

The level of tactics the Indians used against De Soto's men can be gauged by the military operations of the Caddo chief Naguatex. He brought together a number of allied chiefs and their warriors, with himself in command of four units. The first two attacked the Spanish, skirmished, then feigned retreat while two units remained in reserve. When the Spanish pursued the retreating warriors, the reserves attacked from the rear, at which point the retreating force went on the offensive. "The attack represents a fine example of good military tactics; that is, sending in a first wave to draw off the cavalry and then attacking those left in camp with a second force held in reserve. This attack is even more surprising because Naguatex was able to command and coordinate forces from several different 'provinces,' although it is possible that all may have been his subjects" (DePratter 1991, 45).

Fortifications

The earliest fortification building in the Southeast dates to the Late Woodland Period (A.D. 600–1000). Skeletal remains point to increased rates of violent deaths and traumatic injury. It was a time of marked population growth, agricultural intensification, increased sedentism, and the appearance of the bow and arrow.

The Lubbub Creek site on the Tombigbee River in western Alabama exemplifies an early Southeastern fortified site dating to this period. Constructed in a number of phases, the final one featured a palisade with six rectangular bastions at 30-meter intervals and a surrounding defensive

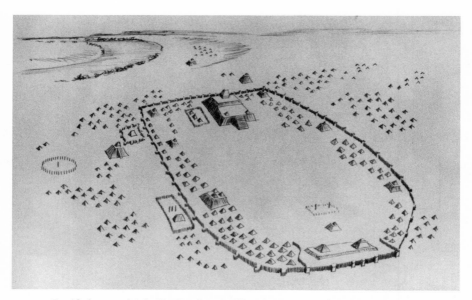

Fortified town of Cahokia. Confluence of Missouri and Mississippi Rivers. 700 A.D.–900 A.D.

ditch. The archaeologists estimated that the palisade comprised 1,332 posts (Blitz 1993, 71–72).

Several hundred years after fortifications were built on the Lubbub Creek site, the town of Cahokia flourished at the confluence of the Missouri and Mississippi Rivers. It covered 5 square miles and was peopled by a population of 30,000 to 50,000. A palisade 2 miles long enclosed 200 acres in the center of the town. Bastions and loopholes were evenly spaced around the walls, which were plastered with clay.

In the years immediately preceding the appearance of De Soto, the fortified town at the Lake George site dominated the Yazoo River valley. Over thirty large pyramid mounds covered a site of 55 acres. A deep defensive ditch surrounded the town, and the dirt from the ditch was piled on the edges and then surmounted by a log palisade. Water from Lake George filled the ditch.

The bow and arrow brought major changes to fortification building (DePratter 1991, 41). Prior to its appearance, when the antagonists used only spears, clubs, and the *atlatl,* widely spaced palisades mounted on earthen berms surrounded by a defensive ditch proved sufficient. With the range of the bow and arrow and its ability to accurately carry fire into a fortified village, fortifications had to be rethought. Defensive ditches became deeper, and the palisades posts were set closer together, often woven

Artist's rendering of Fort King site, Georgia.

together at the top to reinforce the integrity of the wall and plastered to resist fire. Bastions were added, and bark roofs, more resistant to fire than thatch, became standard within fortified villages.

The first Indian fort that De Soto came upon—therefore one of the first to be seen by a European in the Southeast—was the fortified town of Chiaha near present-day Dandridge. But even before that, he had experienced the defensive technology of the Apalachee Indians of north Florida. In the early winter of 1539, the Spanish, pursuing groups of Apalachee warriors, ran into rapidly constructed barricades that the Indians had thrown up to slow the advance of their horsemen. Retreating, the Apalachee again built barricades strong enough that the Spaniards had to hack them down with axes. Following this, the Apalachee lashed branches and poles to standing trees with willow withes to create a horizontal barrier, a fence, to impede the Spanish horses.

In July 1540 De Soto entered the town of Tali, on the south bank of the Little Tennessee River upstream from the mouth of the Tellico River. It was encircled by a log palisade and bastions. On August 21 he arrived at Itaba near present-day Cartersville, Georgia. The town covered 50 acres and was surrounded by a palisade, bastions, and a dry moat 30 feet wide and 10 feet deep. On August 30 the Spaniards reached Ulibahali, near present-day Rome, Georgia. The palisades there stood the height of a lance and were constructed of thick posts, with additional posts set crosswise to the vertical ones. Loopholes for archers were placed at intervals, and the walls were plastered both within and without. On September 3 the Spanish reached the town of Apica, which was surrounded by palisades and a defensive ditch on three sides, while the fourth faced a river.

On Monday, October 18, De Soto led his men toward a fortified town, in the province of Mabila, near present-day Selma, Alabama. In the battle that ensued, De Soto almost lost everything. The Indians had cleared a free-fire zone around their fort for the distance of a crossbow shot and burned several nearby houses to remove cover in case of an assault. As the Spanish scouts watched from a distance, squads of warriors practiced maneuvers in the open area outside the fort.

> Mabila was a small, strongly stockaded village situated in a cleared field. The palisade around Mabila was built out of thick posts set side by side in the ground. Both inside and outside this row of posts, smaller and more flexible poles were bound crosswise with strips of split cane and fiber cordage. The whole of it was plastered over with a mixture of mud and straw, filling up all the cracks. This coating was quite hard. Spaced at intervals of about fifty feet, the palisade had bastions that were each capable of holding seven or eight fighting men. The wall itself had embrasures at a man's height, through which archers could shoot their arrows. (Hudson 1997, 236)

The Battle of Mabila exacted a high price on both Spanish and Indian fighters. According to De Soto's secretary, 22 Spaniards were killed and 148 wounded. Many soldiers were wounded more than once, and it was estimated that De Soto's army sustained a total of 688 wounds. Seven horses were killed and twenty-nine wounded. However, this pales when the Indian losses are considered, for the Spanish estimated that 2,000 to 3,000 were killed.

The Spanish were so worn from their victory at Mabila that they could not move from the area for almost a month, at which time they arranged to winter with the Chicaza (Chickasaw) in Mississippi. De Soto, with his increasingly high-handed manner, antagonized the Chicaza, and they attacked the Spanish winter camp in early March. The Spaniards were again severely damaged and had to wait until late April 1541 before they were able to quit the area.

The day after they left the Chicaza, the Spaniards approached another fort, defended by about three hundred Alibamos Indians. This fort, square in shape, had thick trees as palisade posts. In the outer wall were three doors, all too low to enter on horseback. Inside they discovered another wall, with low doors that stretched from one side of the fort to the other. The wall opposite the entrance reached the edge of a cliff bank, below which ran a deep stream. When attacked, the Indians left the fort and skirmished. As the Spanish pressed them, they withdrew into their fort. When the Spanish breached the front wall, the Indians moved behind the second, and then the third. Finally they crossed a log bridge that placed them on a high embankment that the Spanish horses could not climb.

On June 23 De Soto entered the main town of Casqui, located on the eastern bank of the St. Francis River just below the mouth of the Tyronza River. The village covered 17 acres and was protected on three sides by a palisade and a deep defensive ditch. The fourth side was flush with the bank of the St. Francis River.

Four days later De Soto's group neared Pacaha. The town had strong stockades, defensive towers, and, connected to Wapanocca Bayou, a moat so wide that two large canoes could pass along it side by side. The Spanish chroniclers noted a number of large fortified towns in the immediate area.

Over a hundred years after De Soto had traveled the lower Mississippi, a Louisiana planter, Antoine Le Page du Pratz, wrote of a Natchez fort:

> The walls of these forts are composed of great posts, which are made of the trunks of trees a span in circumference, buried 5 to 6 feet in the earth and extending 10 feet above it, and pointed above. The lines of contact of these posts, however round, are covered inside with other posts a foot in diameter. This wall is provided outside with half towers 40 paces apart. They make them doubtless to prevent scaling. The lower ends of the posts are supported inside by a banquette 3 feet wide by as much in height, which is itself supported by stakes bound together with green branches in order to retain the earth which is in this banquette. The best instructed of these people, as were the Natchez by our soldiers, make about 5 feet above this banquette a kind of penthouse with fragments of trees in order to protect themselves from grenades. They also have loopholes which have only one opening outside and two within which correspond to the one. These loopholes are immediately above the banquette. In the middle of the fort is placed a tree, the branches of which are cut to within 8 or 9 inches of the trunk to serve as a ladder. The tree serves them as a watchtower. (du Pratz 1947, 2:435–437)

Du Pratz wrote that the French had served as advisers to the Natchez in constructing the fort. The basic plan, however, existed many hundreds of years prior to contact, as both archaeological evidence and the De Soto narratives indicate. The Southeastern Indians were inveterate fort builders and very interested in new wrinkles the British, French, and Spanish could show them to strengthen their fortifications. For example, Chief Saturiona examined Laudoniere's fort in 1564: "Upon coming up to the ditch of our fort, he took measurements both within and without; and perceiving that the earth was being taken from the ditch, and laid into the rampart, he asked what was the use of the operation" *(Narrative of Le Moyne 1875, 3).*

Le Moyne also provided an early description of a fortified village of the Timucuan Indians of north Florida, which was clearly more primitive in concept than the forts encountered by De Soto to the north and west some twenty or so years earlier:

> The Indians built their fortified villages in this way: they choose a site near the channel of a swift stream, which they level as evenly as possible. Then they dig a circular ditch round it, into which they drive thick, round palings, placed close together, to a height twice that of a man. This fencing is carried to a point beyond its beginning, spiralwise, making a narrow entrance and admitting not more than two persons at a time. The course of the stream is diverted towards this entrance, and at each end of it a small guardhouse is built. The sentinels in these guardhouses have a highly developed sense of smell. They can detect enemies at a great distance. As soon as they smell them, they follow the scent, and when they discover the disturbers of their peace, they set up a clamor, thus summoning warriors from the town, armed with bows, arrows, and clubs. *(Narrative of Le Moyne 1875, 95)*

In 1700 a French official offered this description of an abandoned Biloxi fort on the Pascagoula River:

> The village [of from 30 to 40 cabins] was surrounded with palings eight feet in height, of about eighteen inches in diameter. There still remains three square watch towers measuring ten feet on each face; they are raised to a height of eight feet on posts; the sides made of mud mixed with grass, of a thickness of eight inches, well covered. There were many loopholes through which to shoot their arrows. It appeared to me that there had been a watchtower at each angle, and one midway of the curtains. (Swanton 1911, 437)

An English trader operating on the headwaters of the Tennessee River in the late 1600s noted the following Yuchi fortification:

[It was] seated on the river side, having the cliffs of the river on one side being very high for its defense. The other three sides trees over two feet wide were pitched on end twelve foot high, and on the tops scaffolds placed with parapets to defend the walls and offend their enemies on which men stand to fight. (Swanton 1911, 437)

In 1715 the English attacked the Catawba, an eastern division of the Siouan family in South Carolina, with cannons. The Indians dug deep trenches behind their strong stockades, into which they withdrew when the English bombarded them. At night the Catawba fighters slipped from their fort and attacked. Finally, the English were forced to lift their siege because they had lost too many men. A relatively unique technique of defense by the Catawba was the "mining" of the ground around their forts with sharp wooden slivers coated with rattlesnake venom.

The English did not disperse the Catawba until their second campaign, when, having learned that cannons and scaling the Indian palisade had not worked, they tunneled under a Catawba village, mined it, and blew it up. The Catawba had no understanding of this type of warfare and immediately sought peace with the English. At the time an Abnaki guide told the English commander:

It will be the same with the Chickasaws, they will know how to protect themselves against the cannons that you will bring to their country only with great difficulty. They are real warriors, even braver than the Catawbas, who are fed in war and instructed by the English. They know the art of defending themselves against the Europeans better. There is no other way to reduce them than to blow their villages up, but that operation will consume a great deal of your provisions because you will have many forts to mine. (Rowland and Sanders 1932, 695)

Twenty years later the French, centered in New Orleans under the command of Governor Bienville, would find reason to echo the observation of the Abnaki scout when they tried to dislodge the Chickasaw from northern Mississippi. In a letter to his superior dated August 20, 1735, Bienville wrote:

I have learned that they [Chickasaw] have five stockade forts, and that in addition every ten individuals had a cabin fortified with three rows of piles with loopholes and covered with earthworks to protect them from fire. All these cabins are placed in such a way that they defend each other. The Natchez, who are about one hundred and eighty men, make a village separate from, but adjacent to, those of the Chickasaws. Besides the fortified cabins they have a large fort with four bastions which they have constructed of trees driven into the ground on the model of the one that we had in their country at the time of their revolt. (Bienville in Rowland and Sanders 1927, 296–297)

In 1736 Governor Bienville set out with his Choctaw allies to defeat the Chickasaw. What he encountered is ample testimony to the Chickasaw's sophisticated fort building and understanding of placement. Bienville's target was Ackia, their principal fortified village, which commanded the natural entrance into the Tombigbee watershed, the heartland of the Chickasaw territory. However, the Indians had in place a number of support installations that made accessing Ackia difficult. The French forces arrived at a wide prairie on which the Chickasaw and Natchez had constructed on the crest of a hill three forts in a triangular arrangement, one of which was Ackia. Each fort supported the others. Bienville realized that he could not simply bypass them without having an enemy force at his back as he attacked Ackia. In addition, a number of fortified "cabins" lined the entrance to Ackia. To reach the walls of the main town, one had to defeat or block the defensive actions of the two surrounding forts, as well as fight from house to house outside the fort as its and the "cabins'" defenders returned fire.

Bienville's forces could not advance from the few "cabins" they had taken because of intense fire from the fort. Understanding that the wind blew in their favor, the Ackia defenders shot flaming arrows into structures outside the fort, and the resulting smoke caused even more difficulty for the French forces in coordinating their efforts. The Choctaw, according to Bienville, simply watched the battle from a safe distance, awaiting the outcome. When Bienville signaled for his forces to retreat, the Choctaw fired several volleys at the fort, and the return fire killed twenty of them.

Governor Bienville described the Chickasaw fort of Ackia in a letter to his superior in Paris:

What may be added about the method of these Indians in fortifying themselves is that after having surrounded their cabins with several rows of large piles they dig holes in the ground inside in order to hide themselves in them

up to their shoulders, and they fire through loopholes that they make almost flush with the ground, but they derive even greater advantage from
the natural situation of their cabins which are separated from each other
and all the shots which cross each other than from all the art of the English
can suggest to them to make them strong. The covering of these cabins is
a wall of earth and wood proof against burning arrows and grenades so that
nothing but bombs can harm them. (Rowland and Sanders 1927, 307)

An indirect indication of the effectiveness of Chickasaw forts can be
seen in a letter from the Ministry of the Colonies which was "laid before
the King, January 1, 1739." It requested weapons necessary to defeat the
Indian fortifications.

As for the artillery, since the Chickasaw villages that are to be attacked are
fortified, it was thought advisable to send four eight-pounder cannon; eight
four-pounders, six of which carry ammunition for three shots; two nine-
pounder mortars of brass; two of iron of six-pound caliber; twelve other
small mortars of wrought-iron which were forged for this purpose; and
powder, bullets, bombs and the tools necessary to make use of them. (Rowland and Sanders 1927, 384)

The English settlers and explorers along the southeast Atlantic coast
saw fortified towns as numerous as the French and Spanish had experienced farther south and west. Along the eastern shore of Maryland and
Virginia, hardened sites appeared during the Late Woodland Period. The
Chicone site, for example, had a circular ditch over 200 feet across that
was associated with a palisade. A number of similar sites in the area dated
between the Late Woodland and Contact Periods (Rountree and Davidson
1997). The English Jamestown colonists mentioned Tockwogh, another
eastern shore fortified town, in 1608. "Entering the River *Tockwogh*, the
savages all armed in a fleet of boats round invironed us . . . they conducted
us to their pallisaded town, mantelled with the barks of trees, with scaf-
fold-like mounts, breasted with barks very formally" (Bushnell 1919, 30).
The Munsee in Delaware and the Nanticoke in Maryland also built fortified villages.

In Virginia on April 7, 1728, Colonel William Byrd visited a Nottoway
fort in Southampton County.

This fort was a square piece of ground, enclosed with substantial puncheons, or strong palisades, about ten feet high, and leaning a little outward, to make scaling more difficult. Each side of the square might be about

a hundred yards long, with loop-holes at proper distances, through which they may fire upon the enemy. Within this enclosure we found bark cabins sufficient to lodge all their people, in case they should be obliged to retire thither. (Bushnell 1919, 57)

A Paski village in 1711 and one of the Pomeoioc were protected in the same manner as the Nottoway site described by Byrd. In 1676 the Susque-hannocks' palisaded fort encompassed approximately 4 acres on the lower Susquehanna River (Grumet 1955, 312).

In North Carolina in the late sixteenth century, English accounts de-scribed a village on Roanoke Island that was simply fortified ("tree trunks set into the ground") but lacking bastions, defensive ditches, and a multi-layered palisade. A town of the Keyauwee near Haw was "fortified with wooden puncheons," as was one of the Eno Indians northeast of present-day Durham (Rights 1947, 82). Likewise, the Cherokee of western North Carolina constructed such palisaded forts (Haywood 1971, 77).

In 1701 John Lawson, the surveyor general of Carolina, traveling through the interior of South Carolina and North Carolina from Charles-ton to Pamlico Sound, observed the larger tribes in fortified villages (Mooney 1894, 90). During their wars with the colonists, the Tuscarora and their allies built palisaded strongholds in North Carolina. A major ex-ample stood about 20 miles west of the town of Newbern.

Tonti, a chronicler with La Salle's expedition in the late 1600s, visited the Taensas on the east bank of the lower Mississippi River. A stockade en-compassed their major temple.

> This fort is not at all regular, but is very well flanked at each angle; there are sentry boxes of hard wood. . . . The temple is surrounded with strong mud walls, in which are fixed spikes, on which they place the heads of their en-emies whom they sacrifice to the sun. At the door of the temple is a block of wood, on which is a great shell, and plaited round with the hair of their enemies in a plait as thick as the arm and about 20 fathoms long. (In Swan-ton 1946, 260)

A possible reason that the Taensas fortified their temple is suggested by the behavior of the Casquis when, with De Soto, they attacked a town of their enemies the Pacaha in June 1541. After the fighting ended, the Casquis entered the holy-of-holies and stripped, and desecrated the in-terior of the temple. They emptied the boxes containing the bones of the Pacaha elite, threw them on the ground, and crushed them (Hudson 1997, 294).

On March 15, 1699, Sieur d'Iberville described a curiously flimsy fortification around a village of the Mugulasha Indians, who lived a short distance from the Mississippi. "I came on and made camp that day 6½ leagues from my last camp, near one of their camp sites, where there are ten huts thatched with palmettos; near it, at a point on the right side of the river, is a small redoubt as high as a man, made of canes in the form of an oval, 25 yards wide and 55 long, having a few huts inside" (McWilliams 1981, 56). The canes were planted about an inch apart and were 10 feet high. In addition, the redoubt had no door that could be closed.

Another rare Southeastern fortification is found on Stone Mountain in De Kalb County, Georgia.

> About half-way up Stone Mountain . . . where the acclivity becomes very marked . . . are the remains of a rock-wall which was originally intended for the protection of the upper portion of the mountain. This wall is still in some places two feet high, and is composed of fragments of rock, all capable of manual motion, piled one upon the other. At either end this wall extended to the precipitous sides of the mountain where—its defensive presence being no longer necessary—access to the summit was either altogether denied or rendered so difficult and perilous as to preclude possibility of anything like a combined attack. Similar rock-walls exist upon Mount Yonah and guard the summits of other solitary peaks within the confines of Georgia. Nor were these rock-defences confined exclusively to the mountains. (Jones 1999, 207)

Shields

Shields of the Southeastern Indians were constructed of rawhide, strips of bark, and a wickerwork of woven split cane. Du Pratz wrote:

> They have in the left hand a buckler, the bow in the right, and arrows in a quiver which is a skin sack. The buckler is made of two round pieces of bison leather bound together, of a diameter of a foot and a half. This buckler is almost confined to those of the north. One does not see it among those of the south. (In Swanton 1911, 368)

In the early 1600s, the Powhatan of Virginia used round, tree-bark shields that "hanged on their left shoulder to cover that side as they stand forth to shoot" (Rountree 1989, 124). They painted them in red-and-black designs.

No wicker shields were mentioned for the Powhatan but were for the Secotan, Roanoke, Pamlico, Pomeioc, and other Algonquin speakers in North Carolina. Charles Hudson noted for the Southeastern Indians in general, "Before the gun was introduced, they used armor and shields made of woven cane and bison leather." Also, "They possessed shields, but there is little evidence that shields played an important role in combat" (1976, 247). The Choctaw are thought to have sometimes made shields from alligator hide (Swanton 1946, 587).

Hodge noted a shield of rod-armor principle:

> At the suggestion of Mosco and the friendly Indians, Captain John Smith, when fighting a tribe on the Chesapeake, made use of the "Massawomek targets," or shields. These the English set "about the forepart of our Boat, like a forecastle, from whence we securely beat back the savages from off the plain without any hurt. These light targets are made of little small sticks woven betwixt strings of their hemp, but so firmly that no arrow can possibly pierce them." (1912, 88)

De Soto's chroniclers noticed wicker shields in war canoes in the spring of 1541 when they arrived on the banks of the Mississippi. Chief Aquijo appeared before De Soto with 7,000 warriors in a fleet of several hundred very large war canoes. Some of the warriors carried wicker shields so tightly woven that a crossbow bolt could not penetrate them. The shield holders protected the bowmen, who stood in a line down the center of the canoes from stem to stern (Hudson 1997, 285). Juan Pardo, exploring along the Tennessee River about a decade after De Soto passed through the area, wrote that the Indians, in describing a river passage to Pardo, told him that to defend himself he would have to lash the canoes together and keep shields at the ready (Hudson 1990, 101).

Milling described, for seventeenth-century North Carolina, "a people so addicted to arms that even their women come into the field and shoot arrows over their husbands' shoulders, who shield them with leathern targets" (1978, 53).

One of the earliest observations of shields came when De Soto's men entered the previously mentioned temple at Talimeco. In addition to the array of weapons in the hands of the statues guarding the entrance to the temple, they found woven cane shields—some large, some small, some round, some oblong. Applying their usual test of enemy defenses, the Spanish found that a crossbow bolt could not penetrate the wicker shields.

Armor

The presence, or relative lack, of armor in the Southeast presents an interesting puzzle. Strikingly, there are two early and very dramatic evidences of its presence in the area. The first returns us to the temple at Talimeco, where the Spanish, in addition to the offensive and defensive weapons orderly arrayed in the temple interior, discovered rawhide cuirasses and helmets. The second is a stone pipe from the Spiro Mounds site, in eastern Oklahoma along the Arkansas River, dating to between 850 and 1450. In very realistic fashion it shows a man with what clearly appears to be a thick turban and wooden armor, preparing to scalp a fallen enemy.

Regardless of the above two examples, John R. Swanton, in his monumental tome *The Indians of the Southeastern United States,* wrote, "References to body armor are so scanty that one wonders whether the few we seem to have are to be relied upon" (1946, 588). And on Hariot's (1893) (in Swanton 1946, 36) observation that the Indians of Carolina had "some armor made of sticks wickered together with thread," he countered that Hariot was possibly looking at a shield and mistaking it for armor. That does not appear to be a tenable critique, however, because wooden armor is found throughout the area Hariot was exploring. The Powhatan in Virginia had rod-armor (Hodge 1969 [1913]). Swanton (1928, 704) indicated wooden breastplates and wicker armor for the Algonquins of Carolina, and the Cherokee used buffalo-hide breastplates (Gilbert 1919, 350). Nevertheless, it is noteworthy that helmets are rarely mentioned in the Southeast.

An interesting breast piece, usually referred to as a gorget, is depicted in the earliest drawings of Indians of both the Southeast and Northeast. It appears to be a plate 8 to 10 inches across, suspended from a cord around the neck. In some cases a matching plate hung on the back. Le Moyne mentions circular metal plates that Timucua Indians wore "to protect the back and breast in war" (in Swanton 1946, 589). Again Swanton challenged, "It is somewhat questionable whether the service rendered in this way was intentional or accidental" (1946, 589). It is true that disks worn on the breast were widespread symbols of the sun for the generally sun-worshipping Southeasterners, but Granganimeo, chief of the Wingandacoa of Virginia, suggested that the circular breastplate can also be viewed

Stone effigy pipe. Spiro Mound. Eastern Oklahoma. 850 A.D.–1450 A.D.

as armor. An English trader wrote: "Of all things that he saw, a bright tin dish most pleased him, which he presently took up and clasped it before his breast, and after made a hole in the rim thereof and hung it about his neck, making signs, that it would defend him against his enemies' arrows" (Quinn and Quinn 1973, 5).

Gorgets were made of wood, shell, and slate, and a thick copper example 10 inches across was found at a site along the Yadkin River in western North Carolina. The abbreviated nature of the gorget-as-breastplate relative to a full cuirass is typical when a piece of armor has over time become stylized and symbolic, for symbolic armor usually adorns only the high-status warrior or leader. In a drawing by Le Moyne, "Outina's Order of March," a highly tattooed (indication of status) warrior in the center wears two gorgets, one slightly lower than the other, each about 8 to 10 inches across. On either side of him march officers, or co-leaders, one with no tattooing and the other with minimal tattooing compared to his. Both wear gorgets. In the background Chief Holata Outina stands within the ranks of his warriors wearing a very large gorget, which might be 12 to 14 inches across. Warriors in the ranks have no gorgets.

Obviously, reaching complex conclusions from drawings by men who were not professional observers of cultures other than their own is fool-hardy or, at best, merely suggestive. However, the relationship of gorget wearing and gorget size to status and leadership roles appears in a number of drawings from the Northeast and the Southeast.

Finally, Indians had no monopoly on wooden armor in the Southeast. When the French soldiers prepared to attack the Chickasaw fort at Ackia they donned wooden breastplates as protection against the Chickasaw arrows they expected to face. Cushman wrote, "No wonder their astonishment was great, when instead of a shower of arrows to rebound from their breast-plates, a hail storm of leaden bullets greeted them, against which their wooden shields were as gossamer" (1899, 372). For a brief moment in history, the European put his faith in wooden armor and found himself defeated by Indians using the gun.

Hough offered the following when compiling his descriptions of armor found in the American Museum of Natural History: "I have not met with accounts of armor among the southern tribes as the Muskogi group and others, but should hesitate to conclude that the idea of a defense for the body against arrows and spears, other than the shield, had not occurred to these progressive tribes" (1895, 650).

Discussion and Summary

The relative absence of armor in the Southeast at the time of contact is puzzling. De Soto's chroniclers made no mention of it, nor did the accounts of later Spanish explorations led by Pardo and de Luna. The preceding information on armor from various cultural areas of North America suggests it should have been present, since elaborate armoring seems to correlate with population density and the necessity to control access to essential resources such as farmland, fishing sites, or trade routes—all factors relevant to quality of life in the Southeast.

A common explanation for its absence stresses the supposed inability of the armored warrior to dodge projectiles or fight with shock-weapons—an observation based on a Western preconception that equates armor with the heavy metal plate worn by the classic European knights. However, a more apt comparison lies in another warrior tradition, one that used leather and wooden armor—the Japanese. Modern-day *kendo,* the "Way of the Sword," offers valuable insights. A *kendo* fighter wears a thickly padded jacket and light canvas pants, the *dogi,* and on the upper body, a cuirass, or *do,* today made of thick plastic. (In earlier times heavy lacquered rawhide was shaped over a bamboo interior structure.) Around the waist is an apron, *tare,* which protects the stomach and hips. Over the *dogi* a multipleated culotte reaches from waist to ankle. Completing the outfit are gauntlets, or *kote,* and a cumbersome helmet, *men.* Even though the *kendo* player is more impeded than an Indian warrior wearing a rod-armor cuirass, or war shirt, well-trained *kendo* competitors can move so quickly that the amateur observer is unable to see their lightning-fast strikes and feints. The speed of the *kendo* fighter strongly throws doubt on the argument that armor was abandoned because it slowed the Indian fighter.

Sparse archaeological evidence and accounts by a few Spanish explorers confirm the presence of armor up until just before contact, and all Southeastern experts assumed, even in the absence of proof, that wood and hide armor was used in the Southeast in early times. How could it be otherwise? How could Indians all over North America have used armor but not the very advanced cultures of the Southeast? The question then becomes, what factors led to armor's virtual abandonment by the very militaristic Indians of the Southeast, assuming that like all other North American groups, they had it at one time?

One strong consideration echoes that which led to the abandonment of armor in Europe. The key factor, of course, was the introduction of a weapon, the repeating rifle, that could easily and repeatedly pierce armor. The rifled barrel enabled guns to shoot farther, straighter, and with more velocity, and mechanisms that allowed repeat shooting positioned the fighter with such a weapon as to be worth several of his predecessors with muzzle-loading long guns. The armored knight finally reached the point where adding thickness to the plate to defeat the new rifles was counter-productive. He became barely able to move under the weight of his armor, even though for a time it could stop a rifle bullet. But this historical account also applies to the Indian archers of the Southwest, who at the time of contact could fairly closely replicate with their bows and arrows the effects of the repeating rifle.

Anecdotal evidence of the force with which a Southeastern warrior could deliver an arrow is found throughout the chronicles of De Soto's travels in the Southeast. And even though the Spaniards in the sixteenth and seventeenth centuries also experienced hostile Indians in the Southwest, Southern Plains, California, and Northwest Coast areas and offered passing comments on their bows and arrows, the entirety of their descriptions is perhaps a third of that written about the bow and arrow among the Southeast Indians.

The Gentleman of Elvas, one of the chroniclers of the De Soto expedition, wrote:

> Where the arrow meets with no armor, it pierces as deeply as the shaft from a cross-bow. There bows are very perfect; the arrows are made of certain canes, like reeds, very heavy, and so stiff that one of them, when sharpened, will pass through a target. Some are pointed with the bone of a fish, sharp and like a chisel; others with some stone, like the point of diamond: of such, the great number, where they strike upon armor, break at the place where the parts are put together; those of cane split, and will enter a shirt of mail, doing more injury than when armed. (In Jones 1999, 18)

The bows of the Indians of Louisiana had a pull weight of 40 to 50 pounds (Kniffen, Gregory, and Stokes 1987, 144), and a 50-pound pull was observed in many parts of the Southeast. The penetrating power of the Southeastern bow and arrow is underscored by an account of an arrow armed with a fire-hardened whittled tip that penetrated the armored leg of a Spaniard and entered the body of his horse. Hardy, in his work on the longbow, wrote:

> But extraordinary penetration has been claimed for some Indian weapons, and sworn to by eye witnesses. During the Florida campaigns, the Spaniards again and again found their breastplates, which would stop musket balls, penetrated by arrows from the bows of Creek Indians, Choctaws and Chickasaws. An Indian captive, made to demonstrate their shooting methods, shot clean through a heavy coat of mail, the arrow dropping to the ground beyond the back of the armor. He also completely penetrated two such mail armors, one hung on top of the other. (1976, 168)

According to Spanish accounts, some Southeastern bows were as thick as a man's arm, often over 6 feet long, and accurate to 200 yards. In an early engagement, ten of De Soto's Spaniards were killed by Indians while foraging, even though most were wearing good armor; the soldiers' bodies were "pierced all the way through" (Steele 1994, 13). In another account, a horse was killed when an Indian arrow passed through its cloth, saddletree, and pack saddle and carried such force that more than a third of it penetrated the rib cage (Hudson 1997, 66).

In an early account from English settlers in Virginia, the power of the bows and arrows of the Indians was tested.

> One of our gentlemen having a target which he trusted in, thinking it would bear out a slight shot, he set it up against a tree, willing one of the savages

to shoot; who took from his back an arrow of an elle long, drew it strongly in his bow, shoots the target a foot through, or better; which was strange, being that a pistoll could not pierce it. (Swanton 1946, 581)

Many testimonials from the Spanish, as well as the early French and English, in the Southeast could be added to the above. One fact is abundantly clear: The arrows of the Southeastern Indians, like the bullets from a rifle, could pierce metal armor. In addition, the manner in which the arrows were armed, or tipped, is crucial in understanding their effectiveness.

In his article "Antler-Pointed Arrows of the Southeastern Indians," Charles C. Willoughby made an astonishing statement. "In studying the arrows of historic primitive peoples of different parts of the world, we find that, excepting among the Indians of central and western North America and in a few other restricted localities, flint points seem to have been the exception" (Willoughby 1901, 431). Additionally, little evidence exists of stone arrow points in New England in historic times. The key is that only certain types of stone can be chipped effectively, and they are not evenly dispersed across North America; however, other suitable arrow-tipping materials are. The major big-game animal hunted by Indians everywhere in North America was, with few exceptions, the deer; and "buckhorn," or deer antler, was widely employed in tipping arrows. British trader John Adair wrote that the Cherokee used arrows pointed with "scooped points of buckhorn," and De Soto's chroniclers observed arrows in the province of Cofitachequi that were tipped with buckhorn "wrought with four corners like a diamond." Archaeological evidence of antler arrows is found throughout the Algonquin area along the Eastern seaboard and from Maine to as far west as Arkansas (Willoughby 1901, 434).

A study by Nathan Lowrey, "An Ethnoarchaeological Inquiry into the Interactive Relationship between Northwest Coast Projectile Point and Armor Variants" (1994), lends insight into the implications of antler-tipped arrows in the Southeast. Lowrey replicated Northwest Coast Indian suits of wooden armor, as well as bows and arrows with stone, slate, and bone points, and learned that the stone- and slate-tipped arrows shattered against the wooden armor, or merely stuck into it. The bone points, however, punched through it.

Significantly, Ames and Maschner observed:

Stone projectile forms and styles are quite variable on the Northwest Coast while bone projectiles are similar across broad regions. These bone points are relatively long and slender, with a wedge-shaped base, and have been found outside the palisades of defensive fortifications. While having a long history on the Northwest Coast, a proliferation in numbers may correlate with the arrival of the bow and arrow in the region. (1999, 213)

The ability of the repeating rifle to fire consecutive shots with enough force to pierce metal armor ended the military use of plate armor in the West. The archers of the Southeast replicated the effects of the repeating rifle. With their bows and arrows, the Southeastern Indians were ahead of the evolution of the repeating rifle in the West. Under these circumstances there is little wonder that the Southeast lacked armor at the time of contact.

An interesting case from samurai history, discussed by Noel Perrin in *Giving Up the Gun: Japan's Reversion to the Sword, 1543–1879* (1979), offers another possible explanation for the abandonment of armor. Guns first appeared in Japan on August 25, 1543, when a Chinese cargo ship carrying about one hundred passengers, including three Portuguese traders armed with matchlock guns, ran aground on the island of Tanegashima, off the west coast of Japan. The governor of the island, Lord Tokitaka, after seeing one of the Europeans shoot ducks with the weapon, bought them for the equivalent of $10,000 apiece and turned them over to his swordsmith with orders to copy them. Within a year Lord Tokitaka's swordsmith had reproduced ten guns, and within a decade swordsmiths all over Japan were selling them. Sixty years after the shipwreck off Tanegashima, a Japanese could buy a better quality gun than the original for about $20.

However, within a century after contact, the samurai, the noble warrior class of Japan, turned against the gun. Some reasons for spurning such a powerful weapon were practical. Since at that time the warrior class numbered only about 8 percent of the population, a majority armed with guns would have threatened the warrior's traditional prerogatives. The samurai could have simply outlawed the use of firearms by anyone but themselves, but they went beyond that. They abandoned the gun for several centuries—part of a general abandonment of all things Western—because it ultimately offended their sense of morals, ethics, aesthetics, and honor. The sword stood as a visible symbol of warrior status; it was "the soul of the samurai." The gun was ugly, ungainly, and democratic: One could learn to shoot it in a few minutes, whereas skill with the sword required a lifetime of practice. The samurai turned from an obviously effective weapon for philosophical, artistic, and religious reasons.

Frederic Gleach discussed a similar situation among the southern Algonquins under the rubric "aesthetic of warfare" and "the moral nature of war."

> The moral nature of Algonquin warfare is illustrated by the Algonquin's attitude toward defense and defeat. Trowbridge described this attitude for the Shawnees in the nineteenth century, noting that they relied on the aid of their tutelar spirits and "war medicines" for defense, rather than armor, and that "if any who were reputed brave met death in battle, the Indians acknowledged themselves mistaken and such persons were set down as cowards, because it would have been impossible to kill them had they possessed true courage." (1997, 22)

The Algonquin aesthetic of warfare assumed a spirit of play. Artistically and religiously correct warfare is not about brute force, but rather the shrewdness of the warrior or the artful utilization of the resources possessed. Michabo, the Algonquin culture hero, conquered his enemies, not by confrontational force, but by "craft and ruse." The Delaware attitude toward war demanded courage, art, and circumspection as essential qualifications of a warrior. Each fighter should strive to display them by stealing upon his enemy unawares to deceive and surprise him in various ways. The "aesthetics" or "morals" of Algonquin warfare seem out-of-sync with the widespread wearing of heavy body armor (Gleach 1997, 24).

As for shields in the Southeast, a number of shapes of leather, wicker, and rawhide were encountered. They apparently played little part in warfare as observed by the Spanish, French, and English, and no evidence of the artistic and religious fascination with shields shown by peoples of the Plains and the Southwest exists. It is clear that shields were mainly used in the northern sections of the Southeast Area.

The ultimate development of Southeastern defensive technology was fortification building, which displayed myriad types from stone and brush breastworks to forts complete with multilayered palisades, bastions, and moats, and from simple, one-layer post forts to temple forts and forts made of cane.

10 Home of the North Wind
The North Pacific Culture Area

The North Pacific Culture Area includes eastern Siberia, the Aleutian Islands, and coastal Alaska from Prince William Sound to Point Hope. On the Siberian side the Chukchee and Yukaghir peoples dominate, with scattered settlements of Asiatic Inuit (Eskimo) found on the southeast edge of the Chukchee Peninsula. Many tribes of the Alaskan Inuit occupy the Alaskan coast, and a variety of Aleutian groups live on the islands that reach from the Alaska Peninsula to Attu Island on the westernmost reaches of the Aleutian chain.

Inhabitants of the North Pacific experience an extremely harsh climate. Temperatures drop to as low as $-100°$ F when a winter storm blows out of the northwest. Even during the three frost-free months of the year, thawing of the permafrost penetrates only a few inches into the frozen earth, resulting in shallow bogs, covering hundreds of square miles, where mosquitoes of prodigious size breed. Vegetation is at best sparse tundra with rare stands of stunted trees growing in sheltered areas.

The most successful animal in this frozen world is the caribou, a prime hunting target from Greenland to Siberia. The native peoples also harvest seal, walrus, lake and river fish, musk ox, small game, and wild plant foods during the brief times of the year when they are available. However, because the North Pacific environment is, in fact, quite varied, the various human groups differ in the emphasis they place on certain species; whereas one group stresses sea mammal hunting, another focuses on the caribou.

The archaeological evidence suggests that humans have been in this part of the world for about 10,000 years and that from the earliest times, cultural connections existed among the various groups. In 8000 B.C. Alaska was a cultural province of Siberia, as it had been in earlier times, occupied by peoples whose ultimate cultural roots lay to the west in the Dyukhtai tradition of Siberia (Fagan 1991, 174). The Inuit and the Aleut, along with the peoples of northern Siberia, are connected by their physical type and by language, in that they speak languages of the same stock.

Likewise, much contact occurred between the "Americans," the Russians' designation for the Inuit and the Aleut, and the Siberian tribes. Ray wrote:

Siberians and Alaskans visited each other across the strait—probably not often and sometimes with war in mind, but they did not live in the isolation often attributed to them. From 2,300-foot Cape Mountain behind Wales [Alaska], Siberia's coastal hills loom high above the horizon and the Diomede Islands appear to ride like rocky whales in a glassy sea on a calm, sunny day. After the *umiak* [open row boat] was invented, the strait became an intercontinental highway, its coastal fringes occupied by people who had more or less the same way of life. (1975, 10)

In the early 1800s Alaskan Inuit traded along the Kolyma River in Siberia, well west of the ranges of the Chukchee and Yukaghir (Ray 1975, 47). Evidence of the deep historical interconnections of the peoples of coastal Alaska, the Chukchee Peninsula, and the Aleutian Islands is relevant because the later survey of the armor, shields, and fortifications of the area suggests a similar conclusion and further indicates the Chukchee Peninsula as a major diffusion point for certain types of armor into the American area.

Warfare was widespread among all groups in the North Pacific area. The Aleut reported that long before the appearance of the Russians on their islands, they had warred both among themselves and with outsiders. "Their disposition involves them in continual wars, in which they always endeavor to gain their point by stratagem" (Coxe 1803, 198, cited in Hrdlička 1945, 144). Another early chronicler stated, "Wars, or more justly, killings and pillage, existed among the Aleut nearly always. Particularly among the Aleut of the later former time, i.e. with the grandfathers and great grandfathers of the present generation, wars were extraordinarily frequent and most destructive" (Hrdlička 1945, 144).

Violence proliferated among the Inuit communities. "Between these Netsilingmiut and other Eskimo groups in former times there was continual war. . . . Klutschak mentions that the Netsilingmiut through long wars had conquered their neighbors the Ukusikssillik Eskimo after greatly depleting their number. Similarly, for a long time the Netsilingmiut and the Aivilingmiut have been in feud" (Weyer 1932, 161).

Concerning the Bering Strait Inuit, Nelson stated, "In ancient times the Eskimo of the Bering Strait were constantly at war with one another. . . . the defeated party was always pursued and, if possible, exterminated. . . .

when possible, night raids were made by the villages on both sides and the people were usually clubbed or speared to death" (1896–1897, 34).

A favorite strategy of Alaskan Inuit warriors involved attacking at night or when they knew that a large portion of the enemy community was gathered in the *kashim* (community hall) for a meeting or ritual. The attackers blocked the door and threw firebrands down the smoke hole. Those inside either suffocated or burned to death, and those who forced their way out the door faced a waiting enemy.

The Chukchee, on the Siberian side, possessed an elaborate culture of warfare, and their oral history abounds with tales of past wars and the "violent men" who led them. As with most North Pacific groups, they preferred surprise night attacks but would also challenge an enemy to a formal fight, in which sides appeared at a prearranged battlefield in equal numbers. They were often involved in fights with the Asiatic Inuit.

Pointing to the singular focus of Chukchee warfare is the expectation that warriors train and condition their bodies for fighting. It was the duty of a semiprofessional class. Waldemar Bogoras, who in the first decade of the twentieth century wrote the definitive ethnography of the Chukchee, offered the following account, taken from oral history, of Chukchee warrior exercises:

> To be fit for fighting, every warrior undergoes hard training, and spends all his leisure in various exercises. . . . The hero must run for long distances, drawing a heavily-loaded sledge. He carries stones and timber, jumps up in the air, but above all, he fences with his long spear. He performs this exercise quite alone; and the chief feature of it is the brandishing of the spear with the utmost force, so that it bends like a piece of raw reindeer leg-skin. He also practices shooting with the bow, and uses for this purpose various arrows, sharp and blunt. From all these exercises he acquires great skill and agility. . . . When he is shot at, he avoids the arrows by springing to one side, or parries them all with the butt-end of his spear, or simply catches them between his fingers and throws them back. (Bogoras 1909, 642)

In the previous chapter, the author argued against the position that armor was often absent from certain areas because it was too cumbersome to allow warriors to dodge enemy arrows, and the blindingly fast attacks and parries of the armored *kendo* fighters of Japan were cited in support. Oral history accounts of the fully armored Chukchee fighter in action enhance this contention. Bogoras wrote, "The combatants are represented as displaying more agility than would seem consistent with the armor"

(Bogoras 1909, 642). Further, the armor of the Chukchee, as will be noted later in this chapter, was many times heavier than that of the *kendo* fighters or the North American Indians.

The most typical warfare over most of the area involved raids by no more than a dozen fighters. They may have been in response to the theft of women, insults to family or community, murder of a kinsman, threats to hunting and fishing territory, maintenance of territorial boundaries, or simply a desire for adventure. Sometimes, however, the combatants could number hundreds on a side and, as with the case of the Alaskan Inuit, form and maneuver battle lines (Burch 1988, 38).

The most impressive weapon of the Aleut, at least from the Russians' point of view, was the spear thrower, or *atlatl*. A Russian traveler writing in 1761 observed:

> They have neither guns nor bows. They have only long arrows or darts, 4 or 4½ feet long, in the head of which a sharp stone point with barbs is inserted. The darts are discharged from throwing boards in which there are slits for that purpose. With these weapons they kill men, beasts, and birds as well as we do with guns. (Hrdlička 1945, 128)

Later travelers observed the Aleut propelling darts with *atlatls* 80 to 90 yards with accuracy and force. They killed whales with them, and an accomplished fighter could arm and fire one so quickly that a dart would still be airborne when the next one was released. The Aleut used two kinds of "stone dirks" in warfare, as well as clubs, adzes, lances (which were sometimes poisoned), and bows and arrows, the latter two being the principal weapons of war.

The Chugach, an Alaskan Inuit group, fought with bows and arrows, daggers, spears, slings, wooden clubs, and a "braining stone" attached to a thong and used either like a bola or thrown. A warrior specialist called a "strong man" entered battle armed only with a club with which he knocked down arrows (Oswalt 1967, 186). More northerly Inuit groups focused on the bow and arrow, lance, knife, and harpoon.

Among the Chukchee, the lance was the major weapon of warfare, and it retains its aura of power among many contemporary Siberian groups. As late as the early twentieth century, Koryak men attached spears to their riding sleighs with special bone rings to suspend them; however, the bow and arrow was a necessary weapon. The lance and the bow and arrow held high status among the Koryak (Jochelson 1908, 558) and the Yukaghir

(Jochelson 1926, 383). The Yukaghir traditionally crafted their war lances from a birch shaft, to which they attached a sharpened elk rib.

The Siberian groups wielded a long knife (50–60 cm.) carried in a sheath on the left side like a sword. The bolalike weapon noted for the Alaskan Chugach Inuit is also found in Siberia. Jochelson referred to it as a "slung-shot."

> Judging from accounts of the customs of former times, the slung-shot must have been used in war. It consisted of a long thong of thong-seal hide, with a stone at its end. In one tradition which I recorded in Nayakhan, in which a battle between two heroes is described . . . it is related that the warrior from Nayakhan had no bow and spear, but only a slung-shot which he wore like a belt. While dodging his adversary's arrows, he hurled his slung-shot at the latter with such force that the line encircled his body several times and cut him in twain. (Jochelson 1908, 561)

Fortification

According to Ray (1975, 134), the Bering Strait Inuit did not build permanent defenses or live in fortified villages; however, stockades were constructed by the Asiatic Inuit, as well as the Koryak, Chukchee, and Kamchadal (Birket-Smith and De Laguna 1938, 375).

A Russian map of the Siberian area from 1765 includes a drawing of an Inuit camp that appears to be fortified with the dense hide coverings of the *umiak* (Inuit open boat). Within the perimeters the mapmaker drew a raised platform upon which four Inuit men stand, each holding a spear. Outside the walls of the refuge, three men hold spears.

When reacting to the threat of a raid, the Nuniwagmiut (Inuit) of Alaska erected breastworks and scattered broken and split caribou bones around their defenses to cut through the boots of attackers. They dug secret tunnels to connect individual houses to the *kashgee* (community hall) and the houses and *kashgee* to secret exits (Oswalt 1967, 186). The Chugach Inuit of Alaska stretched long hide screens that prevented the attacker from knowing exactly where the defenders were. (The Japanese used a similar technique centuries ago. When attacked by a Chinese fleet, they hung miles of silk screens to confuse the Chinese about their precise movements and location.) If the screen technique failed the Chugach, they retreated to provisioned defensive houses located on inaccessible bluffs or ledges.

Hrdlička stated that the Aleut "knew evidently no fortification—nothing of that nature has been reported by the Russians, or found by Dall's, Jochelson's, or our explorations. But they had refuges for time of danger" (Hrdlička 1945, 146). A number of Russian explorers provided additional information on refuge building. The Aleut "forts" tended to be locations on inaccessible islands or ones with steep sides and a flat top. One account described an island fort on top of which trenches had been dug, as well as a breastwork constructed of wooden planks (Hrdlička 1945, 147). There is also mention of "subterranean secret hideouts." When attacked on their high island refuges, the Aleut would pour water down the side that the enemy was pressing to ensure that it was too slippery to climb. They rolled boulders onto the attackers and pelted them with stones.

On the Siberian side, refuge and fortification building was reported for the Koryak and the Chukchee. The Koryak, whenever possible, built their villages on steep-sided islands or along the coast on easily defended sites (Jochelson 1908, 563). When an enemy approached, they moved their boats into the natural fortresses present on the many austere islands in their region. If there were no islands close by, they fortified a good defensive position with an earthen embankment, a stone wall, or a stockade. Jochelson recalled:

> I saw traces of a fortified settlement. It was situated on a rock promontory, with cliffs on three sides rising abruptly from the sea. On the fourth side there is a steep descent to the river-valley. This slope had been protected with a stone rampart. Piles of stones which once formed the wall are still visible. Tradition relates that the Russians were led there by Tungus who were hostile to the Koryak. The latter stubbornly defended the approach to the village. It was winter, and they poured water on the slope to make it slippery. During one night the Russians forged sharp iron ice-creepers, tied them under the soles of their fur boots, and stormed the fort. Many of them perished from the arrows of the Koryak and from the stones which they rolled down. (1908, 564)

If the Koryak were attacked while traveling in the open on sleighs, they would corral their reindeer and tilt their sleighs on edge to form a breastwork. The Chukchee constructed a similar refuge in the mid-1700s to withstand a Russian attack by drawing their sleighs into a circle, covering them with walrus hide, and reinforcing the walls with stones and earth (Bogoras 1909, 695). If they had time, they tied thick hides to the overturned sleighs.

Shields

Shields were not highly developed in the North Pacific area. The Aleut used a simple wooden shield, called the *kuyake* (Hrdlička 1945, 128). Bishop Veniaminov wrote:

> The shield was made simply of two folding slabs, each about 35 inches long and 14 inches broad; with it they protected their head against the flying darts or arrows, holding it in the left hand by a "bridge" raised in its middle. The shield was used only in an open encounter, or in attacks against a fortified place. (In Hrdlička 1945, 135)

Hrdlička's expedition found such shields, in the mummy caves at Kagamil, that were "rather plainly made" and decorated with red paint (Hrdlička 1945, 356). Shields of wooden slats were reported for the Nuniwagmiut Inuit of Alaska (Oswalt 1967, 186), as well as for the Asiatic Inuit (Birket-Smith and De Laguna 1938, 467). A cumbersome wooden shield covered in sealskin was borne by the Bering Strait Inuit (Paterek 1994, 392). Citations for shields on the Chukchee Peninsula likewise indicate simple ones of wood or walrus hide.

In the account of an expedition to the "northern parts of Russia" sponsored by Catherine the Great in the late eighteenth century, the following observation is made concerning a type of shield used by natives in the vicinity of Kodiak Island. The expedition's leader, Commodore Joseph Billings, wrote, "They have very large screens; I was told, (but saw none) of sufficient strength and thickness to withstand a musket-ball, and large enough to shelter twenty or thirty men" (Billings 1802, 198).

Armor

The North Pacific area is rich in armor. A unique hide armor, which does not resemble any armor of North America, was worn by the Chukchee, Asiatic Inuit, and Inuit of St. Lawrence Island. About ten telescoping rings, perhaps 5 inches wide, formed the lower portion from the upper chest to below the knees. The fighter could lift the armor by grasping the bottom ring to free his knees and legs. If he wanted to run for some distance, he would tie the lower ring to a higher one. If he faced a flight of arrows, he could simply crouch, and the armor would envelop him from the ground up. The top portion of this fascinating armor was a rawhide screen of bleached sealskin and wood that rose above the fighter's head and wrapped around his upper back, extending down both arms. When he

Chukchee (Siberia) wearing armor of telescoping rawhide rings.

turned his back to the enemy's projectiles, he was totally covered. Greaves, shin guards of walrus ivory, offered additional protection to the lower legs (Paterek 1994, 392).

Hough included a number of examples of Inuit armor in his classic paper on North American armor. Below is his description of one type from Cape Prince of Wales, Alaska:

> Made of three rows of walrus-ivory plates, averaging 1 inch in width and 6 inches in length. Each plate contains 6 holes, through which pass rawhide thongs, thus lashing the plates together. These plates are slightly overlapping, as are also the different rows, so as to ward off more effectively the weapons of the enemy. The lower row contains 43 plates and the middle 38. The upper row consists of two sections; one containing ten plates, protecting the breast, the other 8 plates protecting the upper part of the back. A rawhide strap passes over the shoulders and supports the armor. The armor very closely resembles that of Japan. Length when spread out: 44 inches. (Hough 1895, 632)

Iron armor plates were excavated from a marsh at Cape Prince of Wales, and plates of iron and copper have been found on St. Lawrence Island (Hough 1895, 633).

The following details a suit of Inuit armor from Diomede, Alaska:

> Made of five imbricating rows of plates of walrus ivory of unequal size in the different rows, pierced with from 6 to 13 holes, lashed with sealskin thongs. The vertical edge of the plates are chambered. The upper row has 40, 3 by 1 $\frac{1}{4}$ inches; second row, 49 plates, 5 by 1 inch; third row 28 plates, 3 $\frac{1}{2}$ by 1 $\frac{5}{8}$ inches. This armor was wrapped around the body after the manner of a cuirass. In the form of lashing and adjustment of the plates, it is identical with certain types of Japanese armor. (Hough 1895, 634)

Slat and ivory-plate armor is reported for the Inupiat along the northern Alaskan coast (Pritzker 1998, 2:777), the Alutiiq from Kodiak Island north (Pritzker 1998, 2:755), and the Inuit of Cape Rodney (Ray 1975, 290). Commodore Joseph Billings described the armor he saw among the natives living near Kodiak Island in the late eighteenth century:

> They have armor of wood, which covers the body of the warrior and his neck; but his arms and legs are exposed. This is made of very neat pieces of wood, about half an inch thick, and near an inch broad, tied very artfully together with fine thread of the sinews of animals; and so contrived, that

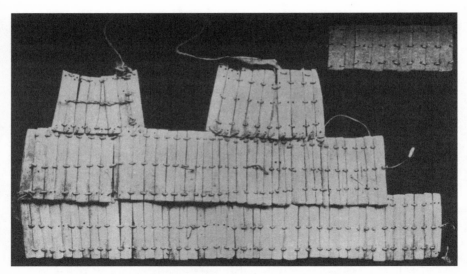

Inuit walrus ivory-plate armor.

they can roll it up or expand it. This they tie round the body, a flap before reaching down their thighs; but so made as to rise or fall, and permit their sitting in baidars: a similar flap hangs on the breast, which may be risen as high as their eyes. Straps fasten this armor on their shoulders, and strings tie it round the body on one side. The head is well guarded with a wooden helmet; some of these are made to resemble the head of a bear, and cover the face completely. (Billings 1802, 198–199)

The Bering Strait Inuit wore armor of wooden slats, bone, and ivory held up by walrus-hide shoulder straps. (Some armor from this area featured a raised back to protect the neck.) The Kotzebue Sound Inuit wore bone or ivory-plate armor and at times only rawhide tunics. Many northern Alaska Inuit groups followed this pattern. The Inuit of southwest Alaska, as well as the Nunivak Island Inuit, constructed bone or ivory-plate armor as a cuirass that hung from the shoulders with rawhide straps (Paterek 1994, 397). The Chugach used wooden slat-armor augmented with a seal-skin cuirass underneath (Burch 1988, 38).

Almost no mention is made of armor among the most northerly of the Inuit groups. Perhaps the many layers of thick hide and fur that people like the Polar Inuit were forced to wear because of the harsh cold supplanted the need for it.

Rod-armor worn under an outer garment was reported for the Fox Island Aleut (Hrdlička 1945, 132). The Kagamil caves, noted above, pro-

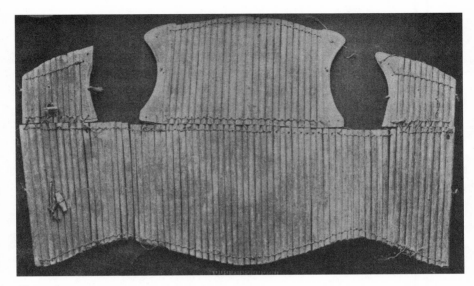

Aleut rod-armor.

duced a thick whalebone breastplate (Hrdlička 1945, 135). Hough (1895, 137) was of the opinion that in form the Aleut armor, instead of following the Eskimo type, belonged with the rod type of the Indians. A "battle *Kamleikas,*" an especially thick, waterproof parka for warfare, as well as helmets, was noted for the Aleut (Paterek 1994, 388).

The Chukchee of Plover Bay made a cuirass of whalebone strips hung vertically and tied tightly together. Additional thin strips blocked any spaces, albeit very small, remaining when the underlayer of strips was sewn together. The cuirass was suspended from shoulder straps and was used when they traded with the often hostile Inuit of St. Lawrence Island (Hough 1895, 635). The Chukchee also wore a helmet of wooden slats sewn together and covered with rawhide. The head protector was tied to the cuirass from the back and both sides (Bogoras 1909, 164). The Giliaks of Siberia replicated this type of helmet in more modern form, though instead of wooden plates they used iron. Greaves and arm guards of hide and/or iron armored the Chukchee fighter. On the borders of the Chukchee, the Yukaghir built a rare style of armor of reindeer antler rings strung on sinew (Graburn and Strong 1973, 163).

An incident from Siberia offers insight into the prevalence of native-made armor during the early historic period. A Russian led an expedition of Chukchee (perhaps Inuit) to King Island to establish trade. When the Chukchee noticed that the King Islanders had sighted them, they stopped

Koryak (Siberia) in armor.

paddling, donned armor, and arranged their spears and bows and arrows so that they were easily accessible. When the Russian leader protested that he wished to trade with the King Islanders, not attack them, the Chukchee responded that they were simply preparing to meet the King Islanders in the customary fashion. The King Islanders greeted the expedition dressed in armor and wielding spears and bows and arrows. After meeting in this fashion, the Russian expedition was feasted and treated in a friendly manner (Ray 1975, 58). This greeting ritual, based around a mock attack, was seen over much of native North America.

Discussion and Summary

The North Pacific area proved bereft of complex fortification building for the most part. Refuges, however, were produced in a variety of ways—from breastworks to isolated island refuges, which provided a natural defensive position, to visual screens, to provisioned houses built in isolated areas. Tunneling and hidden rooms were found in some defensive positions. Shields were infrequently used and were of a generally uninspired construction. In armor making, however, the area excelled. Some of the most complex and effective armor in North America arose from the creative forces operating in the North Pacific area.

The armor styles of the Siberians, in turn, were influenced by surrounding areas—particularly China, Korea, and Japan—and, more recently, by the Cossack invasion in the seventeenth century. However, Black's admonition must be observed. "The problem of cultural relations in the entire North Pacific area is complex, not fully understood, and various aspects of the problem are hotly debated by specialists, primarily archaeologists and physical anthropologists" (Black 1984, 12). He presents a variety of cultural traits which seem to show that the eastern Aleut have been affected by the cultures of Japan, China, and Korea, beginning sometime in the early centuries of the second millennium A.D. Bogoras, in his masterwork on the Chukchee, includes a photograph of a suit of Japanese armor, with helmet, that he purchased from a Chukchee on the O'nmilin tundra (1909, 164). The armor and helmets of the Chukchee Peninsula–dwellers appear inspired by the metal-plate armor worn by the Cossacks when they first raided into Siberia to control the fur trade centuries ago.

The nature of cultural relations in the area under consideration is complex and confusing. However, with so many similarities, in armor making in particular, the evidence of ancient and continuing contact between the

American and Siberian sides is so compelling that diffusion from Siberia into America, and vice-versa, must be considered highly probable.

Hough, with more certainty than most modern experts on the issue of diffusion, makes a statement that at least in its general outline must be accurate:

> Plate armor in America is a clear case of the migration of invention, its congeners having been traced from Japan northeastward through the Ainos, Giliaks, and Chukchee, across the Bering Strait by the intervening islands to the western Eskimo. Here the armor spread southward from the narrowest part of the Strait, passing into the slat armor of the Northwest Coast, which is possibly a development of the plate idea. The plate armor may have spread to the eastern coast of North America. Hence it appears to be conclusive that plate armor in America had Asiatic origins. The date of introduction is not considered. (1895, 651)

Conclusion

Armor may have arisen when projectiles, blades, and clubs evolved enough to cause mortal danger in combat. Covering the body with some sort of protection seemed a logical response. Once the offensive-defensive reaction set in, the spiral began. An offensive weapon was negated by a defensive technique, which was nullified by an enhanced offensive weapon, *ad infinitum*, continuing to the point where the technology of one side superseded, by great lengths, that of the other: metal trumped wood and leather; gunpowder far exceeded the power of the bow or *atlatl*.

The archaeological record offers extensive testimony on the widespread use of fortifications before and after contact, but little insight into the ancient use of armor, because the wood, leather, and twine of Indian armor decayed in the ground. The historical record, containing most of what is known on the subject of Indian armor, reveals a highly varied picture. In the Southeast, armor disappeared shortly before contact (assuming that it existed in earlier times). In the Northwest Coast, area armor that could stop musket balls remained in use into the early nineteenth century. In some cases all warriors wore armor; in others, only military elites did. The one sure fact is that no armor, metal or rawhide, could stand against the rifle. As that weapon entered the picture, armor disappeared.

The relevant literature clearly shows a positive correlation between armor use and arrow poisoning. Wherever arrows were poisoned, armor was inevitably in use. Further, armor appears connected to elite status in many areas, a particularly strange phenomenon, since North American Indian armor is based on easily available materials and construction principles that anyone could employ. In Europe, on the other hand, armor was reserved for elites, originally at least, because of its expense and the specialized knowledge required for construction. In Japan, likewise, armor was highly complex and made of expensive materials by skilled artisans. Perhaps, as the discussion of Plains shields suggested, a major expense involved with the weapon was the rituals performed by the relevant priest or shaman to protect the user in battle. Or perhaps, as the California material suggested, military elites wore armor to preserve themselves as resources and to serve as small, mobile shields for unarmored warriors fighting around them. Reports from the Southeast dating to the time of early contact describe armored war leaders positioning themselves within the ranks of their warriors as a means of protection.

Of the many types of armor worn by the Indians, rod-armor seems—after rawhide shirts and tunics—the most widespread "constructed" armor. Slat-armor was somewhat less widely dispersed. Rod-armor is based on simpler construction principles: fewer pieces, no holes to drill, and little preparation of materials, since unmodified twigs can be used. It may be a safe guess, based on ease of construction, that after hide armor, rod-armor developed and was later augmented and then replaced in some areas by slat-armor, which seems to have emanated from the North Pacific area.

Several examples from the Northeast, Southeast, and Plains indicate that armor usage complied with cultural beliefs on the nature of the afterlife and the proper behavior of warriors facing life-and-death confrontations. An Iroquois warrior's death placed his soul in a dark and lonely place. The Southeasterners' religious beliefs, at least prior to contact, posited the afterlife of the warrior as a glorious extension of this life, without the negative qualities appertaining. The Plains warriors, though having a slight interest, relative to other North American Indians, in the details of the warrior's afterlife, stressed the courting of danger as a source of reputation and honor. Death in battle, given those values, might be considered a good thing. The Shawnee questioned the death of a warrior as perhaps indicative of the failure of his Medicine.

Shields remained on the scene longer than body armor. In a way, it might be said that shields had more variable functions than body armor. Thick rawhide shields could deflect musket and rifle bullets, fired from a distance, that struck at an oblique angle. Shields could hide the body outline from a sharpshooter, as well as present a visual screen for a line of warriors when placed side by side. They were also amenable to ceremonial use and personal religious behavior, especially in the Plains and the Southwest (and also in early Basin cultures). Body armor and helmets might in ancient times have been endowed with mystical qualities. The "clan hats" as helmets and the shamanic helmet-mask of the Northwest Coast peoples suggest this relationship, as do the Zuni helmet-masks.

North American Indian shields were devised from bison, moose, mountain goat, or deer rawhide. Sometimes they were quilted or multilayered, wicker or bark; and sometimes they were made of wooden planks. For the most part they were simple and unadorned, the Plains and the Southwest usage notwithstanding. Round, square, oval, or rectangular in shape, some were only half again as large as a dinner plate, while others covered almost the entire body. They tended to become lighter and smaller toward the end of their history, mainly because of the adaptation to cavalry warfare. In a few rare instances, curtain-shields were devised from a simple deer pelt suspended from a bow or stick.

Evidence of fortification reaches back many centuries before contact, at which time North American Indians built fortifications with bastions, multilayered palisades, and moats. This pattern was so successful that it was still in wide use when Europeans first contacted the Indians. There also existed what appears to be a simpler, perhaps older, type of fortification without bastions, moats, or multilayered palisades. Such forts were generally circular and composed of a single line of pointed logs embedded several feet into the ground.

Many enhancements and variations added to the basic fort plans: shooting platforms, elevated fortified houses, escape tunnels, briar "barbed wire," poisoned stakes, loopholes, water troughs for dowsing fires built against palisade walls, elevated torches for exterior lighting, and the arrangement of forts in what Keegan calls "strategic defenses," where forts defended each other. Noted also were "guard towns," where warriors were lodged, "war lodges," and mountaintop strongholds (Keegan 1994, 139– 142). North American Indians used about every fortification embellishment known worldwide.

However, not all Indians built complex fortifications. The foregoing casual survey suggested that elaborate fortifications were most likely constructed by densely populated, relatively sedentary groups who depended upon resources that could not be moved: land suitable for horticulture, rich fishing and hunting sites—as opposed to territories—and trade route access. Small nomadic hunting bands did not build complex fortifications, nor did the peoples of the Great Basin and the Subarctic.

A style of defensive construction universal in North America is entrenching and breastwork building, which may represent the earliest form of refuge. The two techniques were used individually, together, and as features of complex fortifications.

The cases in my survey support Keegan's model, presented in the Introduction, vis-à-vis refuges, strongholds, and strategic defensive systems. He suggested that refuge building would most likely occur in small-scale, nomadic bands. The information developed in this volume on North American Indian fortifications supports that contention. The defensive technology of the Great Basin and Subarctic bands was of the refuge type. With the tribal (organized multiband) type of society like the Blackfoot, Cheyenne, Comanche, Kiowa, etc., refuge building predominated. The key here is that nomadic groups defended themselves from spontaneous attack through refuge building and entrenching. Generally, instead of defending specific locations, they thought of defense in terms of territory.

Strongholds with palisades, bastions, and moats were, according to Keegan, most prominent in "small or divided sovereignties . . . [where] central authority has not been established, or is struggling to secure itself or has broken down" (Keegan 1994, 142). The elaborately fortified sites, particularly in the Southeast, Northwest, and Northeast, were situated in a context of "small or divided sovereignties."

Finally, Keegan defined strategic defenses as those in which a number of strongholds supported one another or connected in such a way as to control a vaster area than could be accomplished by a single stronghold. Since strategic defenses were complex and expensive, "their existence is always a mark of the wealth and advanced political development of the people" who build them (Keegan 1994, 142). His observations once more prove apt. Strategic defenses were seen mainly in the Southeast and Southwest, the two culture areas in North America that arguably possessed the most complex political organization found among any Indian groups.

North American Indians constructed both complex strongholds and armor before contact. It is also true, however, that they were influenced by some of their neighbors before contact and by the Europeans after contact. The diffusion of plate- and slat-armor in the North Pacific area seems undeniable, given its earlier existence on the Siberian side. Further, the presence of slat-armor diminishes the farther one moves from the North Pacific Area although it is still found as far away as the Atlantic coast.

Clearly, some degree of Mesoamerican culture influenced the Southwest and Southeast. The presence in both areas of maize, beans, and squash suggests that other influences could also have reached into the North American cultural realm. Armored elites stiffening the ranks of the warriors, as seen in several California examples, reflects Aztec warfare and offers an explanation for armor not usually being worn by all fighters. Typical Aztec swords, in which blades of obsidian were set edgewise into a slotted wooden baton, were noted in Georgia by De Soto's group and in the Southwest. Likewise in the Southeast, the common feathered capes, the most elaborate of which were generally worn by men of high status, almost exactly replicated the feathered war coats of the Aztec. Quilting of multiple-layered cotton into armor was also found in both Mesoamerica and North America.

The influence of Europeans on Indian fortification building began at the dawn of contact. Many accounts record Indian leaders visiting European forts and asking probing questions about their construction. The letters of French colonial governors in the early 1700s contain many allusions to Indian forts that had begun to display the effects of European tutelage.

Armor, too, was at certain times and in certain places much influenced by Europeans. In particular, the Plains Indians borrowed horse armor, small shields, and perhaps some facets of the leather cuirass from the Spaniards, although leather vests and jackets were ubiquitous in North America. There was some reciprocal influence with regard to armor. The papers of La Salle's expeditions mention his men donning wooden armor to defend against Indian arrows. Many hapless Frenchmen made the same mistake in the attack on the Chickasaw fortress of Ackia a half century later.

Regarding further research into the area of armor, shields, and fortifications, it might be interesting to elaborate on the psychological advantages of armor; the relationship among armor, horticultural lifeways, and matrilineality; and the diffusion routes of various types of armor. Likewise, the uncanny uniformity of styles of fortifications in native North America begs investigation, as do the systems of Indian martial arts alluded to in many of the earliest contact accounts.

Almost everywhere, at various times, North American Indians used armor, carried shields, and constructed defensive structures both simple and complex, and these behaviors probably stemmed from Late Archaic and Early Woodland times. However, the images of the American Indian held by most do not include an armor-wearing warrior. This is curious in that armor wearing and fortification building were practiced by certain Indian societies from the mid-1500s to the early 1800s.

All Americans are familiar with such emblems of Indian culture as tipis, totem poles, feathered "war bonnets," peace pipes, buffalo hunting, bows and arrows, pottery and basketry, the Snake Dance, pueblos, tomahawks, moccasins, and birch-bark canoes. But the survey of defensive technology in this work argues that the following image must also be added: The fort stands along a river on the northern Plains. The log walls are 18 feet high, lined on the inside with shooting platforms. At intervals bastions and loopholes have been placed, and surrounding the entire structure, a moat. Twenty elite fighters exit the fort and arrange themselves in a defensive position before the barred gate. Dressed in armor and carrying bows and arrows and clubs, they await their attackers. The "Piercers," mounted on armored horses, thunder across the open expanse toward the fort. They wear leather helmets and multilayered rawhide cuirasses as they drive down on the waiting defenders with 12-foot lances tipped by Spanish swords couched under their left arms. Battle cries from the charging warriors are thrown back at them by the fort's defenders. Clouds of arrows fill the air. Lances glisten in the sun. The two sides clash. Golden clouds of dust rise from the fray and swirl around the battle standards fluttering from the walls of the fort as the Indian knights exert their will to defend their people and their land and to claim glory.

Bibliography

Abbott, Charles C. 1885. The Use of Copper by the Delaware Indians. *American Naturalist,* vol. 19.

Abel, Annie Heloise, ed. 1939. *Tabeau's Narrative of Loisel's Expedition to the Upper Missouri.* Norman: University of Oklahoma Press.

Abler, Thomas S. 1970. Longhouse and Palisade: Northeastern Iroquoian Villages of the Seventeenth Century. *Ontario History,* vol. 62.

Ackerman, Robert E. 1990. Prehistory of the Asian Eskimo Zone. In *Handbook of North American Indians,* vol. 5, ed. William C. Sturtevant. Washington, D.C.: Smithsonian Institution.

Ames, Kenneth M., and Herbert D. G. Maschner. 1999. *Peoples of the Northwest Coast: Their Archaeology and Prehistory.* London: Thames and Hudson, Ltd.

Anderson, David G. 1994. *The Savannah River Chiefdoms: Political Change in the Late Prehistoric Southeast.* Tuscaloosa: University of Alabama Press.

Annual Archaeological Report. 1918. *Wood and Wood Products of the Prehistoric Indians of Ontario.* Toronto: L. K. Cameron.

Arai, Hakuseki. 1964. *The Armor Book in Honcho Gunkiko.* Edited by H. Russell Robinson. London: Holland Press; Tokyo: Charles E. Tuttle Co.

Bamforth, Douglas B. 1994. Indigenous People, Indigenous Violence: Precontact Warfare on the North American Great Plains. *Man* 29 (1): 95–115.

Barnett, Homer G. 1955. *The Coast Salish of British Columbia.* Eugene: University of Oregon Press.

Basso, Keith H., ed. 1971. *Western Apache Raiding and Warfare.* Tucson: University of Arizona Press.

Bauman, Robert. 1960. Ottawa Fleets and Iroquois Frustration. *Northwest Ohio Quarterly,* vol. 33.

Bean, Lowell J. 1990. The Gabrielino. In *Handbook of North American Indians,* vol. 8, ed. William C. Sturtevant. Washington, D.C.: Smithsonian Institution.

Bean, Lowell J., and Katherine S. Saubel. 1972. *Temalpakh: Cahuilla Indian Knowledge and Usage of Plants.* Banning, Calif.: Malki Museum Press.

Bean, Lowell J., and Florence C. Shipek. 1990. The Luiseno. In *Handbook of North American Indians,* vol. 8, ed. William C. Sturtevant. Washington, D.C.: Smithsonian Institution.

Beard, Edmund. 1970. Warfare among the Eskimos. *Columbia Essays in International Affairs. The Dean's Papers, 1969,* vol. 5.

Beardsley, Richard K. 1967. Culture Sequences in Central California Archaeology.

In *The California Indians,* ed. R. F. Heizer and M. A. Whipple. Berkeley and Los Angeles: University of California Press.

Beauchamp, William M. 1905. Aboriginal Use of Wood in New York. *New York State Museum Bulletin,* no. 89.

Bell, Robert E., et al. 1974. *Wichita Indian Archaeology and Ethnology: A Pilot Study.* New York: Garland Publishing.

Biddle, Nicholas, ed. 1962. *The Journals of the Expedition under the Command of Capts. Lewis and Clark.* Vol. 2. New York: Heritage Press.

Billings, Joseph. 1802. *An Account of a Geographical and Astronomical Expedition to the Northern Parts of Russia.* London: n.p.

Birket-Smith, Kaj, and Frederica De Laguna. 1938. *The Eyak Indians of the Copper River Delta, Alaska.* København, Denmark: Levin & Munksgaard.

Black, Lydia T. 1984. *Atka: An Ethnohistory of the Western Aleutians.* Kingston, Ont.: Limestone Press.

Blackburn, Thomas C., and Lowell J. Bean. 1990. The Kitanemuk. In *Handbook of North American Indians,* vol. 8, ed. William C. Sturtevant. Washington, D.C.: Smithsonian Institution.

Blitz, John H. 1993. *Ancient Chiefdoms of the Tombigbee.* A Dan Josselyn Memorial Publication. Tuscaloosa: University of Alabama Press.

Boas, Franz. 1909. The Kwakiutl of Vancouver Island. *The Jesup North Pacific Expedition. Memoir of the American Museum of Natural History,* vol. 5, ed. Franz Boas. New York: G. E. Stechert.

———. 1966. *Kwakiutl Ethnography.* Edited by Helen Codere. Chicago: University of Chicago Press.

Bogoras, Waldemar. 1909. The Chukchee. *The Jesup North Pacific Expedition. Memoir of the American Museum of Natural History,* vol. 7, ed. Franz Boas. New York: G. E. Stechert.

Boyd, Robert. 1990. Demographic History, 1774–1874. In *Handbook of North American Indians,* vol. 7, ed. William C. Sturtevant. Washington, D.C.: Smithsonian Institution.

———. 1997. *People of the Dalles: The Indians of Wascopam Mission.* Lincoln: University of Nebraska Press.

Brathwaite, Jean. 1972. The Taking of the Ship *Boston. Syesis,* vol. 5.

Bright, William. 1990. The Karok. In *Handbook of North American Indians,* vol. 8, ed. William C. Sturtevant. Washington, D.C.: Smithsonian Institution.

Brown, Vinson, and Douglas Andrews. 1969. *The Pomo Indians of California and Their Neighbors.* American Indian Map-Book Series, vol. 1. Healdsburg, Calif.: Naturegraph Publishers.

Brugge, David M. 1960. History, Huki, and Warfare: Some Random Data on the Lower Pima. *Kiva* 26, no. 4.

Bullen, Adelaide. 1954. *Florida Indians Past and Present.* Gainesville, Fla.: Kendal Books.

Burch, Ernest S. 1988. *The Eskimos.* Norman: University of Oklahoma Press.

Burpee, Lawrence J., ed. 1908. An Adventurer from Hudson Bay: Journal of Matthew

Cocking, from York Factory to the Blackfeet Country, 1772–1773. *Transactions of the Royal Society of Canada, Vol. 2*. Third Series—1908–1909.

Bushnell, David I. 1919. *Native Villages and Village Sites East of the Mississippi*. Smithsonian Institution Bureau of American Ethnology, Bulletin 69. Washington, D.C.: Smithsonian Institution.

———. 1922. *Villages of the Algonquian, Siouan, and Caddoan Tribes West of the Mississippi*. Smithsonian Institution Bureau of American Ethnology, Bulletin 77. Washington, D.C.: Smithsonian Institution.

Cadzow, Donald A. 1920. *Native Copper Objects of the Copper Eskimo*. Indian Notes and Monographs. New York Museum of the American Indian. Washington, D.C.: Heye Foundation.

Caldwell, Warren W. 1964. Fortified Villages in the Northern Plains. *Plains Anthropologist*, vol. 9.

Callaghan, Catherine. 1990. The Lake Miwok. In *Handbook of North American Indians*, vol. 8, ed. William C. Sturtevant. Washington, D.C.: Smithsonian Institution.

Callaway, Donald. 1990. The Ute. In *Handbook of North American Indians*, vol. 11, ed. William C. Sturtevant. Washington, D.C.: Smithsonian Institution.

Carlson, Roy L. 1965. Eighteenth-Century Navajo Fortresses of the Gobernador District. *University of Colorado Studies. Series in Anthropology, No. 10*. Boulder: University of Colorado.

Carpenter, Edmund, and Royal Hassrick. 1947. Some Notes on Arrow Poisoning among the Tribes of the Eastern Woodlands. *Proceedings of the Delaware County Institute of Science*, vol. 10.

Castañeda, Pedro. 1966. *The Journey of Coronado*. Ann Arbor, Mich.: University Microfilms.

Castile, George Pierre, ed. 1985. *The Indians of Puget Sound: The Notebooks of Myron Eells*. Seattle: University of Washington Press.

Catlin, George. 1868. *Last Rambles amongst the Indians of the Rocky Mountains and the Andes*. London: Sampson Low, Son, and Marston.

Charlevoix, Pierre de. 1866. *History and General Description of New France*. Translated by John G. Shea. New York: John G. Shea.

———. 1966. *Journal of a Voyage to North America*. Ann Arbor, Mich.: University Microfilms.

Clayton, Lawrence A., Vernon James Knight Jr., and Edward C. Moore, eds. 1990. *The De Soto Chronicles: The Expedition of Hernando De Soto to North America in 1539–1543*. Tuscaloosa: University of Alabama Press.

Clifton, James A., et al. 1986. *People of the Three Fires: The Ottawa, Potawatomi and Ojibway of Michigan*. Grand Rapids, Mich.: Grand Rapids Inter-Tribal Council.

Codere, Helen. 1950. *Fighting with Property: A Study of Kwakiutl Potlatching and Warfare, 1792–1930*. Seattle: University of Washington Press.

Colnett, James. 1787. The Journal Aboard the Prince of Wales. Manuscript ADM 155/146. Public Records Office, London.

Cook, S. F. 1943. *The Conflict between the California Indian and White Civilization.* Berkeley and Los Angeles: University of California Press.

Couture, B., and J. O. Edwards. 1940. *Origin of Copper Used by Canadian West Coast Indians in the Manufacture of Ornamental Plaques.* National Museum of Canada Bulletin, vol. 194. Ottawa: National Museum of Canada.

Covington, James W. 1975. Relations between the Eastern Timucuan Indians and the French and Spanish, 1564–1567. In *Four Centuries of Southern Indians,* ed. Charles M. Hudson. Athens: University of Georgia Press.

Cox, Isaac J. 1922. *The Journey of Rene Robert Cavelier Sieur de La Salle.* Vol. 1. New York: Alberton Book Company.

Cremony, John C. 1868. *Life among the Apaches.* Lincoln: University of Nebraska Press.

Crimmins, M. L. 1932. The Aztec Influence on the Primitive Cultures of the Southwest. *Bulletin of the Texas Archaeological and Paleontological Society* 4 (September).

Cushing, Frank Hamilton. 1894. Primitive Copper Working: An Experimental Study. *American Anthropologist* 7, no. 1.

Cushman, H. B. 1899. *History of the Choctaw, Chickasaw and Natchez Indians.* Greenville, Tex.: Headlight Printing House.

Cusick, David. 1848. *David Cusick's Sketches of Ancient History of the Six Nations.* New York: Lockport.

Dall, W. H. 1877. On Succession in the Shell-Heaps of the Aleutian Islands and the Tribes of the Extreme Northwest. In *Tribes of Western Washington and Northwestern Oregon,* ed. George Gibbs. Contributions to North American Ethnology, vol. 1. Washington, D.C.: Department of the Interior.

De Laguna, Frederica, and Catharine McClellen. 1990. Ahtna. In *Handbook of North American Indians,* vol. 8, ed. William C. Sturtevant. Washington, D.C.: Smithsonian Institution.

Demetracopoulou, D. 1939. Wintu War Dance. *Proceedings—Pacific Science Congress* 6, no. 4.

Denniston, Glenda. 1990. Sekani. In *Handbook of North American Indians,* vol. 6, ed. William C. Sturtevant. Washington, D.C.: Smithsonian Institution.

DePratter, Chester B. 1991. *Late Prehistoric and Early Historic Chiefdoms in the Southeastern United States.* New York: Garland Publishing.

Dictionary of Daily Life of Indians of the Americas. Vol. 1. 1981. Newport Beach, Calif.: American Indian Publishers.

Dixon, Roland B. 1905. The Northern Maidu. *Bulletin of the American Museum of Natural History* 17, no. 3.

Dobie, J. D. 1950. Indian Horses and Horsemanship. *Southwest Review,* vol. 35.

Dobyns, Henry F., Paul H. Ezell, Alden W. Jones, and Greta Ezell. 1957. Thematic Changes in Yuman Warfare. In *Proceedings of the 1957 Annual Spring Meeting of the American Ethnological Society.* Seattle: Washington University Press.

Dorsey, James O. 1920. *Omaha Sociology.* New York: Johnson Reprints.

Douglas, F. H. 1936. *Copper and the Indian*. Denver Art Museum, Department of Indian Art Leaflet 2, no. 2.

Dufour, Charles L. 1967. *Ten Flags in the Wind: The Story of Louisiana*. New York: Harper & Row.

du Pratz, Antoine Le Page. 1947 [1774]. *History of Louisiana, or of the Western Parts of Virginia and Carolina*. New Orleans: Pelican Press.

Edmunds, David R., and Joseph L. Peyser. 1993. *The Fox Wars: The Mesquakie Challenge to New France*. Norman: University of Oklahoma Press.

Elsasser, Albert B. 1990. The Wiyot and the Athabascans. In *Handbook of North American Indians,* vol. 8, ed. William C. Sturtevant. Washington, D.C.: Smithsonian Institution.

Emmons, George T. 1908. Copper Neck-Rings of Southern Alaska. *American Anthropologist,* vol. 10.

Evans, Philip W. 1997. *The Arms and Armor of Raleigh's Roanoke Voyages, 1584–1590*. Fort Raleigh National Historic Site. Manteo, N.C.: National Park Services.

Ewers, John C. 1943. Primitive American Commandos. *Masterkey for Indian Lore and History,* vol. 17.

———. 1944. The Blackfoot War Lodge: Its Construction and Use. *American Anthropologist,* vol. 46.

———. 1957. Hair Pipes in Plains Indian Adornment: A Study in Indian and White Ingenuity. *Smithsonian Institution, Bureau of American Ethnology, Bulletin 164.* Anthropological Papers, no. 50.

———. 1958. *The Blackfeet: Raiders of the Northwestern Plains*. Norman: University of Oklahoma Press.

———. 1980. *The Horse in Blackfoot Indian Culture*. Washington, D.C.: Smithsonian Institution Press.

Ezell, Paul H. 1961. The Hispanic Acculturation of the Gila River Pimas. *American Anthropologist Memoir 90,* vol. 63, no. 5, part 2.

Fagan, Brian M. 1991. *Ancient North America: The Archaeology of a Continent*. London: Thames and Hudson.

Fahey, John. 1974. *The Flathead Indians*. Norman: University of Oklahoma Press.

Farmer, Malcolm F. 1957. A Suggested Typology of Defensive Systems of the Southwest. *Southwestern Journal of Anthropology,* vol. 13.

Fathauer, George H. 1954. The Structure and Causation of Mohave Warfare. *Southwestern Journal of Anthropology,* vol. 10.

Feder, Norman. 1932. *New England Indian Houses, Forts and Settlements*. Denver Art Museum, Department of Indian Art Leaflet, no. 39.

Feiler, Seymour, trans. and ed. 1962. *Jean-Bernard Bossu's Travels in the Interior of North America, 1751–1762*. Norman: University of Oklahoma Press.

Fletcher, Alice C., and Francis La Flesche. 1972. *The Omaha Tribe*. Vols. 1 and 2. Lincoln: University of Nebraska Press.

Forbes, Allan. 1971. Two and a Half Centuries of Conflict: The Iroquois and the Laurentian Wars. *Pennsylvania Archaeologist,* vol. 30.

Forbes, Jack D. 1960. *Apache, Navaho, and Spaniard.* Norman: University of Oklahoma Press.

———. 1965. *Warriors of the Colorado: The Yumas of the Quechan Nation and Their Neighbors.* Norman: University of Oklahoma Press.

Garbarino, Merwyn S., and Robert F. Sasso. 1994. *Native American Heritage.* Prospect Heights, Ill.: Waveland Press.

Garth, T. R. 1990. The Atsugewi. In *Handbook of North American Indians,* vol. 8, ed. William C. Sturtevant. Washington, D.C.: Smithsonian Institution.

Gebhard, D. 1965. The Shield Motif in Plains Rock Art. *Society for American Archaeology,* vol. 31.

Gibbs, George. 1877. *Tribes of the Extreme Northwest.* Contributions to North American Ethnology, vol. 1. Washington, D.C.: Government Printing Office.

Gibson, Arrell M. 1963. *The Kickapoos.* Norman: University of Oklahoma Press.

———. 1971. *The Chickasaws.* Norman: University of Oklahoma Press.

Gibson, Jon L. 1974. Aboriginal Warfare in the Protohistoric Southeast: An Alternative Perspective. *American Antiquity,* no. 39.

Gifford, E. W. 1940. California Bone Artifacts. *Anthropological Records,* vol. 3, no. 1. Berkeley and Los Angeles: University of California Press.

Gilbert, William Harlen. 1919. *The Eastern Cherokee.* Smithsonian Institution Bureau of American Ethnology Bulletin 133. Washington, D.C.: Smithsonian Institution.

Given, Brian J. 1981. The Iroquois Wars and Native Firearms. In *Papers from the Sixth Annual Congress: Canadian Ethnology Society.* Ottawa: Canadian Ethnology Society.

Gleach, Frederic W. 1997. *Powatan's World and Colonial Virginia: A Conflict of Cultures.* Lincoln: University of Nebraska Press.

Goddard, Pliny Earle. 1931. *Indians of the Southwest.* Handbook Series, no. 2. New York: American Museum of Natural History.

Goldschmidt, Walter. 1951. *Nomlaki Ethnography.* University of California Publications in American Archaeology and Ethnology, vol. 42, no. 4. Berkeley and Los Angeles: University of California Press.

Goldschmidt, Walter R., and Harold E. Driver. 1947. The Hupa White Deerskin Dance. University of California Publications in American Archaeology and Ethnology, vol. 35. Berkeley and Los Angeles: University of California Press.

Graburn, Nelson H. H., and B. Stephen Strong. 1973. *Circumpolar Peoples: An Anthropological Perspective.* Pacific Palisades, Calif.: Goodyear Publishing Company.

Grant, Campbell. 1978. Eastern Coastal Chumash and Interior Chumash. In *Handbook of North American Indians,* vol. 8, ed. William C. Sturtevant. Washington, D.C.: Smithsonian Institution.

Grant, W. L., ed. 1907. *Voyages of Samuel De Champlain: 1604–1618.* New York: Barnes & Noble.

Graymont, Barbara. 1988. *The Iroquois.* New York: Chelsea House Publishers.

Griffen, William B. 1988. *Apaches at War and Peace: The Janos Presidio, 1750–1858.* Albuquerque: University of New Mexico Press.

Grinnell, George B. 1922. Who Were the Padouca? *American Anthropologist,* vol. 22.

Grumet, Robert S. 1995. *Historic Contact.* Norman: University of Oklahoma Press.

Gunther, Erna. 1972. *Indian Life of the Northwest Coast of North America (As Seen by the Early Explorers and Fur Traders during the Last Decades of the Eighteenth Century).* Chicago: University of Chicago Press.

Hackett, Charles W., intro. and annotations. 1942. *Revolt of the Pueblo Indians of New Mexico and Otermin's Attempted Reconquest: 1680–1682.* Albuquerque: University of New Mexico Press.

Hadlock, Wendell S. 1947. War among the Northeastern Woodland Indians. *American Anthropologist,* vol. 49.

Hajda, Yvonne. 1990. Southwestern Coast Salish. In *Handbook of North American Indians,* vol. 7, ed. William C. Sturtevant. Washington, D.C.: Smithsonian Institution.

Haley, J. E. 1928. Charles Goodnight's Indian Recollections. *Plains-Panhandle Historical Review,* no. 20.

Haley, James L. 1981. *Apaches: A History and Cultural Portrait.* Garden City, N.Y.: Doubleday & Company.

Hanson, C. 1967. The Deadly Arrow. *Museum of the Fur Trade Quarterly* 3, no. 4.

Hardy, Robert. 1976. *Longbow: A Social and Military History.* New York: Arco Publishing Company.

Harmon, E. M. 1945. The Story of the Indian Fort near Granby. *Colorado Magazine* 22 (4): 167–171.

Haywood, John. 1971. *Civil and Political History of the State of Tennessee from Its Earliest Settlement up to the Year 1796.* New York: Arno Press.

Heizer, Robert F. 1942. Aconite Poison Whaling in Asia and America: An Aleutian Transfer to the New World. *Smithsonian Institution Bureau of American Ethnology Bulletin 133, No. 24.*

———. 1945. Introduced Spearthrowers in California. *Masterkey for Indian Lore and History,* vol. 19.

———. 1947. The California Indians, 1579. *University of California Publications in American Archaeology and Ethnology,* vol. 42, no. 3.

———. 1951. Francis Drake and the California Indians, 1579. In *University of California Publications in American Archaeology and Ethnology,* vol. 42 (1945–1951), ed. Ralph L. Beals, Harry Hoijer et al. Berkeley and Los Angeles: University of California Press.

———. 1970. How Accurate Were California Indians with the Bow and Arrow? *The Masterkey* 44, no. 3.

Heizer, R. F., and M. A. Whipple. 1967. *The California Indians.* Berkeley and Los Angeles: University of California Press.

Hill, W. W. 1936. Navaho Warfare. *Yale University Publications in Anthropology,* vol. 5.

Hodge, Frederick Webb. 1924. Kwakiutl Sword. *Museum of the American Indian,* vol. 1. Washington, D.C.: Heye Foundation.

Hodge, Frederick Webb, ed. 1912. *Handbook of American Indians North of Mexico.* Washington, D.C.: Government Printing Office.

———. 1969 [1913]. *Handbook of Indians of Canada.* Ottawa: C. H. Parmelee.

Hoig, Stan. 1993. *Tribal Wars of the Southern Plains.* Norman: University of Oklahoma Press.

Holm, Bill. 1990. Tlingit Art. In *Handbook of North American Indians,* vol. 7, ed. William C. Sturtevant. Washington, D.C.: Smithsonian Institution.

Holm, Tom. 1996. *Strong Hearts, Wounded Souls: Native American Veterans of the Vietnam War.* Austin: University of Texas Press.

Honigmann, John J. 1946. *Ethnography and Acculturation of the Fort Nelson Slave.* Yale University Publications in Anthropology, no. 33. New Haven, Conn.: Yale University Press.

———. 1954. The Kaska Indians: An Ethnographic Reconstruction. Yale University Publications in Anthropology, no. 51. New Haven, Conn.: Yale University Press.

Hoover, Robert L. 1972. Industrial Plants of the California Indians. *California Academy of Science* 25, no. 5.

Hough, Walter. 1895. Primitive American Armor. *Report of the National Museum.* Washington, D.C.: Government Printing Office.

Howard, James H. 1995. *The Ponca Tribe.* Reprint. Lincoln: University of Nebraska Press.

Howay, F. W. 1925. Indian Attacks upon Maritime Traders of the Northwest Coast, 1785–1805. *Canadian Historical Review,* vol. 6.

Hrdlička, Ales. 1945. *The Aleutian and Commander Islands and Their Inhabitants.* Philadelphia: Wistar Institute of Anatomy and Biology.

Hudson, Charles. 1976. *The Southeastern Indians.* Knoxville: University of Tennessee Press.

———. 1990. *The Juan Pardo Expeditions: Exploration of the Carolinas and Tennessee, 1566–1568.* Washington, D.C.: Smithsonian Institution Press.

———. 1997. *Knights of Spain, Warriors of the Sun: Hernando de Soto and the South's Ancient Chiefdoms.* Athens: University of Georgia Press.

Hudson, Charles, and Carmen Chaves Teser. 1994. *The Forgotten Centuries in the American South, 1521–1704.* Athens: University of Georgia Press.

Hultkrantz, Ake. 1987. *Native Religions of North America: The Power Visions and Fertility.* Prospect Heights, Ill.: Waveland Press.

Hunt, George T. 1940. *The Wars of the Iroquois.* Madison: University of Wisconsin Press.

Hurst, A. E. 1968. On the Source of Copper at the Etowah Site, Georgia. *American Antiquity,* vol. 24.

Irving, Washington. 1961. *The Adventures of Captain Bonneville in the Rocky Mountains and the Far West.* Norman: University of Oklahoma Press.

Jefferson, James, Robert W. Delaney, and Gregory C. Thompson. 1972. *The Southern Utes: A Tribal History.* Ignacio, Colo.: Southern Ute Tribe.

Jennings, Jesse D. 1989. *Prehistory of North America.* Mountain View, Calif.: Mayfield Publishing Company.

Jochelson, Waldemar. 1908. The Koryak. *The Jesup North Pacific Expedition. Memoir of the American Museum of Natural History,* vol. 6, ed. Franz Boas. New York: G. E. Stechert.

———. 1926. The Yukaghir and the Yukaghirized Tungus. *The Jesup North Pacific Expedition. Memoir of the American Museum of Natural History,* vol. 9, ed. Franz Boas. New York: G. E. Stechert.

———. 1933. *History, Ethnology, and Anthropology of the Aleut.* Washington, D.C.: Carnegie Institution of Washington.

Johnson, Patti J. 1990. The Patwin. In *Handbook of North American Indians,* vol. 8, ed. William C. Sturtevant. Washington, D.C.: Smithsonian Institution.

Jones, Charles C. 1999. *Antiquities of the Southern Indians, Particularly of the Georgia Tribes.* Tuscaloosa: University of Alabama Press.

Jopling, Carol F. 1989. The Coppers of the Northwest Coast Indians: Their Origin, Development, and Possible Antecedents. *Transactions of the American Philosophical Society* 79, no. 1.

Kane, Paul. 1925. *Wanderings of an Artist among the Indians of North America.* Toronto: Radisson Society of Canada Limited.

Keegan, John. 1994. *A History of Warfare.* New York: Vintage Books.

Keesing, Felix M. 1987. *The Menomini Indians of Wisconsin: A Study of Three Centuries of Cultural Contact and Change.* Madison: University of Wisconsin Press.

Kehoe, Alice Beck. 1992. *North American Indians: A Comprehensive Account.* Upper Saddle River, N.J.: Prentice-Hall.

Kelly, William H. 1949. The Place of Scalps in Cocopa Warfare. *El Palacio,* vol. 56.

Kenner, Charles L. 1969. *A History of New Mexican–Plains Indian Relations.* Norman: University of Oklahoma Press.

Kinnaird, Lawrence. 1958. *The Frontiers of New Spain: Nicolas De Lafora's Description (1766–1768).* Berkeley, Calif.: Quivara Society.

Knapp, Frances, and Rheta Louise Childe. 1896. *The Thlinkets of Southeastern Alaska.* Chicago: Stone and Kimball.

Knaut, Andrew L. 1995. *The Pueblo Revolt of 1680.* Norman: University of Oklahoma Press.

Kniffen, Fred B., Hirman F. Gregory, and George A. Stokes. 1987. *The Indian Tribes of Louisiana from 1542 to the Present.* Baton Rouge: Louisiana State University Press.

Koch, Ronald P. 1977. *Dress Clothing of the Plains Indians.* Norman: University of Oklahoma Press.

Kroeber, Alfred L. 1917. Yahni Archery. *University Publications in American Archaeology and Ethnology,* vol. 13.

————. 1939. *Cultural and Natural Areas of Native North America.* Berkeley and Los Angeles: University of California Press.

————. 1967. A Kato War and Elements of Culture in Native California. In *The California Indians,* ed. R. F. Heizer and M. A. Whipple. Berkeley and Los Angeles: University of California Press.

————. 1976 [1925]. *Handbook of the Indians of California.* New York: Dover Publications.

Lafitau, Joseph François. 1977 [1724]. *Customs of the American Indians Compared with the Customs of Primitive Times.* Vol. 2. Toronto: Champlain Society.

Lane, Robert B. 1990. The Chilcotin. In *Handbook of North American Indians,* vol. 6, ed. William C. Sturtevant. Washington, D.C.: Smithsonian Institution.

Lapena, Frank R. 1990. The Wintu. In *Handbook of North American Indians,* vol. 8, ed. William C. Sturtevant. Washington, D.C.: Smithsonian Institution.

Laubin, Reginald, and Gladys Laubin. 1980. *American Indian Archery.* Norman: University of Oklahoma Press.

LeBlanc, Steven A. 1999. *Prehistoric Warfare in the American Southwest.* Salt Lake City: University of Utah Press.

Liberty, Margot. 1961. Fights with the Shoshone, 1855–1870: A Northern Cheyenne Indian Narrative. *Occasional Papers, Montana State University,* no. 2.

Linton, Ralph. 1944. Nomad Raids and Fortified Pueblos. *Society for American Archaeology,* vol. 10.

Lisiansky, Urey. 1814. *A Voyage around the World in the Years, 1803–1806 . . . in the Ship Neva.* London: John Booth.

Lowie, Robert H. 1909. The Northern Shoshone. *Anthropological Papers of the American Museum of Natural History,* vol. 11, part 2.

————. 1913a. Crow Military Societies. *Anthropological Papers of the American Museum of Natural History,* vol. 11.

————. 1913b. Societies of the Crow, Hidatsa and Mandan Indians. *Anthropological Papers of the American Museum of Natural History,* vol. 11, part 3.

————. 1915. Societies of the Arikara Indians. *Anthropological Papers of the American Museum of Natural History,* vol. 11, part 8.

————. 1916. Societies of the Kiowa. *Anthropological Papers of the American Museum of Natural History,* vol. 11, part 11.

————. 1935. *The Crow Indians.* Lincoln: University of Nebraska Press.

————. 1954. *The Indians of the Plains.* Garden City, N.Y.: Natural History Press.

Lowrey, N. S. 1994. An Ethnoarchaeological Inquiry into the Interactive Relationship between Northwest Coast Projectile Point and Armor Variants. Ph.D. diss., University of Wisconsin, Madison.

McCorkle, Thomas. 1990. California Warfare. In *Handbook of North American Indians,* vol. 8, ed. William C. Sturtevant. Washington, D.C.: Smithsonian Institution.

McGinnis, Anthony. 1990. *Counting Coup and Cutting Horses: Intertribal Warfare on the Northern Plains, 1738–1889.* Evergreen, Colo.: Cordillera Press.

McKennan, Robert A. 1959. The Upper Tanana Indians. *Yale University Publications in Anthropology,* no. 55. New Haven, Conn.: Department of Anthropology, Yale University.

———. 1965. The Chandalar Kutchin. *Arctic Institute of North America Technical Papers,* no. 17.

Mackenzie, Alexander. 1891. Descriptive Notes on Certain Implements, Weapons, etc., from Graham Island, Queen Charlotte Islands, B.C. *Proceedings and Transactions of the Royal Society of Canada* 9, no. 2.

McNitt, Frank. 1972. *Navaho Wars: Military Campaigns, Slave Raids, and Reprisals.* Albuquerque: University of New Mexico Press.

McWilliams, Richebourg G., trans. and ed. 1953. *Fleur de Lys and Calumet: Being the Penicaut Narrative of French Adventure in Louisiana.* Tuscaloosa: University of Alabama Press.

———. 1981. *Iberville's Gulf Journals.* Tuscaloosa: University of Alabama Press.

Mainfort, Robert C., and Lynne P. Sullivan. 1998. *Ancient Earthen Enclosures of the Eastern Woodlands.* Gainesville: University of Florida Press.

Malinowski, Sharon, and Anna Sheets, eds. 1998. *The Gale Encyclopedia of Native American Tribes.* Detroit: Gale.

Martin, Paul. 1967. *Arms and Armour: From the 9th to the 17th Centuries.* Rutland, Vt.: Charles E. Tuttle Company.

Martin, Paul S., George I. Quimby, and Donald Collier. 1947. *Indians before Columbus: Twenty Thousand Years of North American History Revealed by Archaeology.* Chicago: University of Chicago Press.

Mason, J. Alden. 1946. Notes on the Indians of the Great Slave Lake Area. *Yale University Publications in Anthropology,* no. 34. New Haven, Conn.: Yale University Press.

Mathews, John J. 1961. *The Osages: Children of the Middle Waters.* Norman: University of Oklahoma Press.

Matthews, Washington. 1883–1884. The Mountain Chant. *Annual Report of the Bureau of Ethnology.* Washington, D.C.: Smithsonian Institution.

Maud, Ralph, ed. 1978a. The Local Contribution of Charles Hill-Tout, Volume 2: The Squamish and the Lillooet. Vancouver: Talonbooks.

———. 1978b. The Salish People: The Local Contribution of Charles Hill-Tout, Volume 2: The Squamish and the Lillooet. Vancouver: Talonbooks.

Maximilian, Prince of Wied. 1843. *Travels in the Interior of North America.* London: n.p.

Mayer, Joseph R. 1943. Flintlocks of the Iroquois. *Research Records of the Rochester Museum of Arts and Sciences,* no. 6.

Miller, Jay, and William R. Seaburg. 1990. Athabascans of Southwest Oregon. In *Handbook of North American Indians,* vol. 7, ed. William C. Sturtevant. Washington, D.C.: Smithsonian Institution.

Miller, Polly. 1967. *Lost Heritage of Alaska: The Adventure and Art of the Alaskan Coastal Indians.* New York: Bonanza Books.

Milling, Chapman J. 1978. *Red Carolinians.* Columbia: University of South Carolina Press.

Milloy, John S. 1988. *The Plains Cree: Trade, Diplomacy and War, 1790 to 1870.* Winnipeg: University of Manitoba Press.

Mooney, James. 1894. *The Siouan Tribes of the East.* Smithsonian Institution Bureau of Ethnology. Washington, D.C.: Smithsonian Institution.

Moore, Warren. 1967. *Weapons of the Revolution.* New York: Funk & Wagnall's.

Morfi, Juan Agustin. 1935. *History of Texas: 1673–1779.* Translated by Carlos Eduardo Castañeda. Albuquerque, N.Mex.: Quivara Society.

Morgan, Louis H. 1901. *League of the Ho-De-No-Sau-Nee or Iroquois.* New York: Burt Franklin.

———. 1952. Reports on the Fabrics, Inventions, Implements, and Utensils of the Iroquois. *Annual Report of the State University of New York,* no. 5.

———. 1965 [1881]. *Houses and House-Life of the American Aborigines.* Chicago: University of Chicago Press.

Morice, A. G. 1889. The Western Dene. *Proceedings of the Canada Institute,* vol. 25.

Moss, Madonna L., and Jon M. Erlandson. 1992. Forts, Refuge Rocks, and Defensive Sites: The Antiquity of Warfare along the North Pacific Coast of North America. *Arctic Anthropology,* vol. 29.

Murie, James R. 1914. Pawnee Indian Societies. *Anthropological Papers of the American Museum of Natural History,* vol. 11, part 7.

Narrative of Le Moyne. 1875. Translated from the Latin by De Bry. Boston: James R. Osgood and Company.

Nelson, E. W. 1896–1897. The Eskimo about Bering Strait. *Annual Report of the Bureau of American Ethnology,* vol. 18.

Nequatewa, Edmund. 1944. A Mexican Raid on the Hopi Pueblo of Orabai. *Plateau* 16, no. 3.

Newcomb, W. W. 1978. *The Indians of Texas: From Prehistoric to Modern Times.* Austin: University of Texas Press.

Newcombe, W. A. 1931. *A Large Salish Earthwork.* Victoria, B.C.: Provincial Museum of Natural History.

Nuttall, Thomas. 1819. *Journal of Travels into the Arkansas Territory during the Year 1819.* Philadelphia: Thomas W. Palmer.

O'Callaghan, Edmund R. 1850. *The Documentary History of the State of New York.* Albany, N.Y.: n.p.

Olmsted, D. L., and Omer C. Stewart. 1990. The Achumawi. In *Handbook of North American Indians,* vol. 8, ed. William C. Sturtevant. Washington, D.C.: Smithsonian Institution.

Olson, Ronald L. 1936. The Quinault Indians. *University of Washington Publications in Anthropology* 6, no. 1.

Olson, Wallace, and Marie M. Olson. 1991. *The Tlingit: An Introduction to Their Culture and History.* Auke Bay, Alaska: Heritage Research.

Oswalt, Wendell H. 1967. *Alaskan Eskimos.* San Francisco: Chandler Publishing Company.

Owen, M. 1951. Indian Wars in Alabama. *Alabama Historical Quarterly,* vol. 13.

Palmer, Rose A. 1929. *The North American Indian.* Smithsonian Scientific Series, vol. 4. Washington, D.C.: Smithsonian Institution.

Parker, Arthur C. 1918. Champlain's Assault on the Fortified Town of the Oneidas, 1615. *New York State Museum Bulletin,* vol. 207.

Paterek, Josephine. 1994. *Encyclopedia of American Indian Costume.* Santa Barbara, Calif.: ABC-CLIO.

Peers, Laura. 1994. *The Ojibway of Western Canada: 1780–1870.* St. Paul: Minnesota Historical Society Press.

Perrin, Noel. 1979. *Giving Up the Gun: Japan's Reversion to the Sword, 1543–1879.* Boston: D. R. Godine.

Plog, Stephen. 1997. *Ancient Peoples of the American Southwest.* London: Thames and Hudson Ltd.

Post, Richard H., and Rachel S. Commons. 1938. Material Culture. In *The Sinkaietk or Southern Okanagon of Washington,* ed. Leslie Spier. General Series in Anthropology, No. 6. Contributions from the Laboratory of Anthropology, Vol. 2. Menasha, Wis.: Banta Publishing Company.

Pratt, Peter P. 1963. A Heavily Stockaded Late Prehistoric Oneida Iroquois Settlement. *Pennsylvania Archaeologist. Bulletin of the Society for Pennsylvania Archaeology* 33, nos. 1–2.

Pritzker, Barry M. 1998. *Native Americans: An Encyclopedia of History, Culture, and Peoples.* 2 vols. Santa Barbara, Calif.: ABC-CLIO.

Quinn, David B., and Alison M. Quinn, eds. 1973. *Virginia Voyages from Hakluyt.* London: Oxford University Press.

Ramsey, J. G. M. 1971. *The Annals of Tennessee to the End of the Eighteenth Century.* New York: Arno Press.

Ratti, Oscar, and Adele Westbrook. 1973. *Secrets of the Samurai: A Survey of the Martial Arts of Feudal Japan.* Rutland, Vt.: Charles E. Tuttle Company.

Ray, Dorothy Jean. 1975. *The Eskimos of the Bering Strait, 1650–1898.* Seattle: University of Washington Press.

Ray, P. H. 1886. Manufacture of Bows and Arrows among the Natano (Hupa) and Kenuck (Klamath) Indians. *American Naturalist,* vol. 20.

Ray, Vernon R. 1938. Lower Chinook Ethnographic Notes. Vol. 7, no. 2. Seattle: University of Washington.

Richard, T. 1939. The Use of Iron and Copper by the Indians of British Columbia. *British Columbia Historical Quarterly* 3, no. 1.

Richter, Daniel K. 1983. War and Culture: The Iroquois Experience. *William and Mary Quarterly,* 3d series, vol. 15, no. 4.

Riddell, Francis. 1990. The Maidu and Kunkow. In *Handbook of North American Indians,* vol. 8, ed. William C. Sturtevant. Washington, D.C.: Smithsonian Institution.

Rights, Douglas L. 1947. *The American Indian in North Carolina.* Durham, N.C.: Duke University Press.

———. 1953. Copper Specimens from Yadkin River in Piedmont, North Carolina. *American Antiquity* 18, no. 4.

Roberts, Frank H. H. 1967. Early Man in California. In *The California Indians,* ed. R. F. Heizer and M. A. Whipple. Berkeley and Los Angeles: University of California Press.

Rodack, Madeleine T., trans. and ed. 1981. *Adolph F. Bandelier's "The Discovery of New Mexico by the Franciscan Monk Friar Marcos de Niza in 1539."* Tucson: University of Arizona Press.

Roe, Frank G. 1962 [1955]. *The Indian and the Horse.* Norman: University of Oklahoma Press.

Rountree, Helen C. 1989. *The Powhatan Indians of Virginia.* Norman: University of Oklahoma Press.

Rountree, Helen C., and Thomas E. Davidson. 1997. *Eastern Shore Indians of Virginia and Maryland.* Charlottesville: University Press of Virginia.

Rowland, Dunbar, and Albert G. Sanders, trans. and eds. 1927. *Mississippi Provincial Archives: French Dominion, 1729–1740.* Vol. 1. Jackson: Press of the Mississippi Department of Archives and History.

———. 1929. *Mississippi Provincial Archives, 1701–1729: French Dominion.* Vol. 2. Jackson: Press of the Mississippi Department of Archives and History.

———. 1932. *Mississippi Provincial Archives.* Vol. 3. Jackson: Press of the Mississippi Department of Archives and History.

Ruby, Robert H., and John A. Brown. 1976. *The Chinook Indians: Traders of the Lower Columbia River.* Norman: University of Oklahoma Press.

Ruppe, R. J. 1953. Acoma Archaeology: A Preliminary Report of the Final Season in the Cebolleta Mesa Region, New Mexico. *El Palacio* 60, no. 7.

Russell, Howard S. 1980. *Indian New England before the Mayflower.* Hanover, N.H.: University Press of New England.

Ruttenber, E. M. 1872. *History of the Indian Tribes of Hudson's River.* Port Washington, N.Y.: Kennikat Press.

Sauer, Carl O. 1971. *Sixteenth-Century North America: The Land and the People as Seen by the Europeans.* Berkeley and Los Angeles: University of California Press.

Schaafsma, Polly. 2000. *Warrior, Shield, and Star.* Santa Fe: Western Edge Press.

Schulman, Albert. 1950. Pre-Columbian Towers in the Southwest. *American Antiquity* 15, no. 4.

Seaburg, William R., and Jay Miller. 1990. The Tillamook. In *Handbook of North American Indians,* vol. 7, ed. William C. Sturtevant. Washington, D.C.: Smithsonian Institution.

Secoy, Frank R. 1951. The Identity of the "Paduca": An Ethnohistorical Analysis. *American Anthropologist,* vol. 53.

———. 1992 [1953]. *Changing Military Patterns of the Great Plains Indians.* Monographs of the American Ethnological Society, no. 21. Lincoln: University of Nebraska Press.

Schmalz, Peter S. 1991. *The Ojibwa of Southern Ontario.* Toronto: University of Toronto Press.

Shotridge, L. 1919. War Helmets and Clans Hats of the Tlingit Indians. *Museum Journal* 10, nos. 1–2.

Silver, Shirley. 1990. The Shasta. In *Handbook of North American Indians,* vol. 8, ed. William C. Sturtevant. Washington, D.C.: Smithsonian Institution.

Skinner, Alanson. 1915a. Ponca Societies and Dances. *Anthropological Papers of the American Museum of Natural History,* vol. 11.

———. 1915b. Societies of the Iowa, Kansa, and Ponca Indians. *Anthropological Papers of the American Museum of Natural History,* vol. 11, part 9.

Slaughter, Thomas P., ed. 1996. *William Bartram: Travels and Other Writings.* New York: Library of America.

Slobodin, R. 1960. Eastern Kutchin Warfare. *Anthropologica,* vol. 2.

Smith, Dwight L. 1960. Provocation and Occurrence of Indian-White Warfare in the Early American Period of the Old Northwest. *Northwest Ohio Quarterly,* vol. 33.

South Dakota State Department of History. 1914. South Dakota Historical Collections, vol. 7.

Spaulding, Albert C. 1953. Statistical Techniques for the Discovery of Artifact Types. *American Antiquity* 18, no. 4.

Spicer, Edward H. 1962. *Cycles of Conquest: The Impact of Spain, Mexico, and the United States on the Indians of the Southwest, 1533–1960.* Tucson: University of Arizona Press.

Spier, Leslie. 1928. Havasupai Ethnography. *Anthropological Papers of the American Museum of Natural History,* vol. 29, part 3.

Spinden, Herbert Joseph. 1974. *The Nez Perce Indians.* Memoirs of the American Anthropological Association, part 3. Milwood, N.Y.: Kraus Reprint Company.

Spring, Christopher. 1993. *African Arms and Armor.* Washington, D.C.: Smithsonian Institution Press.

Starkey, Armstrong. 1998. *European and Native American Warfare, 1675–1815.* Norman: University of Oklahoma Press.

Steele, Ian K. 1994. *Warpaths: Invasions of North America.* New York: Oxford University Press.

Stewart, Kenneth M. 1947. Mohave Warfare. *Southwestern Journal of Anthropology,* vol. 3.

Stone, George Cameron. 1961. *A Glossary of the Construction, Decoration and Use of Arms and Armor.* New York: Jack Brussel, Publisher.

Sturtevant, William C., General Editor. 1990. *Handbook of North American Indians.* Washington, D.C.: Smithsonian Institution.

Suttles, Wayne P. 1974. *Coast Salish and Western Washington Indians.* Vol. 1. New York: Garland Publishing Inc.

———. 1990. The Central Coast Salish. In *Handbook of North American Indians,* vol. 7, ed. William C. Sturtevant. Washington, D.C.: Smithsonian Institution.

Suttles, Wayne P., and Barbara Lane. 1990. The Southern Coast Salish. In *Handbook of North American Indians,* vol. 7, ed. William C. Sturtevant. Washington, D.C.: Smithsonian Institution.

Sutton, Mark Q. 2000. *An Introduction to Native North America.* Boston: Allyn and Bacon.

Swanton, John R. 1911. *Indian Tribes of the Lower Mississippi Valley and Adjacent Coast of the Gulf of Mexico.* New York: Dover Publications.

———. 1928. Religious Beliefs and Medical Practices of the Creek Indians. *Forty-Second Annual Report of the Bureau of American Ethnology.* Washington, D.C.: Government Printing Office.

———. 1937. Historic Use of the Spear-Thrower in Southeastern North America. *American Antiquity,* vol. 3.

———. 1942. Source Material on the History and Ethnology of the Caddo Indians. *Smithsonian Institution Bureau of American Ethnology Bulletin 312.*

———. 1943. Relations between Northern Mexico and the Southeast of the United States from the Point of View of Ethnology and History. *Sociedad de Mexicana de Anthropologaia.*

———. 1946. *The Indians of the Southeastern United States.* Bureau of American Ethnology Bulletin No. 137. Washington, D.C.: Smithsonian Institution.

Teit, James A. 1900a. The Lillooet Indians. *Memoir of the American Museum of Natural History, Vol. 2. The Jesup North Pacific Expedition,* ed. Franz Boas. New York: G. E. Stechert.

———. 1900b. The Thompson Indians of British Columbia. *Memoir of the American Museum of Natural History, Vol. 1. The Jesup North Pacific Expedition,* ed. Franz Boas. New York: G. E. Stechert.

Tello, José Espinosa. 1967. The Monterey Bay Costanoans. In *The California Indians,* ed. R. F. Heizer and M. A. Whipple. Berkeley and Los Angeles: University of California Press.

Temple, Wayne C. 1958. Indian Villages of the Illinois Country. *Illinois State Museum Scientific Papers,* vol. 2, part 2.

Terrell, John Upton. 1975. *The Plains Apache.* New York: Thomas Y. Crowell Company.

Thomas, Alfred B. 1932. *Forgotten Frontiers: A Study of the Spanish Indian Policy of Don Juan Bautista de Anza, Governor of New Mexico: 1777–1787.* Norman: University of Oklahoma Press.

———. 1935. *After Coronado: Spanish Exploration Northeast of New Mexico (Documents from the Archives of Spain, Mexico, and New Mexico).* Norman: University of Oklahoma Press.

Thompson, David. 1916. *David Thompson's Narrative of His Explorations in Western America: 1784–1812.* Edited by J. B. Tyrrell. Toronto: Champlain Society.

Thwaites, Reuben Gold, ed. 1959a. *The Jesuit Relations and Allied Documents, Vol. 1. Acadia: 1610–1613.* New York: Pageant Book Company.

———. 1959b. *The Jesuit Relations and Allied Documents, Vol. XLVI. Lower Canada: 1659–1661.* New York: Pageant Book Company.

Tobey, Margaret L. 1990. The Carrier. In *Handbook of North American Indians,* vol. 6, ed. William C. Sturtevant. Washington, D.C.: Smithsonian Institution.

Tollefson, Kenneth D. 1987. The Snoqualmie: A Puget Sound Chiefdom. *Ethnology* 26, no. 2.

Tooker, Elisabeth. 1964. An Ethnography of the Huron Indians, 1615–1649. *Smith-*

sonian Institution Bureau of American Ethnology Bulletin 190. Washington, D.C.: U.S. Government Printing Office.

Van Horne, Wayne William. 1993. The Warclub: Weapon and Symbol in Southeastern Indian Societies. Ph.D. diss., University of Georgia, Athens.

Vanstone, James W. 1974. *Athapaskan Adaptations*. Chicago: Aldine Publishing.

Verne, F. 1938. Lower Chinook Ethnographic Notes. *University of Washington Publications in Anthropology* 7, no. 2.

Wagner, Henry R. 1971. *Spanish Exploration in the Strait of Juan De Fuca*. New York: AMS Press.

Wagner, Henry R., ed. and trans. 1936. Journal of Tomas de Suria of His Voyage with Malaspina to the Northwest Coast of America in 1791. *Pacific Historical Review* 5, no. 3.

Waldman, Carl. 1985. *Atlas of the North American Indian*. New York: Facts on File Publications.

Wallace, Ernest, and E. Adamson Hoebel. 1952. *The Comanches: Lords of the South Plains*. Norman: University of Oklahoma Press.

Wallace, William J. 1949. *Hupa Warfare*. Southwest Museum Leaflets, no. 23. Los Angeles: Southwest Museum.

———. 1990. The Hupa. In *Handbook of North American Indians*, vol. 8, ed. William C. Sturtevant. Washington, D.C.: Smithsonian Institution.

Wallis, Wilson D., and Ruth Sawtell Wallis. 1955. *The Micmac Indians of Eastern Canada*. Minneapolis: University of Minnesota Press.

Weslager, Clinton A. 1983. *The Nanticoke Indians: Past and Present*. Newark: University of Delaware Press.

West, George A. 1928. *Copper: Its Mining and Use by the Aborigines of the Lake Superior Region. Report of the McDonald-Massee Isle Royale Expedition, 1928*. Westport, Conn.: Greenwood Press.

Weyer, Edward M. 1932. *The Eskimo*. New Haven, Conn.: Yale University Press.

Willoughby, Charles C. 1901. Antler-Pointed Arrows of the Southeastern Indians. *American Anthropologist*, vol. 3.

———. 1922. Feather Mantles of California. *American Anthropologist*, vol. 24.

Wissler, Clark. 1910. Material Culture of the Blackfoot Indians. *Anthropological Papers of the American Museum of Natural History*, vol. 9, part 1.

———. 1912. Societies and Ceremonial Associations in the Oglala Division of the Teton-Dakota. *Anthropological Papers of the American Museum of Natural History*, vol. 11, part 1.

———. 1913. Societies and Dance Associations of the Blackfoot Indians. *Anthropological Papers of the American Museum of Natural History*, vol. 11, part 4.

———. 1916. Societies of the Plains Indians. *Anthropological Papers of the American Museum of Natural History*, vol. 11.

Wood, W. R. 1967. An Interpretation of Mandan Culture History. *Bureau of American Ethnology, Bulletin 198, River Basin Survey Paper, No. 39*.

Woodbury, Richard B. 1958. A Reconsideration of Pueblo Warfare. *International Congress of Americanists, 33rd*. San José, Costa Rica.

Worcester, D. E. 1945. The Weapons of American Indians. *New Mexico Historical Review,* vol. 20.

Wright, Barton. 1976. *Pueblo Shields (From the Fred Harvey Fine Arts Collection).* Albuquerque: Northland Press.

Wright, J. Leitch. 1986. *Creeks and Seminoles: The Destruction and Regeneration of the Muscogulge People.* Lincoln: University of Nebraska Press.

Index